# HOSPITALITY AND TOURISM

# HOSPITALITY AND TOURISM

**B.S. Badan**
**Harish Bhatt**

COMMONWEALTH

[*The responsibility for the facts stated, conclusions reached and plagiarism, if any, in this book is entirely that of the Author. And the Publisher bears no responsibility for them, whatsoever.*]

**Hospitality and Tourism**



First Published : 2007

ISBN 81-311-0068-5

*Published by* :

**Ajay Verma**
**For COMMONWEALTH PUBLISHERS**
4831/24, Prahlad Street,
Ansari Road, Darya Ganj,
New Delhi - 110002
Ph. : 23272541, 23257835
Fax : 91- 011- 23257835
e-mail : campusbooks@hotmail.com

*Printed at :*
**Roshan Offset Printers**
Delhi

# Preface

Tourism can be defined as the act of travel for the purpose of recreation, and the provision of services for this act. It is a service industry, comprising a number of tangible and intangible components. The tangible elements include transportation systems—air, rail, road, water and now, space; hospitality services, accommodation, foods and beverages, tours, souvenirs; and related services such as banking, insurance and safety and security. The intangible elements include: rest and relaxation, culture, escape, adventure, new and different experiences.

Travel and tourism is a major industry in the world and is at the top of the league of invisible earners of foreign currency. Many sovereignties, along with their respective countries and states, depend heavily upon travel expenditures by foreigners as a source of taxation and income for the enterprises that sell services to these travellers. Consequently the development of tourism is often a strategy employed either by a non-governmental organization or a governmental agency to promote a particular region for the purpose of increasing commerce through exporting goods and services to non-locals.

During recent years the tourism industry has witnessed unprecedented growth. Increasing consumer demand for educational and participatory travel experiences has resulted in a variety of specialty niche markets such as ecotourism, cultural-heritage tourism, and agritourism. New paradigms link strategic tourism planning with sustainable development.

The leisure and tourism industry is one of the leading global economic activities, a multi-billion-dollar industry with

700 million international travellers per year around the world. Tourism is a motor for employment and income creation and, especially in poor countries, a vehicle for development. But today it is not sufficient to simply create employment without regard for the quality of jobs and the social and environmental effects of tourism in vulnerable areas. A growing number of organizations, including the tourism industry leadership, are increasingly conscious of the risks and are adopting a more responsible attitude.

The present publication provides an authoritative look at how to manage travel and tourism industry in a better way. It introduces the complexities of the tourism system so that they will be better positioned to eventually assume the managerial challenges and responsibilities in a diverse and challenging industry. The latest advancements in tourism theory and thinking, retaining the thoroughness of content, diversity of applications, regional and international issues, economic significance, tourism operators and the role of technology in the tourism industry etc. are also described elaborately. Numerous regional and global case studies and examples are included to provide an appropriately broad geographic context. This work will be highly informative and useful to students, researchers, policy makers, managers and working groups of travel and tourism industry.

*B.S. Badan*
*Harish Bhatt*

# CONTENTS

# CONTENTS

# 1

# INTERNATIONAL TOURISM

## Introduction

In his comprehensive review of 85 international tourism forecasting studies, Crouch (1994b) noted. 'A reading of the past research leads one to conclude that income is the single most important determinant of demand for international tourism' (p. 12). The income of the residents of a nation can affect outbound travel in two ways. First, it provides the financial resources to fund this travel, especially for leisure purposes. Second, national income is an indicator of the business activity of a nation. If income is high and rising, it is quite likely that the business activity is growing and stimulating business travel to foreign markets.

Population has been a less popular explanatory variable in international tourism forecasting studies. Crouch (1994a) found that population was employed as an explanatory variable in only 15% of the 85 international tourism demand forecasting studies he reviewed (p. 50). However, population is an appealing instrument in the tourism demand forecaster's toolkit for at least two reasons. One is that it is people who do the travelling. And just as we usually deflate economic values stated in currency terms to remove inflation, we should deflate visitor volumes over time to remove that growth due simply to more people. This is common in studies of other national economic and social variables, such as income, automobile and telephone ownership, crime and disease stated on per resident ('per capita') bases.

Second, population for most countries has the distinction of being the socio-economic variable easiest to forecast with accuracy over the medium to long-term: for 80% or more of all the people expected to be living a decade hence are already born. Demographers usually know a great deal about trends in birth rates and mortality rates by age, so that the number of people in each age cohort can be forecast ten years or so out with a relatively high degree of accuracy.

In this study, I investigate what past fluctuations in national income (represented by countries' real GDPs) and population sizes and structures can reveal about outbound travel from 20 countries. The intent is to discover relationships that can be used to forecast long-haul visitor volumes from these countries to 2010. These forecasts are necessarily long-term trends rather than annual point estimates. A host of other explanatory factors often push a country's outbound travel volumes off their long-term trends for brief periods of time (e.g. Frechtling, 1996, p. 135).

**Purpose and Use**

This chapter reports on efforts to discern the impact of population and income trends on outbound international travel over the past decade, in order to indicate trends in the first decade of the new millennium. Time series on outbound long-haul international travel from 20 countries, population trends by age grouping and real Gross Domestic Product (GDP) are analysed over the 1989 – 98 period to suggest major relationships among these variables. Projections of population by age group and real GDP for these countries are then used to project outbound international long-haul travel for these countries to 2010. Finally, some conclusions are drawn about the future of long-haul international travel.

To my knowledge, informed by extensive literature reviews by Crouch (1994a, 1994b) and Witt and Witt (unpublished paper, 1992, pp. 16 – 29), no published studies have investigated the change in individual age cohorts as an explanatory factor in international travel demand. The present study, then, is exploratory, providing the results of an initial investigation of these variables to aid understanding of international travel demand.

This study should be of interest to marketers planning where to devote their resources to develop visitor markets from an array of origin countries. The findings herein could be used in a two-stage model of inbound visitor forecasting suggested by Smeral (1998). In the first stage, the total volume of outbound visitors or visitor spending is estimated for major originating countries. In the second stage, the distribution of this outbound tourism among destination countries is estimated, based on marketing expenditures, relative prices, air fares, exchange rates, etc.

Finally, this study should provide additional intelligence on a tourism generating factor largely ignored in tourism demand literature; the age structure of national populations. The world's rate of population growth is declining, and the inhabitants of this planet are collectively growing older. The volume of residents of some countries has already begun to decline, with more countries projected to enter these ranks in the decade ahead.

**Definitions and Base Data**

I employ here the definitions of international travel adopted by the United Nations Statistical Commission in 1993 in response to the World Tourism Organisation's (WTO) report on tourism statistics (UN/WTO, 1994, p. v) In this system of classification, the central statistical unit is the 'visitor'. 'International visitor' is defined as 'any person who travels to a country other than that in which he/she has his/her usual residence but outside his/her usual environment for a period not exceeding 12 months and whose main purpose of visit is other than the exercise of an activity remunerated from within the country visited' (UN/WTO, 1994, p. 29). By extension, the terms 'international trip' or 'international visit' describe any travel to a place outside the country in which the visitor resides (UN/WTO, 1994, p. 42).

This report focuses on the 'outbound' visitors a country generates, that is, the number of trips recorded by residents of the country under study to all other countries of the world (UN/WTO, 1994, p. 11). Outbound travel is further classified by the spatial extent of the international trip. 'Long-haul' is used to indicate that an outbound visitor has travelled to one or more countries outside the multi-country region in which the visitor lives as defined by the World Tourism Organisation (Travel Industry Association of America, 1999, p. 47). Complementarily, 'short-haul' indicates outbound travel by the residents of a country to other countries within the same region, as defined by the WTO. 'Total outbound' travel is the sum of long-haul outbound travel and short-haul outbound travel from a country (1999, p. 47).

All estimates of long-haul visitors for each of 20 generating countries used in this study were derived from the most recent Travel Industry Association of America report (1999), covering the years 1989 – 98. Note that these visitors/trips are computed as the residences reported by visitors to each receiving country as compiled by the WTO. Since a given international visitor may visit two or more countries on a single trip, the total outbound estimates for individual generating countries used in this study are likely to exceed the estimates of outbound visitors or trips reported by the countries of visitors' residences. The aggregate of outbound trips by residents of these 20 countries comprised over 62% of total world arrivals in 1998.

'Gross Domestic Product' (GDP) is defined as 'equal to the total gross expenditure on the final uses of the domestic supply of goods and services valued at purchasers' values less imports of goods and services valued c.i.f.' (Organisation for Economic Co-operation and Development, 1999, p. 7). It is thus a standard measure of the net output of goods and services within the political borders of a country. This study employs annual estimates of 'real' GDP for the 20 countries analysed published by the OECD at 1990 prices and exchange rates (Organisation for Economic Co-operation and Development, 1999, p. 138) for the years 1989 through 1997. The 1997 GDP estimates were updated to 1998 for each country by the figures provided to the author by the WEFA

Group. GDP represents national income herein, since it is also the sum of incomes to all factors of production residing within the country's borders.

Estimates of each country's total population and population by three major age groups were collected from the US Bureau of the Census International Data Base as listed on the Internet at http://www.census.gov/ggi-bin. The data for Canada were incomplete, so the author obtained these population estimates from Statistics Canada at www.statcan.ca/datawarehouse/cansim/cansim.cgi.

The WTO database published by TIA includes data on the 20 countries listed in Table 1.1 with their WTO regions. The only exception to this convention is that while Israel is

**Table 1.1**
**Countries included in the present study by WTO region and economic status**

| *Generating country* | *WTO region* | *Economic status* |
|---|---|---|
| Argentina | South America | Developing |
| Australia | East Asia/Pacific | Industrialised |
| Belgium | Europe | Industrialised |
| Brazil | South America | Developing |
| Canada | North America | Industrialised |
| France | Europe | Industrialised |
| Germany | Europe | Industrialised |
| Israel | Middle East | Industrialised |
| Italy | Europe | Industrialised |
| Japan | East Asia/Pacific | Industrialised |
| Korea, Republic of | East Asia/Pacific | Developing |
| Mexico | North America | Developing |
| Netherlands | Europe | Industrialised |
| Spain | Europe | Industrialised |
| Sweden | Europe | Industrialised |
| Switzerland | Europe | Industrialised |
| Taiwan | East Asia/Pacific | Developing |
| United Kingdom | Europe | Industrialised |
| United States | North America | Industrialised |
| Venezuela | South America | Developing |

*Source:* Travel Industry Association, 1999; World Tourism Organisation, 1997a, pp. 256–57.

included by WTO in the Europe region, in this study, long-haul trips comprise those visits to countries outside WTO's Middle East region. The 'economic status' of the country is as provided by the World Tourism Organisation's Compendium of Tourism Statistics (WTO, 1999).

## The Present

Figures 1.1 presents the 1998 estimates of outbound visitors for each of the 20 generating countries.

The United States leads all countries of the world by far in current outbound long-haul visitors, supplying one-third of the total for all 20 countries. Japan and the United Kingdom form a second tier of long-haul generating countries, with Germany and France following.

As Figure 1.2 indicates, generally, outbound long-haul travel varies with the population size of the countries. However, Mexico and Brazil produce considerably fewer long-haul visitors than their populations would indicate, suggesting the impact of relatively low income and/or an extremely unequal distribution of income among residents are among factors dampening this demand. Japan, on the other hand, is producing considerably more long-haul visitors than

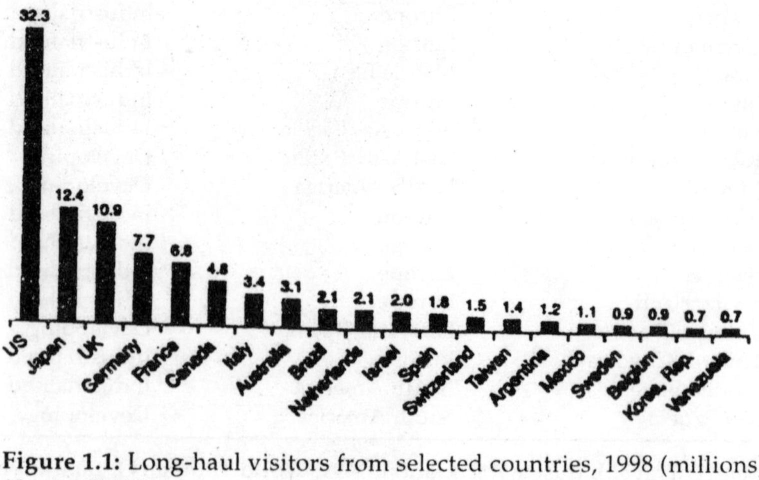


**Figure 1.1:** Long-haul visitors from selected countries, 1998 (millions). (*Source:* WTO)

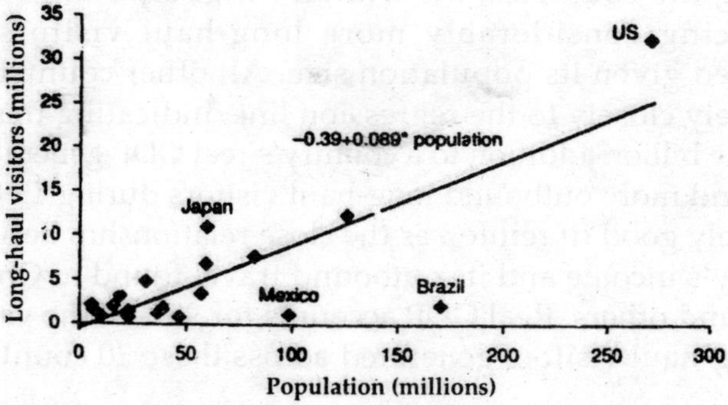


**Figure 1.2:** Long-haul visitors and population of selected countries, 1998. (*Source:* WTO and US Census Bureau)

its population size, suggests the effects of an island nation with a large economy and a government encouraging outbound travel. For all 20 countries in 1998, population size accounted for about 64% of the variance in long-haul visitors generated.

Figure 1.3 shows the relatively close relationship between real GDP in 1998 and volume of long-haul outbound trips.

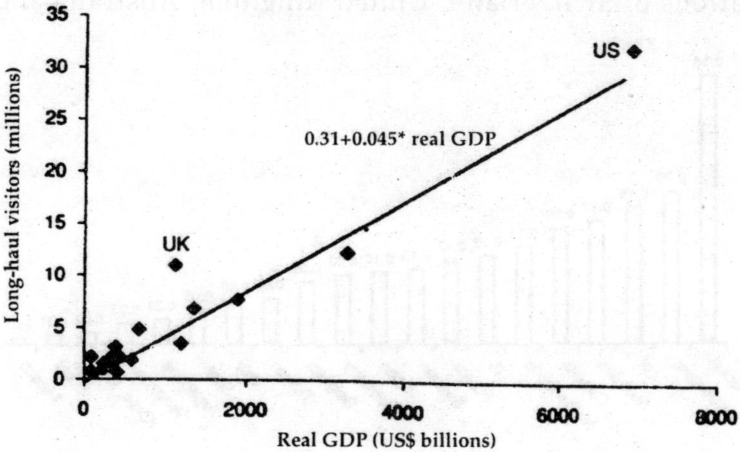


**Figure 1.3:** Long-haul visitors and real GDP of selected countries, 1998 (millions). (*Source:* WTO and US Census Bureau)

Among the countries, the United Kingdom stands out as producing considerably more long-haul visitors than expected given its population size. All other countries fall relatively closely to the regression line, indicating that each US$ one billion addition to a country's real GDP generated 4.5 thousand more outbound long-haul visitors during 1998. The relatively good fit reinforces the close relationship between a country's income and its outbound travel found in Crouch's study and others. Real GDP accounts for 95% of the variance on long-haul visitors generated across these 20 countries in 1998.

Of course, outbound travel among nations may vary only because resident populations differ: a large population country could be expected to produce more outbound visitors annually than a country with a small population. This relationship could obscure other factors explaining outbound visitors volumes.

Figures 1.4 ranks the 20 countries on the basis of outbound travel intensity, that is, the average number of visitors generated per resident of the country. This shows a considerably different ranking from that in Figure 1.1. Israel surpasses all other countries by far, with the industrialised nations of Switzerland, United Kingdom, Australia and

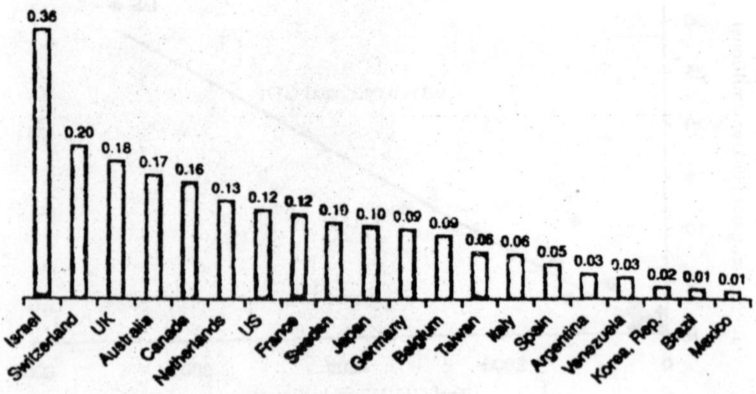


**Figure 1.4:** Long-haul visitors per resident for selected countries, 1998 (millions). (*Source:* WTO, US Census Bureau, author's estimates)

Canada forming a second tier. Most of the developing nations fall at the end of this scale.

Long-haul visits per resident is a useful measure for tourism demand forecasting. It indicates how active the individual resident is in travelling abroad. Although not conclusive, the measure suggests how widespread international travel is among the population. We could expect that a larger percentage of Israel's population travels abroad in a year than of the United States' population, for example. Destination marketers attempting to access the most productive outbound markets could expect greater success promoting to Israeli residents than to US residents as a whole.

In addition, this measure of travel intensity helps us avoid problems of multicollinearity, which plague attempts to forecast international travel (Witt and Witt, unpublished, 1992, p. 17). In regression analysis, when two or more explanatory variables are highly correlated with one another (i.e., are multicollinear), regression analysis has difficulty assigning coefficients to them, and these estimates become highly unstable i.e., have high standard errors (Frechtling, 1996, p. 242). Population by itself is likely to be multicollinear with several other socio-economic variables of interest to the

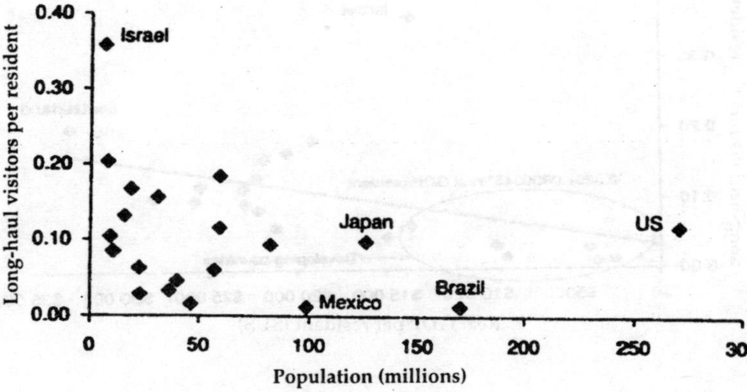


**Figure 1.5:** Long-haul visitors intensity and population of selected countries, 1998. (*Source:* WTO and US Census Bureau, author's estimates)

forecaster (e.g., Frechtling, 1996, p. 143). Adjusting outbound visitor volumes over space and time by population removes one source of multicollinearity in this demand forecasting. Moreover, little correlation was found between these countries' absolute long-haul visitor volumes and their intensities of this travel for 1998, indicating that the latter is a new variable that may shed light on important income and population relationships to this travel.

Figure 1.5 indicates that there is no discernible relationship between countries' population sizes and intensities of long-haul travel generated. For example, regardless of population size, the developing nations in the sample produce low long-haul travel intensities. The relatively small country of Israel produces an intensity three times that of the large USA.

There is a weak relationship between long-haul travel intensity and real income per capita (Figure 1.6). The regression line for these 20 countries explains only about 22% of the variance in long-haul visitors per resident in 1998. The six developing countries in the sample all produced lower outbound long-haul intensities than the average for the group.

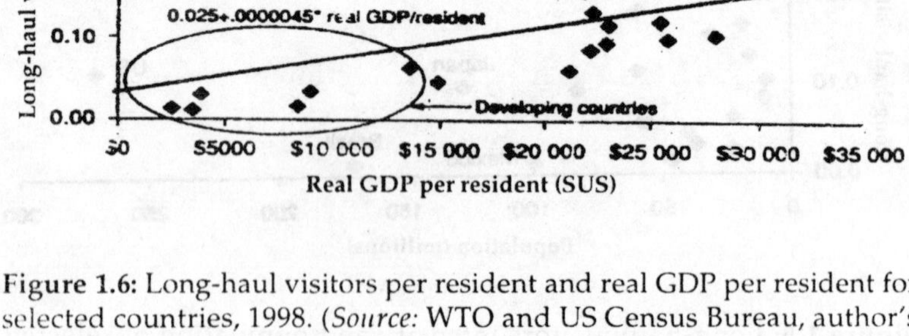


Figure 1.6: Long-haul visitors per resident and real GDP per resident for selected countries, 1998. (*Source:* WTO and US Census Bureau, author's estimates)

### Age cohorts

Figure 1.7 ranks the selected countries by population size and shows the volume of residents by three age cohorts: 19 years of age and under, 20 – 64 years of age and 65 and older. These roughly conform to youth, working age and retired populations, respectively. The cohoris vary widely in absolute size among the nations profiled.

Figure 1.8 more clearly distinguishes the age structures of these populations by proportion, beginning with Italy with less than one-fifth of its population in the youth category, to Venezuela and Mexico, each with more than one-third. Investigations of possible relationships between the age cohorts and intensity of long-haul travel by regression analysis produced no significant relationships for these countries for 1998.

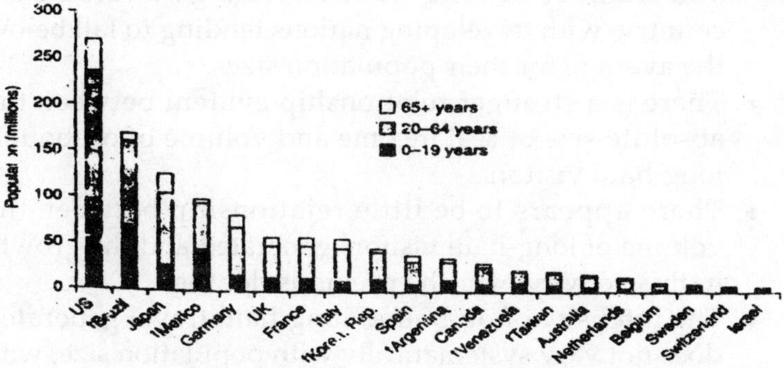


**Figure 1.7:** Age cohorts of resident population of selected countries, 1998: †denotes developing country. (*Source:* US Census Bureau)

## Conclusions on the Present

For 1998, the following conclusions can be drawn regarding outbound long-haul travel for these 20 countries:

- The volume of long-haul outbound visitors varies considerably, with developing nations tending to produce the smallest absolute numbers.

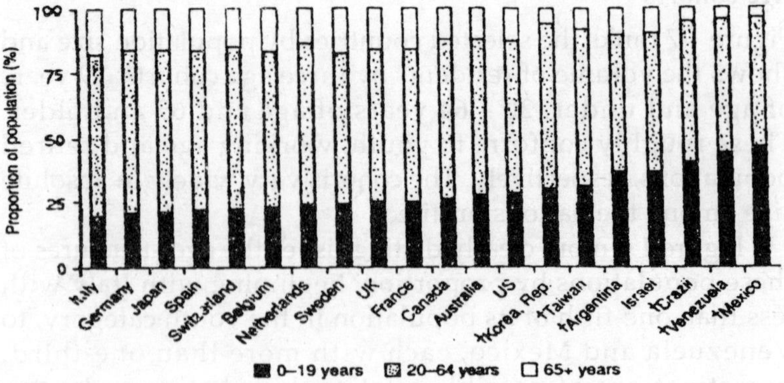


**Figure 1.8:** Resident population of selected countries by age cohort, 1998: †denotes developing country. (*Source:* US Census Bureau)

- There is a moderate relationship between population and number of long-haul visitors generated by a country, with developing nations tending to fall below the average for their population sizes.
- There is a stronger relationship evident between the absolute size of real income and volume of outbound long-haul visitors.
- There appears to be little relationship between the volume of long-haul visitors generated and the growth in this activity over the previous decade.
- The intensity of outbound long-haul travel generated does not vary systematically with population size, with developing countries falling below the averages for their population sizes.
- There is a weak relationship between long-haul travel intensity for the generating countries and real income per resident with developing countries falling below the averages for their per-capita incomes.
- The relative sizes of young, middle and upper age groups vary considerably among the countries with developing countries tending to show the highest proportions for the youngest age cohort.

- There is no discernible relationship between the age structure of a country's population and long-haul travel intensity.

These conclusions relate only to 1998. The next section analyses the changes over the past decade in these magnitudes.

**The Past**

Trends over the past decade can further inform us of the relationships between population and national income on the one hand, and changes in outbound long-haul visitor volumes for the selected countries.

Figures 1.9 shows the growth in outbound long-haul visitors by country for the 1989 – 98 decade. Taiwan is the major outlier, but the developing countries of the Republic of Korea, Argentina and Venezuela also lead the sample with growth rates of 100% or more over this period. Switzerland, Australia, Sweden, Mexico and Canada lag the rest with growth rates below 50%.

There is no statistical relationship between population growth over the past ten years and growth in long-haul travel for these countries (Figure 1.10). Five of the six developing

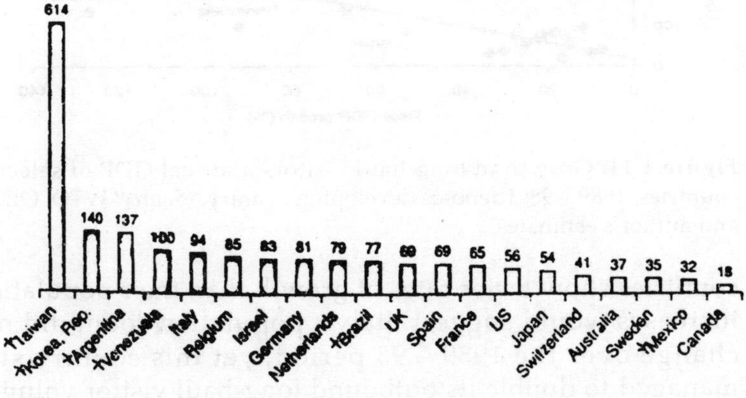


**Figure 1.9:** Long-haul visitor growth (%) for selected countries. 1989 – 98: †denotes developing country. (*Source:* WTO and author's estimates)

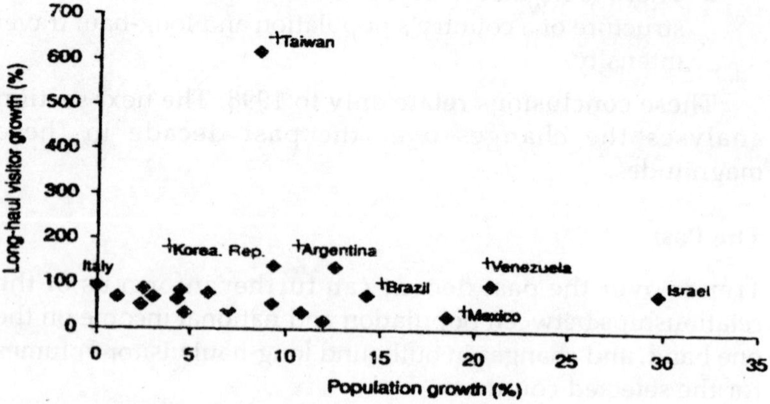


**Figure 1.10:** Growth in long-haul visitors and population of selected countries, 1989 – 98: †denotes developing country. (*Source:* WTO, US Census Bureau, author's estimates)

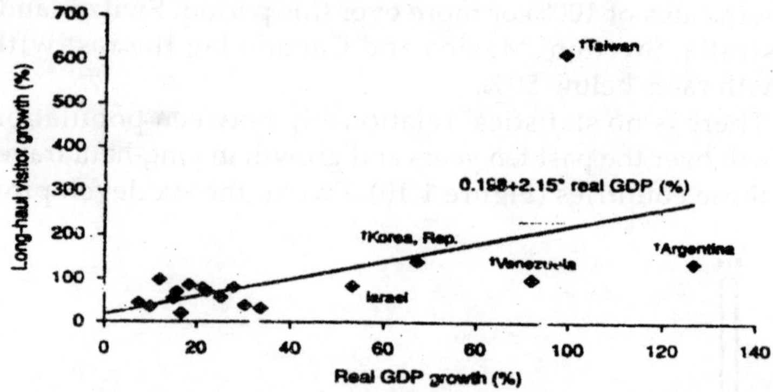


**Figure 1.11:** Growth in long-haul visitors and real GDP of selected countries, 1989 – 98: †denotes developing country. (*Source:* WTO, OECD and author's estimates)

countries show faster rates of growth than their population increases would suggest. Italy's population count did not change over the 1989 – 98 period, yet this country still managed to double its outbound long-haul visitor volume. Clearly, something more than total population growth drove the long-haul travel increases.

Income growth is one of these driving factors. The regression trend line in Figure 1.11 explains about one-third of the variance in long-haul visitor growth over the past decade. Taiwan again dominates, even though its real GDP grew more slowly than Argentina's. Except for Taiwan, the developing countries selected followed the sample in relating long-haul travel growth to rising income.

If Taiwan is removed from the sample, the trend line accounts for nearly one-half of the variance of the 19 countries' long-haul visitor growth, but it also shifts downward to show a more moderate relationship between income growth and long-haul visitors generated (trend line becomes 0.472 + 0.724* real GDP%).

As per capita incomes rise in a country, we could expect the per capita incidence of long-haul travel to rise as well. The population is better off financially, and this should translate into additional spending on luxuries such as long-haul travel. Figures 1.12 indicates this is the case for the countries under analysis here. The regression line slopes upward and explains about one-quarter of the variance in real

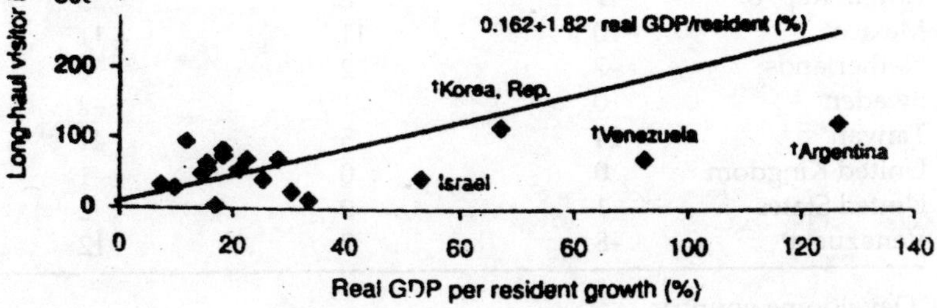


**Figure 1.12:** Growth in long-haul visitor intensity and real GDP per resident, 1989 – 98: †denotes developing country. (*Source:* WTO, OECD and author's estimates)

income per resident growth rates. In this case removing Taiwan does not appreciably increase the regression's explanatory power. Except for Venezuela and Argentina, the developing countries produced long-haul visitor growth equal or exceeding what would be expected from their income growth rates.

Population estimates by age cohort are available for the entire decade for 16 of the countries, as shown in Table 1.2. It is evident that the proportion of the total comprised by the youth cohort has fallen for most countries, and substantially for several of the underdeveloped countries and Japan. On the other hand, the proportion comprised by the retired age cohort has risen significantly for all nations but the United States, Sweden and the United Kingdom show declines.

**Table 1.2**
**Change in incidence of total population of three age cohorts for selected countries, 1989 – 98**

| | *0 – 19 years (%)* | *20 – 64 year (%)* | *65+ years (%)* |
|---|---|---|---|
| Argentina* | –4 | 1 | 11 |
| Australia | –8 | 2 | 12 |
| Belgium | –6 | –1 | 14 |
| Brazil* | –11 | 9 | 25 |
| Canada | –5 | 0 | 13 |
| France | –8 | 1 | 13 |
| Israel | –9 | 6 | 7 |
| Japan | –21 | 2 | 37 |
| Korea, Rep. of* | –17 | 8 | 33 |
| Mexico* | –10 | 11 | 11 |
| Netherlands | –7 | 2 | 6 |
| Sweden | 0 | 1 | –2 |
| Taiwan* | –14 | 5 | 41 |
| United Kingdom | 0 | 0 | –1 |
| United States | –1 | 0 | 2 |
| Venezuela* | –8 | 7 | 12 |

*Developing country.

*Source:* US Bureau of the Census

Investigation of the statistical relationships between the age cohort changes and the intensity of outbound long-haul travel for these 16 countries shows that the retired age group accounts for more than one-third of the variance in long-haul travel intensity changes over the decade. Figure 1.13 indicates the relationships. The developing nations in the sample show about the same sensitivity to the retired cohort's growth as do the rest of the selected countries.

***Conclusions on the past***

The analysis of changes in population, income and outbound long-haul travel over the past decade suggests the following:

- Developing nations tended to lead the growth rates of long-haul travel.

Total population growth does not provide a very satisfactory explanation for this travel growth among the nations studied over the past decade, but developing nations produced greater growth rates in outbound long-haul visitors than their population growth rates would indicate.

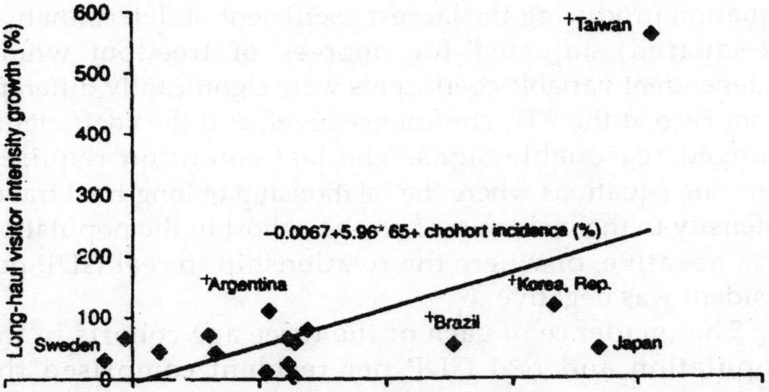


**Figure 1.13:** Change in long-haul visitor intensity and incidence of 65+ age cohort for selected countries, 1989 – 98: †denotes developing country. (*Source:* WTO, US Census Bureau and author's estimates)

- Growth in real national incomes was much more powerful in explaining long-haul visitor growth over the past decade than population growth; developing nations shared this relationship with the industrialised nations in the sample.
- The elasticity of long-haul visitor growth to income growth was about two for both absolute visitors and the intensity of long-haul travel generated by the sample.
- Two of the three age cohorts for which data are available over the past decade show no relationship to the growth in outbound long-haul travel, but the 65 and over age group did demonstrate a significant relationship.

**The Future**

Based on these findings, various regression equations were tested to find the one that best explained the course of outbound long-haul visitors per resident for each country over the 1989 – 98 period. 'Best explained' was defined as the equation producing the largest coefficient of determination (R-squared) adjusted for degrees of freedom where independent variable coefficients were significantly different from zero at the 95% confidence level, and the coefficients showed reasonable signs. The last condition required ignoring equations where the relationship of long-haul travel intensity to the incidence of an age cohort in the population was negative, or where the relationship to real GDP per resident was negative.

The incidence of each of the three age cohorts in the population and real GDP per resident comprised the explanatory variables tested for each country. The impact of the Gulf War was also tested for the 1991 period and was found to be significant (at the 90% confidence level) for eight of the countries. Israel's generation of outbound long-haul travel was found to be significant for 1991 and 1992.

Table 1.3 indicates population changes over the past decade and projected to 2010 for the selected countries.

**Table 1.3**
**Populations and rates of change for selected countries, 1989 – 2010**

| *Generating country* | *2010 forecast (millions)* | *1998 – 10 CARC (%)* | *1989 – 98 CARC (%)* |
|---|---|---|---|
| Argentina* | 42.0 | 1.2 | 1.3 |
| Australia | 20.4 | 0.8 | 1.2 |
| Belgium | 10.1 | –0.1 | 0.3 |
| Brazil* | 191.0 | 1.0 | 1.5 |
| Canada | 34.3 | 0.9 | 1.3 |
| France | 59.7 | 0.1 | 0.5 |
| Germany | 81.0 | –0.1 | 0.5 |
| Israel | 6.7 | 1.4 | 3.0 |
| Italy | 55.3 | –0.2 | 0.0 |
| Japan | 127.1 | 0.1 | 0.3 |
| Korea, Rep. of* | 51.2 | 0.8 | 1.0 |
| Mexico* | 118.8 | 1.6 | 1.9 |
| Netherlands | 16.2 | 0.3 | 0.6 |
| Spain | 39.2 | 0.0 | 0.1 |
| Sweden | 9.1 | 0.2 | 0.5 |
| Switzerland | 7.4 | 0.1 | 0.8 |
| Taiwan* | 24.2 | 0.8 | 0.9 |
| United Kingdom | 60.0 | 0.1 | 0.3 |
| United States | 298.0 | 0.8 | 1.0 |
| Venezuela* | 27.3 | 1.5 | 2.1 |
| Total | 1.279.0 | 0.6% | 0.9% |

CARC = compound annual rate of change.
*Developing country.
*Source:* US bureau of the Census

Compound annual rates of change are employed for this comparison since the two time periods differ in length.

Whereas Italy was alone in posting no increase in population in the past decade, Italy, Belgium, Germany and Spain are projected to show no growth or decline to 2010. Indeed, no country is expected to increase its resident population in the future as fast as it did in 1989 – 98. Even the developing countries will post significantly lower population gains in the next decade or so. Overall, population for the group will grow only two-thirds as fast as it did in the past decade.

Compound annual rates of change (CARC) in outbound long-haul visitors forecast for 1998 to 2010 are shown in Figure 1.14. The developing countries of the Republic of Korea and Taiwan are projected to lead all others in the rate that they generate these outbound trips, with Germany close behind. At the other end of the scale, Switzerland is projected to produce only negligible rises in this outbound travel over the next 12 years.

Table 1.4 summarises the projected growth of outbound long-haul travel for each of the 20 countries selected for this study, alongwith comparisons of growth rates over the ensuing 12 years compared to the historical period. Compound annual rates of change are employed for this comparison since the two time periods differ in length.

For these 20 countries in aggregate, long-haul outbound travel is projected to grow to 2010 only two-thirds as fast as over the 1989 – 98 period. Argentina, Belgium, France, Italy, Sweden, Switzerland, Taiwan, the United States and Venezuela are projected to grow at less than half their previous rates in generating long-haul visitors.

On the other hand, Australia, Canada and Mexico are forecast to grow at a faster pace than in the past, and Germany

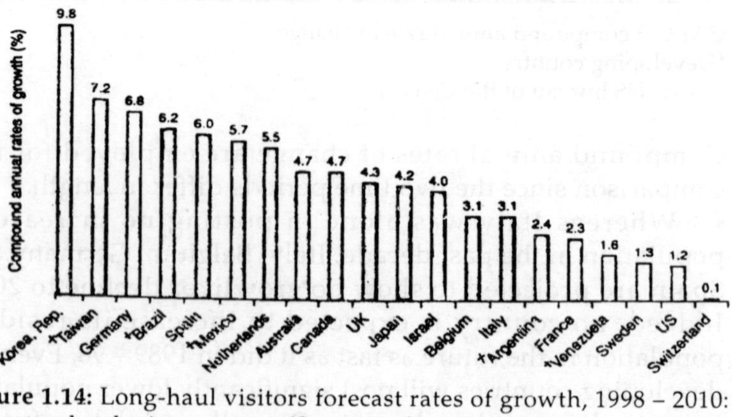


**Figure 1.14:** Long-haul visitors forecast rates of growth, 1998 – 2010: †denotes developing country. (*Source:* author's estimates)

**Table 1.4**
**Long-haul visitors and rates of change for selected countries, 1989 – 2010**

| *Generating country* | *2010 forecast (000)* | *1998 – 2010 CARC (%)* | *1989 – 98 CARC (%)* |
|---|---|---|---|
| Argentina* | 1639 | 2.4 | 10.1 |
| Australia | 5391 | 4.7 | 3.6 |
| Belgium | 1249 | 3.1 | 7.1 |
| Brazil* | 4324 | 6.2 | 6.6 |
| Çanada | 8300 | 4.7 | 1.8 |
| France | 8874 | 2.3 | 5.7 |
| Germany | 16933 | 6.8 | 6.8 |
| Israel | 3229 | 4.0 | 7.0 |
| Italy | 4925 | 3.1 | 7.7 |
| Japan | 20138 | 4.2 | 4.9 |
| Korea, Rep. of* | 2262 | 9.8 | 10.2 |
| Mexico* | 2063 | 5.7 | 3.2 |
| Netherlands | 3923 | 5.5 | 6.7 |
| Spain | 3637 | 6.0 | 6.0 |
| Sweden | 1076 | 1.3 | 3.4 |
| Switzerland | 1500 | 0.1 | 3.9 |
| Taiwan* | 3158 | 7.2 | 24.4 |
| United Kingdom | 18002 | 4.3 | 6.0 |
| United States | 37391 | 1.2 | 5.1 |
| Venezuela* | 814 | 1.6 | 8.0 |
| Total | 148828 | 3.6% | 5.5% |

CARC = compound annual rate of change.
*Developing country.
*Source:* WTO and author

and Spain will maintain their previous rates of outbound long-haul travel growth.

It should be emphasised that these are long-term trend projections based upon the most powerful population and income explanatory variables investigated. The actual long-haul visitor totals may differ from these in 2010 due to the impact of political, economic, socio-cultural and technological variables not considered here.

No correlation was found between the projected rates of outbound long-haul visitor growth to 2010 and total

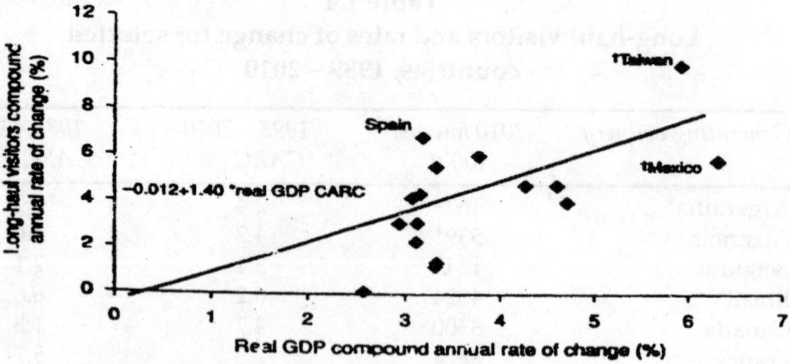


**Figure 1.15:** Forecast growth rates for real GDP and long-haul visitors, 1998 – 2010: †denotes developing country. (*Source:* WEFA Group and author's estimates)

population growth or absolute size of these visitors in 1998 for the 20 countries studied. However, these rates of growth are somewhat related to projected growth in real GDP for these countries, as projected by the WEFA Group. This relationship is presented in Figure 1.15 for the 16 countries for which WEFA provided estimates (missing are the developing countries of Argentina, Brazil, Republic of Korea and Venezuela). The regression line shown accounts for somewhat more than one-third of the variance of the visitor estimates.

**Conclusions on the Future**

This forecasting exercise suggests the following about the future of long-haul visitor generation over the next 12 years:

- The volume of outbound long-haul visitors will continue to grow over the initial decade of the 21st century for all countries, even though populations will increase at slower rates for all countries studied, and decline for a few.
- The rate of long-haul visitor growth will slow for most countries, developing and industrialised alike, to 2010.
- Projected age cohorts and real incomes in some countries, however, are expected to boost rates of

growth in long-haul visitors generated over the next decade from their rates over the past ten years.

- The rates of growth forecast are not related to current long-haul visitor volumes, rates of growth over the past decade, or population projections for the next.

The rates of growth forecast appear to be related to projected growth in real GDP for most countries to 2010.

**Implications**

Other data, such as the US Department of Commerce's In-flight Survey of International Air Travellers, indicate that long-haul travellers are especially lucrative sources of spending for destinations and international transport modes. They tend to stay longer at the destinations they visit than the average visitor, and often spend more per day. Consequently, the following overall conclusions should be of particular interest to destinations and business firms seeking to attract this lucrative market:

- Long-haul travel generated by the Republic of Korea, Taiwan, Germany, Brazil, and Spain will be especially robust in the first decade of the 21st century, offering good prospects for destination and international transportation marketers.
- The United States will remain by far the largest source of such travel, with Japan, the UK and France in the second tier.
- Despite rapid growth rates, developing countries will remain relatively small generating markets for long-haul travel.
- The retired market is a large and growing segment generating long-haul travel.

The author expresses his special thanks to the World Tourism Organisation and the Travel Industry Association of America for providing historical data on international travel essential to this chapter. He also appreciates the generousity of the WEFA Group of Eddystone, PA 19022, USA for providing forecasts of GDP for selected countries.

# 2

# ROLE OF HOSPITALITY IN TOURISM

Experience has taught us that the future is usually not what we would have expected from extrapolating past developments, but rather what we make of it. Jacques de Bourbon-Busset once wrote: 'What we want is not to guess at the probable future, but to prepare one that is desirable and perhaps even to got that bit further and try to make the desirable future the probable one.' To do so, we have to focus on the future, something that seems appropriate at the dawn of a new millennium.

**The Challenges of Our Time**

A backward glance reveals that tourism development has always fluctuated, though since the Second World War this fluctuation has been very slight, with trends pointing steadily upwards. What is more, all forecasts indicate tremendous growth in international tourism.

Numerous, particularly turbulent changes are currently taking place in the immediate and wider context of leisure and travel. Not only has the new consumer gone into top gear, society as a whole has become ever more fragmented. Political boundaries are being abolished to be replaced by others. In contrast, as the result of worldwide globalisation mechanisms, our planet is turning into a 'global village' with a uniform, commercialised culture. And lastly, what was regarded as ecological stability appears to be becoming increasingly unstable. Although we know more and more about our world, travel it extensively, study and investigate it, interrelations are becoming more and more complex and less comprehensible. To put it in a nutshell, we face tremendous challenges.

### *The Challenge of Globalisation*

Dealing with world-wide globalisation trends is new to all of us. Everything is in a state of flux: demand, labour, know-how and capital are all flowing to where the biggest hopes for the future lie, with the resultant standardisation of production technologies, business strategies, marketing plans and management styles. Although tourist production is tied to local conditions, the tourism industry cannot avoid being affected by globalisation. Tourist products, and even whole destinations, are becoming interchangeable; continental and inter-continental transport networks determine the direction and speed of development; distribution channels and/or reservation systems are increasingly a decisive factor in success.

Worldwide excess capacity in all departments of tourism – carriers, accommodation, adventure and leisure parks, sports facilities, cultural events, etc. – is a key driving force in globalisation. Drops in tourism figures in highly differentiated national economies (Austria, Switzerland, Germany, etc.) are largely due to the fact that almost all national economies worldwide have discovered tourism as a development-promoting factor and been drawn into the globalisation maelstrom through the competitive situation.

### *The Challenge of the Changing Climate*

The environmental discussion is hotting up from two sides. On the one hand, many places are already virtually at their ecological limits, and the consequences will become increasingly visible and tangible over the next few years. On the other, the process of environmental awareness is continuing among broad segments of the population. Holidaymakers too are becoming more and more environment conscious, but in an opportunistic fashion: they are particularly sensitive to environmental damage when it threatens to spoil their holiday pleasure.

The consequences of the changing climate are crucial for tourism. Not only the rising snow line or higher sea levels, but also the increasingly capricious weather with a greater tendency towards natural disasters, changes in the permafrost areas, adjustments by flora and fauna as well as the melting glaciers represent major challenges for mountain and coastal regions.

Thus, the dilemma facing tourism is particularly great because tourism, with its high transport energy consumption, generates a large proportion of greenhouse gases (especially $CO_2$) and because the distances travelled are growing longer and longer while stays are becoming progressively shorter.

### *The Challenge of an Ageing Population*

Setting aside the fact that the populations of highly industrialised countries may be considerably influenced by influxes of refugees, the assumption can (or must) be that the population of the industrialised countries is stagnating. On the other hand, the population's demographic composition will change radically. While the proportion of young people will fall drastically in the coming years, the percentage of senior citizens will increase by up to 1% per year. With the contraceptive pill we started an experiment that is unique in human history and whose consequences will leave their mark on the 21st century. There will be fewer and fewer young people and more and more active 'younger senior citizens' with time and money on their hands who will set the tone in the leisure and travel market.

### *The Challenge of Changing Values*

The process of changing values is equally turbulent. It is characterised by a basically hedonist attitude (desire, enjoyment, living out one's dreams) which, however, goes hand in hand with a certain pessimism about the future. The system of shared basic values that makes for social cohesion has now virtually disappeared. Our live-for-the-moment society is characterised not only by individualism but also by many sub-groups with their own value patterns, each of them claiming to represent society. Cultural identity seems to be increasingly reduced to leisure behaviour, and travel with its utopian, ritual and mythical nature is steadily becoming the last common identity area (Thiem, 1994). The so-called 'mega generation' makes itself head loud and clear, and its values are mainly as follows:

- substantial material demands;
- little willingness to do anything special to merit these;
- call for more freedom in all areas of life;
- growing escapism;
- growing unwillingness to take orders from others;
- fewer inhibitions;
- individualisation of the masses.

In mega-generation 'scenes', it is becoming ever more difficult to choose between burn out (exhaustion) and drop out (exclusion). The division between 'the knows' and 'the don't-knows' is obvious. Sings of these behavioural patterns can be detected in the alpine snowboard scene, for instance, or at the beach with Ballermann.

Matthias Horx (1995, p. 43) has detected a mega-trend which could be essential for tourism, namely 'soft individualism'. He describes the basic shift in values of our time as follows:

- the 'economic miracle' phase with the values of fulfilment, duty, discipline, family, loyalty and piety has been replaced by
- the 'ego era' with the values of adventure, performance, desire, 'number one', eros, materialism and fun, which is followed by
- the 'soft individualism' phase with the values of experience, commitment, calm, friendship, honesty, spirituality and responsibility.

Basing one's argument on Horx, it could be said that whenever everything becomes commercialised, materialised, rationalised and technical, people more and more come to long for 'spirituality'.

### *The Challenge of Mobility*

The fact that a growing number of people can drive combined with the individualisation of society is leading to greater motorisation in all Western European countries, despite intensive debates about the ecological aspects. The willingness to be mobile, and hence the need for greater mobility during leisure time, will also continue to increase. For instance, leisure-time mobility in Switzerland rose from approximately 35% in the 1960s to over 50% at the end of the 20th century.

With little probability of major adjustments to transport infrastructure and in view of the poor coordination of school holiday arrangements in Europe, this will involuntarily but inevitably result in even greater traffic problems and in total traffic chaos, particularly when it comes to holiday traffic. Nevertheless, little change in mobility patterns can be expected from the majority of people. Holiday traffic jams have established themselves as part of the vacation ritual. The percentage of people suffering from 'mobility exhaustion' will rise more and more.

### *The Challenge of Mass Leisure*

On the whole, people in employment will have more leisure time, in particular through additional free days and as the result of longer (unpaid) breaks among young people. It appears that in addition to its mass prosperity, mass mobility and mass tourism, a kind of mass leisure is the hallmark of our society.

For more and more people, using their leisure time is becoming a problem. This time is increasingly used for media addiction, further consumption based on the 'shopping, cinema, eating outside' formula, frenzied activity or mobility addiction. Only few people manage to interpret leisure time as social time, culture and education time or 'time really for themselves'. In other words, yesterday's working society runs the risk of becoming tomorrow's mass leisure society with media, consumption, activity and mobility time as its salient features. Leisure time – even during holidays – should be upgraded to social, cultural, educational and personal time.

## Two Contrasting Social Development Patterns

Against the background of the emerging challenges of the 1990s, various social development patterns – on the lines of scenarios – are conceivable. The following remarks describe two opposing pictures of societal development developed as presented in an experts' report submitted to the Swiss Federal Council (BFK, 1991, p. 28 et seq.)

### *The 'Totally Mobile Singles Society'*

The trend towards individualism further intensifies, moving towards a society of people interested solely in their own welfare and 'self-fulfilment'. They are in love with themselves, tolerant in the sense of indifferent, consumption-oriented and live by the motto 'Everything has its price', even social services delegated to the state and private suppliers. Political commitment is confined to 'involvement democracy'.

This 'totally mobile singles society' is not tied to one place, so it relates little to local communities, requires a lot of living space and travels longer and longer distances. A majority of economically competitive people stand over and against a growing minority of less well-trained people, the elderly and disabled who, while they receive financial support, are relegated to the fringes of society. The growing number of people in need of care are 'professionally' looked after. The question of what social expenditure is to be borne by which social groups becomes the main political conflict.

### *The 'Partnership with Commitment'*

The tendency towards 'going it alone' is triggering growing unease, thus reinforcing counter-trends on the lines of upgrading partnerships with commitments. Individuals are increasingly prepared to take on social responsibility. Partnerships on traditional or less conventional lines are gaining an importance. However, in parallel with this collective sense of responsibility, social control and intolerance of 'incorrect' behaviour are also intensifying, for instance in the field of ecology.

The non-material components in quality of life are becoming increasingly significant, and with them the willingness to become involved in social and political issues. On the scale of values that is emerging, political and social services constitute an essential part of a person's 'life's work'. Both sexes are moving towards a holistic approach to life in which professional and social work complement each other. This strong link to residential environment and neighbourhood encourages new forms of ownership promotion, with a decrease in mobility and a shift to public transport. The immediate residential area becomes the main point of reference, both politically and socially, encouraging the development of small networks spanning the generations and the related social services.

## Changing Travel Habits

Upheavals in the immediate and less immediate environment of leisure-conscious persons also affect their travel and holiday habits. Horst W. Opaschowski (1995, p. 22) described the holiday of the future as follows:

- Attractive natural setting and clean landscapes are automatically expected.
- People will continue to seek sun, beaches and the sea.
- Artificial holiday paradises will become tomorrow's standard holiday venues.
- Holiday hopping ('here today – there tomorrow') will spread.
- Vacations will become the ultimate adventure.
- The holiday world of the future must be as exotic as possible.
- More and more young families will discover indoor luxury bathing complexes.
- Culture and study trips will develop into a stable market segment.
- Holiday clubs will lose their attraction as something out of the ordinary.

This description of the tourism of the future highlights the fact that some conflicts are bound to become more acute, in particular:

- growing pressure on the remaining nature reserves;
- the distances travelled are becoming longer and longer, consuming more and more energy, with serious consequences;
- the growing risk that holiday destinations will be downgraded to the fast-food articles of the throw-away society;
- the continuing trend towards 'exoticism' with its cultural and health risks for travellers and host populations.

The ongoing long-haul travel boom was summed up in figures in a Delphi study entitled 'Fernreisen 2005' conducted in Germany, Austria and Switzerland. At approximately 5% the annual growth rates for long-haul tourism are far higher than those for domestic tourism (0.5 – 1%)

In addition to these changes in respect of future holiday models, there are also signs of changes in booking and travel habits:

- *Trend towards adventure-oriented holiday behaviour* – seeking a more intensive leisure experience.
- *Trend towards going it alone* – seeking even more independent holidays in line with personal ideas, with a preference for more flexible holiday products.
- *Trend towards more sophisticated travel products* – seeking trips that offer culture and education, as well as variety; both passive recreation and hyperactive sport are 'out'.
- *Trend towards more wellness during holidays* – seeking forms of travel that offer overwrought modern man holistic relaxation, with a healthy diet, gentle exercise, beauty and body care and a wide variety of therapies as the keywords.
- *Trend towards 'second homes'*– seeking cosy holiday accommodation as home-like refuges with a high degree of comfort.

- *Trend towards sunny travel destinations* – seeking holiday destinations with guaranteed sunshine – above all during cold, wet winters.
- *Trend towards cheaper travel* – seeking (cheap) products that represent value for money: holidays at rock-bottom prices and growing market transparency thanks to the Worldwide Web encourage this tendency.
- *Trend towards more frequent, shorter trips* – seeking products that offer occasional variety.
- *Trend towards spontaneous travel decisions* – seeking offers that can be booked at the last minute (or even at the last second) and which are not only cheap but also comprise an element of surprise.
- *Trend towards more mobile travel patterns* – seeking products with frequent changes of location, with travelling as the major attraction.

This spotlight-like future analysis leaves considerable scope for interpretation about the future openings for tourism. Making the most of these trends calls for visionary innovation, targeted cooperation, clear marketing strategies and careful nurture of existing core attractions.

## New Lines of Thrust in Tourism Development

Trends point to changes and determine the future. In order to prepare a desirable future, we should not only analyse trends but also find a joint approach. That is why I should like to conclude with a few requirements to serve as guidelines for tourism professionals and policy designers in making the desirable future the probable one.

### *Tourism must become more Efficient*

Although tourism has achieved a high degree of development in our part of the world, structures in many destinations are still inefficient. Desperate efforts are made to create profiles for far too many brands in order to survive in a keenly competitive environment. In so doing, people overlook the fact that guests are not very interested in structures, which have grown up over the years. What they are looking for is a comprehensive, well coordinated service package. Consequently, joint regional and interest-focused tourism ventures or even mergers should be encouraged. Individual places and tourism associations should be persuaded to combine as destinations proper in the sense of strategic business areas.

***Tourism must Improve its Quality***

People have long been talking about developing quality in tourism. What is required, however, is the implementation of comprehensive quality management at operational and destination level. For today's increasingly demanding guests, it is important for the quality of the total local package to be coordinated. The Total Quality Management (TQM), guest satisfaction, employee expectations, the outcome for the environment and society as well as economic success are the focus of efforts, calling for intelligent process control and a high standard of leadership.

***Tourism must become more Environmentally Aware***

The sources of ecological danger in tourism development have long been identified, so all that remains is to take them seriously and undertake preventive action so as to side-step environmental problems. The aids developed in recent years such as environmental compatibility reports, environment management systems, environmental audits or environment officers should be used to disclose conflicts and seek sustainable solutions. The discrepancy between knowledge and action should be constantly reduced.

***Tourism must Allow Greater Participation***

In tourism, there are not only 'winners' but also many people negatively affected by external effects. In highly developed tourism areas, a kind of 'tourism weariness' is spreading, with people talking of inadequate tourism awareness. To prevent the resultant defensive attitudes, those affected must be given an active role. This presupposes greater participation in tourism development, particularly at destination – but also at operational level.

*Tourism Needs to be Slowed Down*

Tourism requires mobility. 'The more transport is available, the more tourism there will be' was – and still is – the branch motto. But in time, transport has become a key problem, undermining the attractiveness of tourism. Tourism's own threat to itself has taken on a new dimension. However, there is only one key to the mobility issue – namely deceleration – because in the long-term, speed is the only variable in the mobility system. If there were speed limits like 400 km/h for planes, 200 km/h for trains, 100km/h for cars, 30km/h in built-up areas and in holiday resorts, areas where pedestrians can stroll around, the $CO_2$ goals could be easily reached.

*Tourism must be made more Authentic*

For many years, many tourism destinations were famous for their situational pioneering; unique natural and cultural characteristics were skilfully turned to best advantage. But these 'organic' values are increasingly being cast overboard. Under pressure from globalisation, products are becoming standardised and unique characteristics levelled out. In the new century, potential guests will be on the lookout for the natural, organic, unmistakable and authentic.

*Tourism must become more Human*

Pressure to make profits and competitive outlooks have left their mark on many of us. Supported by methods such as lean management or re-engineering, many people have become hard-hearted, strategy-conscious tourism professionals focused on rational action. However, sustainable tourism development is based on human qualities such as emotions, empathy, cordiality or intuition. In a branch that attaches maximum importance to emotional values, human warmth and situational empathy, such qualities should be encouraged and nurtured more.

If visionary design skills are combined with sensitive responsibility, tourism can look forward to a hopeful future in this new century.

# 3

# ROLE OF LEISURE TIME IN TOURISM

## Introduction: Post-industrial Society

Seeing the title of this chapter, some of you may remember seminars back in the 1970s that looked forward to an age of leisure for all, supported by information technology and robotics. As we all know it has not worked out like that. Here, I shall try, based on some recent work for the World Tourism Organisation (WTO), to outline what is happening to leisure time, why, how it affects tourism and finally take a look at prospects for the future.

Post-industrial society was first discussed in the United States in the 1950s. The golden age of postwar prosperity inspired the hope that a good life for all could be built, in a great society, which would abolish poverty, and be increasingly egalitarian. (Patterson, 1998). That dream now seems remote, and the phrase has subsequently been used more modestly to suggest that we have become a post-industrial society simply in the sense that, in the case of Britain, less than one-sixth of employees still earn their living in manual jobs (Roberts, 1999). Balancing that decline has been the dramatic rise in professional and managerial employment, which, in the case of the United States, is now 60% of the workforce.

Underlying these radical changes in employment, which have been accompanied by rising levels of education and income, the Harvard economist Juliet Schor identifies the emergence of 'post materialists' who are less concerned with getting and spending, and more interested in quality of life and leisure. Perhaps, in these workaholic times, some of them have in mind Oscar Wilde's comment that work is the refuge of those with nothing better to do.

**Background**

Be that as it may, in tourism we have generally assumed that as incomes rise people will increasingly buy experiences, such as travel, rather than goods and that the leisure time available to do this is increasing. But is it?

To find out WTO commissioned us to study the prospects for leisure time. WTO noted that in recent years the attention of governments and industry around the world has been on responding to globalisation by improving competitiveness, rather than on improving the conditions of employment, such as paid holiday entitlements. The WTO wanted to know whether as a result the growth in leisure time has been cancelled or at least deferred and if so how the industry should respond. To answer those questions we gathered information on leisure time and tourism in 18 of the world's most important tourism-generating countries. Those countries are – Americas: Brazil, Canada and the United States; Asia Pacific: Australia, China, Japan, Korean Republic, Malaysia, Singapore; Europe and Africa: Austria, France, Germany, Italy. Netherlands, Sweden, Switzerland, UK and South Africa. They include today's leading tourism generators – Western Europe, America and Japan – and some major generating countries of the future and represent about three-quarters of world tourism spend.

In most of these countries leisure time is shaped by laws defining working hours, public holidays and paid holidays and often, within that framework, by agreements between employers and employees. But globalisation is creating new pressures on leisure time, particularly through reduced staffing levels, the intensification of work and more flexible working practices. To explore the implications for tourism we consulted governments, the travel industry, employers's organisations, trade unions and a number of international bodies.

The tourism growth of the past 40 years reflected rising incomes, cheaper travel and increasing leisure time. The working week became shorter. Holiday entitlements grew. Working life tended to start later and finish earlier. But in recent years for many people reductions in working time slowed or reversed. The world economy has become fiercely competitive and employment less secure. The working hours, particularly of many full-time, skilled employees, have risen.

**Youth Tourism**

But what about the years before we face the challenges of working life? The leisure of the more fortunate young in prosperous countries is constrained by limited income rather than time. Twenty per cent of travellers are students. Many take the opportunity to travel before or after as well as during their years at university. They may well see travel as a necessary preparation for a high-flying career. Once embarked on their careers the changing pattern of employment, with less emphasis on lifetime careers, encourages them to take further breaks between periods of work. There are also indications that the young are determined to achieve a better balance between work and leisure than their parents do.

On the other hand, young people are entering a much more competitive employment market, and are often in debt at the end of their studies. So they are likely to take earning a living more seriously than earlier generations. In addition they are told they must maintain their employability and begin saving immediately for a long retirement.

Despite this, the youth travel market is buoyant, well developed in terms of products and targeted marketing, and will grow in the years ahead, mainly because of the rising proportion of young people entering tertiary education.

**The Years of Employment**

Once people enter employment, their leisure comes as either paid leave, public holidays or weekends. These vary around the world but countries fall into three broad categories. Those with paid holidays as a legal entitlement include all Western European countries. Among countries where paid holiday depends on individual employment contracts, with no statutory rights, the United States is the most important, possibly the only country in this category. Countries with strong traditions of public holidays but where legal entitlement to paid holiday is relatively new include many Asian Pacific countries. So holiday taking during working life differs widely. Let us look at the position in some of the 18 countries.

**The United States of America**

The United States is the world's largest economy but paid annual leave is typically some 10 days American productivity has tripled since the 1950s but Americans have largely taken this in pay rather than more free time. In a long hours culture it is difficult to trade income for more leisure and a dramatically increased standard of living has been bought at the cost of a very demanding lifestyle.

Over a 20-year period there has been a reduction in leisure time of 140 hours per year for the average employee. Many opinion surveys suggest that some Americans would sacrifice an element of income if they could have more leisure. The countervailing factor is the commercial pressure on employers to minimise employee numbers and all related costs, including employment related taxes, and holiday and pension benefits.

Juliet Schor argues that there is a failure in the employment market, which creates a structural bias towards spending and against free time. An alternative equilibrium is blocked off by the large career sacrifices an individual must make to get shorter hours. In addition she argues that many Americans are more concerned to purchase goods than experience (Schor, 1998).

These factors, together with a rigorously liberal economic policy and the weakness of trade unions, help explain why American leisure time lags behind European. Nevertheless, in response to the pressure for more leisure time some employers enable employees to work extra hours above the normal schedule to build up an occasional three-day weekend. Others make no distinction between sick leave and vacation, giving employees an overall total to use as they wish.

Yet even taking 2 weeks leave together may be seen as lacking commitment and research by Hilton showed that one-third of Americans took only 50 per cent or less of their vacation. Despite continuing debate on the need for a better work-leisure balance it seems likely that the American travel industry will continue to offer tourism products to meet the needs of a time pressed market, which takes multiple short trips with high daily spend. Until retirement, lack of time will continue to bolster the enormous domestic tourism market and inhibit overseas travel. However, incentive trips, the ultimate reward in a time-squeezed culture, will surely continue to flourish.

**Japan and the Asian Tigers**

In Japan, the world's second largest economy, average statutory holiday entitlement is 17 days: 9.5 days are taken. A regular two-day weekend is still only enjoyed by some 50% of employees. The 14 public holidays continue to be the central focus of Japanese leisure, recently reinforced by reallocating two of them to create two more Happy Mondays – three-day weekends.

At present recession and job insecurity have led to gloom and in the words of the Japan Travel Bureau, a general disinclination to travel abroad. Nevertheless a view is emerging, championed by the Japanese Association of Travel Agents that, in the longer term, a more relaxed attitude towards taking holidays must be encouraged, perhaps by new legislation, to ensure that employees take their holiday entitlements. But rising unemployment and anxiety about pensions make any increase in spending on leisure travel unlikely until economic conditions improve.

Before the 1998 crash, the Korean Republic, Singapore and Malaysia were building up strong outbound markets, albeit on the basis of limited holiday entitlements. That growth received a substantial setback and recovery is likely to be slow.

**Western Europe**

Western Europeans enjoy some 24 days annual paid leave, generous public holidays and a five-day working week. The EU Working Time Directive 1993 gives all employees a minimum of 4 weeks paid holiday and Europeans are, of course, the world's biggest outbound market.

But there is another side to the European position. The chairman of Lufthansa has commented that it cannot be right for employees to have some 8 weeks holiday, more than anywhere else in the world. There is anxiety about the international competitiveness of an economy that supports such generous employment related benefits.

In Europe – as in America – work pressure and job insecurity, which make people reluctant to be away from work too long, encourage shorter breaks. The new statutory holiday rights in the EU cannot be exchanged for money. But, as in America, some employers are now offering flexible employee benefits. So, above the statutory minimum, individuals may have to choose between, for example, more holiday or an enhanced pension contribution or childcare vouchers. The demands of work can be so intense that people simply opt not take their leave. In the Netherlands, in response to this, employees have won a right to sell some holiday back to their employers.

In the United Kingdom, 25 per cent of employees do not take their full holiday. The main reason given is pressure of work. The Institute of Personnel Development recent report *Living to Work?* highlighted the health and family life consequences of the excessive hours worked by many management employees.

Today European trade unions rather than seeking more paid holiday want more family-friendly working hours to ease the strains on family life and make flexible working a two-way street. They are also interested in sabbaticals, as a means of bringing more reality to the idea of lifelong learning. So future discussions on leisure time are likely to be very broadly based and to reflect some of the changes in the relationship between work and leisure.

Only in France, with the introduction of the 35-hour week, is an attempt being made to reduce working hours. The objective is to create more jobs but it is not clear whether this will be achieved. The scheme is strongly opposed by French employers. Nevertheless it is being used to increase flexibility by annualising working time and therefore will often result in extra days off rather than simply shorter hours each week. We should watch the new French policy closely. If it does succeed, further raising France's high levels of productivity and increasing leisure time, as well as creating some employment, it will certainly influence policy elsewhere.

**Paid Leave and Public Holidays**

Table 3.1 summarizes paid leave and public holidays in all 18 countries. The Japanese and Americans have significantly less holidays available than Europeans.

**Retirement**

For the retired, leisure time is abundant. The better off retired have become the key tourism growth market. All 18 countries have an increasing proportion of people over 60 years old and in many they are retiring earlier, fitter and with wide leisure interests. But whilst this market will go on growing and is largely free of time constraints there are some clouds on the horizon.

Governments are reducing pensions, raising the retirement age, requiring increased pension contributions and encouraging people to save more towards their retirement. The American Commission on Retirement Policy has proposed raising the retirement age from 65 to 71. Last year the British National Association of Pension Funds suggested that the

**Table 3.1**
**Paid leave and public holiday entitlement in 18 selected countries**

| | *Paid leave* | *Public holidays* |
|---|---|---|
| Austria | 30 | 13 |
| Italy | 30 | 12 |
| Korean Republic | 22 | 18 |
| Sweden | 25 | 11 |
| France | 22 | 11 |
| Germany | 24 | 11 |
| Brazil | 24 | 10 |
| Netherlands | 25 | 8 |
| Japan | 17 | 14 |
| UK | 23 | 8 |
| Australia | 20 | 8 |
| Switzerland | 20 | 8 |
| South Africa | 14 | 12 |
| Canada | 15 | 11 |
| Korean Republic (actual) | 7 | 18 |
| Malaysia | 12 | 13 |
| Japan (actual) | 10 | 14 |
| Singapore | 10 | 11 |
| United States | 10 | 9 |
| China | 10 | 7 |

retirement age for state pensions in Europe should be 70. Similar changes are happening elsewhere. They will take effect slowly but are already influencing behaviour, as younger age groups, for example Baby Boomers, begin to save more for their old age. In Singapore, the retirement age is also being raised and the important point is made that this will be good for tourism because older people way have less time but will have more money to spend on travel.

## The Prospects of Leisure

So, competition in the world economy is putting a brake on increases in leisure time. Employees are more worried about security of employment and income than long holidays. Increasing life expectancy and control of public expenditure are leading governments to reduce and defer pensions, making the retired ever more value conscious. What then are the prospects for leisure time?

Globalisation seems set to continue. Economic policies around the world are increasingly liberal, including policies within the European Union, where the social market approach has enshrined high levels of leisure time in statutory rights. In these circumstances governments will go on sharpening economic performance. Businesses will continue to minimise employee numbers and all benefit costs. The pressure on employees' time, especially the time of more senior staff will continue. These employees are not normally paid overtime and are usually outside the protection of working hours legislation. Their leisure time can be squeezed at no cost to their employer. How are these pressures reflected in lifestyles?

In the UK the number of non-working hours in a week has reduced substantially over a four-year period – by 100 hours a year. Yet there are increasing demands on that reduced leisure time. The rise in the number of women working and in the number of families dependent on dual incomes greatly reduces family leisure time. It also complicates holiday planning. Husband and wife must co-ordinate their holidays and for parents school holidays are a further complication. Increasingly, flexible working hours, including the substantial rise in those working at weekends, are changing the rhythm of leisure time. The working and leisure time of individuals through the week and through the year is increasingly variable, more fragmented, less predictable. Working hours are being annualised to fit work peaks and troughs more closely. More people are employed on fixed term contracts and simply take time off between work commitments.

**Time for Holidays?**

What do these changes in leisure time mean for tourism? Overall, the response is a move towards shorter, more frequent and more intensive holidays, spread more evenly through the year. Shorter because people cannot or do not wish to be away from work too long. More frequent because holidays are needed to get away from it all and to recover. More intensive because the more their leisure time is squeezed the more people value it and the more they want to get out of it. In addition, many have more to spend. So there are lots of opportunities. Demand is more constant, less peaked. Higher-spend, shorter-stay visitors means a better return on investment.

But there are also challenges for tourism. Holidays need a lot of time so the time squeeze strengthens competition from in the home and near to home attractions. The leisure windows in consumers' lives are targeted from every angle.

**The Blurring of Leisure Boundaries**

There is a blurring of leisure boundaries while leisure options continue to expand. This widening range of leisure time activities – increasingly active, stimulating and varied – is interlinked. There is a boom in fitness centres and fitness enthusiasts are prime prospects for activity holidays. Cultural interests developed at home stimulate the market for an ever-widening range of cultural tourism products.

There are many opportunities to develop relationship marketing by analysing clients' holiday purchases and then presenting them with tempting future holidays. Products can be offered which reinforce travel as an essential element of their personal lifestyle – for which time must be found.

Strengthening the motivation for tourism is important because people feel short of time many are already well travelled, and because leisure industry investors in the tourism-generating countries are creating a wide range of leisure facilities near to home. Examples include the many new combinations of shopping complexes with other leisure facilities and theme parks close to conurbations. These add to the range of day trip possibilities, offer lots of enjoyment and encourage a high spend in a short time. Then there are the substitutes for international travel – like Center Parcs in Europe and the safari park – Animal Kingdom – in Florida, based on Serengeti. So much more convenient, so much less time-consuming and, it may be argued, ecologically preferable to forcing tourists onto possibly reluctant local communities.

**Segmenting the Holiday Market**

In a market increasingly segmented by time as well as money we have the time-poor, money-rich interested in a wide range of shorter breaks – upmarket cultural packages, being pampered, the exotic, the fashionable. Their time is more valuable to them than their money. They expect excellent products, which can be tailored to tight schedules and will maximise the value of their precious leisure time.

The money – and time-rich, open to enjoying several holidays each year, also have many home-based interests competing for their time.

Then there are those with less money who seek a wide range of affordable holidays. Many also have work pressures and take opportunities to get away when those pressures permit.

Finally, those free of time constraints, but with limited income, will be interested in extended but inexpensive trips.

Behind this analysis, in addition to changes in leisure time, the other factor accelerating the segmentation of the market is the increasing polarisation of incomes, those with the highest income often having the least time.

**Travel Hassles**

The squeeze on leisure time adds to the importance of efficient services for selecting and purchasing holidays on ever-shorter lead times. This presents many opportunities for creative marketing, including modular packages and e-commerce, tailoring products to individual requirements.

The time squeeze adds to the value placed upon hassle-free, efficient journeys. There are many opportunities here for nearby destinations, exploiting same country, region, or time zone advantages. The time-pressed do not want avoidable jet lag, slow ground services or accommodation with poor communications links. Many are never truly off duty. Even on holiday they must keep in touch with work, reachable and ready for action.

For governments it will be important to facilitate travel (for example, visa complications do not attract the time-pressed) and to respond to the premium on time efficiency by improving transport, in particular the quality of airport and related surface infrastructure. This is a challenge indeed, particularly in the United States, Europe and Japan.

**Conclusions**

In contrast to the leisure oriented society so widely forecast we find a leisure squeeze for many, arising from work pressure and changes in family structures and lifestyle. At the same time there are debates in the United States, Europe and Japan on the economic issues involved in improving the balance between work and leisure and growing recognition that high standards of living are not necessarily accompanied by a high quality of life.

Better information is certainly needed about what is happening to leisure at a time of rapid economic change. Happily Eurostat has recently settled a blueprint for time use surveys which will provide much better information on holiday nights spent away from home in the European Union countries. There are plans for similar work by the Federal Government in America.

Looking to the future, the prospects for leisure time depend on whether strongly deregulatory economic policies continue to dominate the global economy as we move into the new century or are challenged. Such a challenge might come from Western Europe where there is scepticism about whether economic growth measured in terms of GDP, especially when accompanied by congestion, pollution and the postponement of leisure is an accurate measure of the growth of welfare and an improved quality of life.

Certainly the European Union seems to be searching for a model of social and economic development which combines economic dynamism with a humane working time regime.

The World Trade Organisation's embarrassment at Seattle suggests that there is now wide recognition of the need for globalisation to have a human face and, in the words of the United Nation's Human Development Report of 1999, to be seen to improve the quality of life.

Looking to the future, the leisure industries should participate in these broader debates, focusing particularly on how to ensure that economic growth, as well as raising incomes also enables people to achieve a sensible balance between work and leisure. Meanwhile, the more immediate challenge is to meet the needs of markets, which are increasingly segmented by available time as well as by income.

# 4

# RESEARCH IN TOURISM

## Introduction

This chapter sets out to review 20th century tourism research and theories and to consider their relevance, including new directions, for the tourism industry in the 21st century. The chapter is mostly concerned with the latter, directions for the future, and it comes in the form of five observations about tourism research, together with a series of lessons for research doers, or *producers*, and research users, or *consumers*, which correspond with these five observations. But before these observations and lessons for the 21st century, I provide a brief overview of the growth of research in tourism.

The following data are taken largely from the work of Professor Chuck Goeldner, the well-known and respected editor-in-chief of *Journal of Travel Research (JTR)*. In a keynote paper presented in late 1999 at an international tourism conference in Hong Kong, Goeldner (1999) gave the following as indicators of the explosion of tourism research since the early 1960s.

The first scholarly research journal in tourism was *The Tourist Review*, the official publication of the Association International d'Experts Scientifiques du Tourisme (AIEST), in its 55th year of publication by the year 2000. This was followed by *JTR*, which commenced publication in 1972, and was joined by *Annals of Tourism Research*, which started publication in 1973. The next several years saw just a handful of other new research journals in tourism. The explosion in new tourism research journals came in the late 1980s and in the 1990s, coinciding with the growth of tourism courses and academics teaching and researching in tourism at universities. In 1999, there were some 50 refereed journals being published globally which focused on hospitality, tourism and leisure research. If we assume an average of four issues per journal per year, this represents some 200 journal issues. Of course, additional studies with a tourism focus are also published in the research journals of disciplines such as marketing, consumer behaviour, economics, psychology, sociology, anthropology, geography and transportation studies.

Then there are the tourism research conferences. As Goeldner (1999) points out, there are several international and national research conferences held around the world every year, as well as tourism 'sessions' run at disciplinary conferences such as geography, sociology and marketing. The proceedings of these conferences, together with the publications of university and other research centres, government departments and now web-sites make up the so-called grey literature of tourism research, which is probably even more vast than the published research literature.

An annotated bibliography of tourism research was published in the mid 1960s, and was 371 pages long (Goeldner, 1999: 34). Even if it were possible to produce a bibliography of all the tourism research now being published, the sheer diversity of studies suggests that no one individual could possibly have the expertise to conduct a fair and objective critical evaluation. Consider, for example, the kinds of knowledge required to analyse research on tourism forecasting, consumer behaviour, cost-benefit analyses, advertising images and environmental impacts of tourism.

Eight years ago, Professor Jafar Jafari, the editor-in-chief of the international journal *Annals of Tourism Research,* set out to document the state of tourism research and scholarship with a colleague (Graburn and Jafari, 1991). However, he very wisely recognised that a comprehensive and critical review of all tourism research was beyond the scope of any single human being, indeed, even beyond the capacities of the long-term editor of a very prestigious journal in the early 1990s when there were far fewer academics active in tourism research.

What Jafari did is produce a special issue of *Annals* in which he invited 20 eminent scholars to review the research in their respective disciplines, identify the best tourism research in their discipline and critically evaluate their contribution. Anyone who is serious about gaining even a basic awareness of the scope of research and its contribution to our understanding of tourism phenomena should read Graburn and Jafari's introductory paper and the ten papers in that issue of *Annals* (Vol. 18, No. 1) as well as the 25th anniversary issue of *Annals* (Vol. 27, No. 1), in which a number of authors endeavour to provide a status report on tourism research to 2000.

Both Goeldner and Graburn and Jafari offer valuable insights into how tourism research has matured, and what direction tourism research might take in the next few years. In this chapter I address one issue that I believe has been largely neglected: the gap that still exists between tourism research producers and research consumers. I believe this gap has widened in recent years due to the trends I have just outlined. The number of specialist tourism research publications, specialist tourism research conferences, and the vast number of academics who now work in university departments of tourism, has led to a great reduction in cross-fertilisation both with academics in other disciplines and with industry. The 'new' generation of tourism academics is much more likely to have an undergraduate and postgraduate tourism qualification, rather than grounding in another discipline. They are less likely to have an industry background or work experience in the tourism industry, and are therefore less comfortable with interacting with those in the 'real world' of tourism.

I present my analysis of this gap between tourism research producers and tourism consumers as a series of observations, together with what I believe are some salient lessons for each of the 'research partners'. I believe partnership is the essence of what is needed in order to enhance tourism research in the 21st century. I know this view is shared by many of my research colleagues. To advance tourism research in the 21st century, research consumers and research producers need to make more of an effort *to dance together.* And just as dancing partners must move in response in one another's rhythm, so must research partners respond to the reality of each other's tendencies. As my observations will indicate, research producers and research consumers need to make an effort to dance together, and this includes learning each other's favourite music and steps.

**Observation 1**

*Tourism research has exploded globally, and this growth of qualified researchers and research centres focused on tourism has increased the psychological and even physical distance between research producers and research consumers.*

Why? Tourism research is no longer atheoretical (Jafari, 1990), but with theory and academic legitimacy comes a price: alienation by industry. There are now regular tourism research conferences, which are attended largely by academic staff and students, while those in the tourism industry attend separate conferences, with very few academics in attendance. The volume and sophistication of research publications means that people in industry find it increasingly difficult to keep apace with research methods and findings.

Then there are the government and business persons who believe that theoretical ideas are just 'excess baggage' (Lynch and Brown, 1999: 74), of little value to the practical realities of tourism management.

The reactions of my research colleagues and peers, those who do research, to the explosion of tourism research output is to narrow their focus and lay claim to an area of specialisation in which they feel confident to undertake and critically evaluate research. Unfortunately, in many cases this has tended to result in a distancing from the real and increasingly complex realities of the tourism industry. Like their counterparts in industry and government, researchers fear the unknown, and unless forced to do so, will often stay within their comfort zone of the ivory tower and specialist tourism research conferences and events.

*Lessons for Research Consumers*

- Respect tourism research for what it is – a field of specialisation every bit as complex as managing a hotel or a major international event – and appreciate the fact that there is good research and there is poor research, just as there are tourist facilities and attractions and events that are managed well and there are those that are managed badly.
- Respect the fact that there are specialisations in tourism research – just as a tour operator is not in a position to judge how well a particular hotel is being managed an individual researcher with expertise in the environmental impacts of tourism may not be able to evaluate the reliability of forecasts of visitation in the next century.
- Respect does not mean 'avoid' – stretch your comfort zone, talk to tourism researchers, find out what they do, invite them to your parties, dance with them!
- Be open to what research may have to offer and be willing to change as a result of it.

*Lessons for Research Producers*

- Respect your professional colleagues in industry, and let them know when you think they are doing a good job, and why; support industry award schemes.
- Learn their language and read industry publications; talk about your research in ways that relate to their immediate work environments.
- Respect does not mean 'avoid – stretch your comfort zone, talk to people in industry, invite them to classes and university events, participate in industry events,

give them opportunities to get involved in joint research activities; dance with them!
- Believe in the practical benefits of theoretically informed research and work at demonstrating these benefits to industry players.

**Observation 2**

*Despite the growth in research output, tourism research consumers still feel that research is not meeting their needs.*

Why? The major obstacle lying between them is the difference in the reward systems within which they work. Private industry relies on indicators of profit and growth, and in both the private and public sectors job security depends on quality service to key constituencies or customers. For academics, job security depends on research output, usually in the form of refereed publications. 'Research publications are the path to travel, financial rewards, promotion, prestige and job offers. These are powerful incentives to produce quality research' (Goeldner, 1999: 41). Increasingly, however, there is recognition and reward for applied research than provides benefits to industry, and where these reward systems exist, there are researchers willing and able to do industry-relevant research.

Another difference between the two parties is the timelines within which they work. Research grants often have application-and-decision lead times of several months, and the final output from research projects may take years. Governments and industry work on different financial years, and accountability for research funds may require answers to research questions and research publications within very short timelines and usually less than a year.

***Lessons for Research Consumers***

- Find out what expertise and resources providers have (e.g. qualified and student researcher time and enthusiasm, computer hardware/software, communication and publication outlets) and target those that have what you need.

- Partner with research providers and communicate often and regularly what your research needs are (e.g. lists of potential student projects; short-term and long-term research priorities).
- Actively seek opportunities to serve on university advisory boards related to your research needs. Tell these people that you want to be involved. They will welcome you with open arms, and they will ask for your financial support to conduct research for you. But with that support comes control, including control over the questions the research addresses and control over your publication needs. Dance not only with researchers, but also with university administrators, deputy-vice chancellors and university presidents.
- Build short-term research outputs into projects in order to meet your needs, but do not hamstring researchers by ignoring or rejecting their need also to publish in academic journals in the longer-term. They must do that regularly or you won't have them around for very long.

*Lessons for Research Producers*

- Provide information about your expertise and capacity (including student researcher capacity) in various and accessible forms (e.g. web-sites) and keep your communications up-to-date.
- Consolidate by collaborating with other research providers and select areas of specialisation in order to eliminate duplication within and between universities. Make use of expertise and resources in non-tourism departments such as economics, business/management, cultural and environmental studies, etc. – in other words, dance not only with industry, but also with colleagues in other departments and at other universities!
- Select industry partners who can benefit from your particular areas of expertise and who can provide in-kind support.

- Build in short- and long-term research outcomes that allow for student participation and that meet the immediate needs of industry, while facilitating your long-term research goals.
- Actively and aggressively seek feedback from industry about the use and relevance of your research and learn from it.
- Give industry partners some control in exchange for their support. Engage them not only in funding, but conceptualisation and evaluation of your research. Their control will improve your research, not hinder it.

**Observation 3**

*The rapid growth in tourism researchers and publication outlets may lead to excess quantity and a compromise in quality, which has the potential to widen the gap between research producers and consumers.*

Why? Because journals need research manuscripts in order to survive, and because the headlong rush to produce academics who can teach in the ever-increasing number of university tourism programmes may have encouraged less-than-rigorous research training at the postgraduate level. Moreover, the days of one-on-one apprenticeship-style mentoring of a postgraduate student are gone, due to academic staff carrying much heavier workloads – more classes, larger classes, more postgraduate students to supervise, more administration – together with increasing pressure to bring in research and consultancy funds to their universities.

Some organisations such as the Council for Australian University Tourism and Hospitality Education (CAUTHE) have worked very hard at improving communications between industry and academia and between tourism academics and their counterparts in the more traditional disciplines, and maintaining high research standards. Some of the lessons for research producers below are outcomes of a workshop organised by CAUTHE (Bushell *et al.*, 1997).

***Lessons for Research Consumers***

- Learn where research is published and how to identify quality publication outlets.
- Learn how to read and critically evaluate research: in other words, take dancing lessons.
- Employ people who already know the dancing steps, i.e. who can review and provide bureaucrat-friendly reports on published research results and pay them to do this on a regular basis.

***Lessons for Research Producers***

- Teach students of all levels (future industry personnel) to be able to read, critically evaluate and apply research findings.
- Uphold the peer-review process, educate students and industry about its purpose and continue to be rigorous in setting and maintaining standards for publication in refereed outlets.
- Invite chairs of funding organisations and grant programmes to your dances, to address tourism research conferences. Invite critical review and use it to improve quality.

## Observation 4

*A growing body of relevant and useful research findings exists but is rarely tapped, because too often academics use media, formats and writing styles that are alienating to industry.*

Why? In academia and professional research circles, the name of the game is publication in refereed journals. Researchers are rarely rewarded for anything else. In refereed journals and at research conferences, academics are taught and evaluated to communicate with *each other*, not with applied practitioners. One hundred plain-language reports to industry count for virtually nothing as compared to even a single article in a respected scholarly journal. This is not the researcher's choice. As it is for the applied side of industry, it is simply the way real human beings must perform in order to keep their jobs.

However, in some countries this is changing: if current proposals become Commonwealth government policy in Australia, then universities will be required to demonstrate that their research is collaborative with and relevant to industry as part of their funding conditions.

*Lessons for Research Consumers*

- Require that industry-sponsored research (i.e. research you pay for in cash or in-kind) be reported in media and formats and language that meet your needs.
- Provide incentives and opportunities for researchers to present findings at industry-based events and in industry publications (e.g. waive registration fees if presenting at industry conferences: pay researchers to publish in industry magazines and newsletters).
- Learn to use the new dance steps, electronic literature searches and research databases, to search quickly for subjects/topics. Better yet, develop partnerships with universities that require them to provide this type of training to your employees.

*Lessons for Research Producers*

- Learn to present research in non-technical ways and give research students the skills to do this. There is a whole literature just on this topic and you have a responsibility to concern yourself with it. David Attenborough and Carl Sagan are archetypes of eminent scientists who have changed the world by making esoteric science approachable and understandable – and thereby important – to non-scientists. There should be a little of David and Carl in each of us I believe.
- Use multiple outlets and media (e.g. verbal, written, web-based).
- Budget time and money for each research project for wide dissemination including industry events and to various sectors of the industry and various levels of government.

- Show research benefits to industry, decision-makers and policy-makers often and regularly, e.g., media releases.
- Provide incentives for researchers to publish in trade journals and other publication outlets appropriate for practitioners. Build these incentives into annual performance evaluations and promotion reviews.
- Give dance lessons: organise workshops for industry and government personnel that teach how to access, read and use research.

**Observation 5**

*Gaps remain in our understanding of tourism phenomena and a need for more research, particularly at the community and regional levels and in developing countries.*

Why? I mentioned earlier the enormous number of referred journals and other publication outlets for tourism research. Yet gaps remain in our understanding of tourism phenomena, and a return for a closer look at the 50 tourism, hospitality and leisure research journals provides evidence of one very real weakness. The publishers, editors and authors of tourism research are largely from developed countries. For example, 40% of the 50 research journals are published in the United States, 26% in the UK, 20% in Canada and Australia, 8% in Europe, and only 6% in the developing world. Although there have been an increasing number of published studies about tourism in less-developed countries, the vast majority of the authors and editorial board members of these journals are from the developed world. TRINET, the major international electronic list used by active researchers in tourism, is made up of researchers largely from the developed world; there are still many research producers and consumers in developing countries who do not have regular access to e-mail. In keeping with my first four observations, there is a need for more collaborative research with both industry and with academics in these countries, particularly at the community and regional levels.

Also, it should be noted that much of the scholarly interaction, both written and verbal, is in English, with little evidence that researchers from predominantly English speaking countries are attempting to communicate their findings to the non-English speaking world.

Research knowledge is growing laterally, but depth is still in short supply. Replicating somebody else's research (and even our own) is sometimes seen as mundane and uninsightfal. This stems from the incorrect assumption both on the part of consumers and researchers that a single study provides definitive evidence. It does not.

### *Lessons for Research Consumers*

- Provide opportunities and in-kind support for the kind of research you need and want, e.g., access to databases, employee time, access to visitors and visitor data, feedback/input into research focus and outcomes, accommodation and transportation assistance.
- Provide incentives to producers to collaborate with local universities and NGOs (e.g. student scholarships, prizes, awards, etc.) to undertake research that will directly benefit your region. Give prizes for the best dance teams. And don't forget that your direct financial support for research puts you in the driver's seat!
- Budget for cash support: e.g. data collection costs (travel, mail surveys, wages for research assistants).
- Capitalise on non-tourism grant programmes and organisations in your region that can help you meet your needs.
- Do not assume that research findings produced for another organisation will apply to your situation. Support and advocate the replication of research.

### *Lessons for Research Producers*

- Encourage and provide incentives for replicative and case study research by staff and postgraduate students.

- Provide incentives for students to do industry-relevant research (e.g. build it into assessment criteria) and showcase their results; have a competition for the best dancers.
- Provide incentives for academic staff to collaborate with partners in developing countries and to undertake industry-relevant research (e.g. build into performance appraisal, promotion criteria, criteria for study leave, etc.).
- Learn to adapt your dance steps to local conditions, adopt new styles of doing research, and find ways to communicate your findings to non-English speaking users.

**Conclusions**

This chapter has attempted to demonstrate that those who do tourism research and those who use research have grown further apart in recent years, and thus 'partnership' is an indispensable ingredient for research in the new millenium. Partnership between academia and industry requires a shift in thinking and approach by both tourism research consumers and research producers. Research consumers cannot sit back and wait for researchers to come to them, *i.e. to invite them to dance.* They must provide incentives and rewards for collaborative and industry-relevant research, they must be prepared to adapt to the timelines and reward systems of academia, attend their conferences, step onto their campuses, and generally work with academics and research students in all aspects and stages of the research process. As in other more mature industries, production of research knowledge must become a part of the culture of tourism businesses and government agencies (Lynch and Brown, 1999).

By the same token, research producers in all disciplines, even in prestigious well-funded research centres such as the Smithsonian Tropical Research Institute or Australia's Commonwealth Scientific and Industrial Research Organisation (CSIRO) are actively developing strategies to better disseminate their research findings to a range of target audiences. Tourism research producers need to *take dance lessons* from these other industries. They need to step out of their comfort zone, learn the language of industry, attend and present at industry conferences and events, and above all respect the reward systems of the private sector and their need to stay competitive in order to survive. *In short, they must become better dance partners for their counterparts in industry.*

The challenge for researchers is to meet the needs of research consumers, without loss of theoretical integrity and methodological rigour and therefore publishability (Lynch and Brown, 1999). Over time, the best research will be research that is theoretically informed and stands up to replication and practical application in the 'real world'. And the best researchers will be those who get personal satisfaction from making a difference in the real world of tourism business, not those who are content to be alone with their lofty ideas, disconnected from the things that improve the human condition. *Dancing well requires grace and rhythm, but it also requires learning, practice and adaptation to the needs and tendencies of a willing partner.* To the extent that research producers and research consumers work at adapting to one another's needs and tendencies in the next millennium, the contribution of research to advancing global tourism will reach unprecedented proportions. *Keep dancing.*

# 5

# HOSPITALITY RESEARCH AND THEORIES

## Introduction

This chapter is about research in the field of hospitality management over the 20th century. It is a limited view of the epistemology of a relatively young field of study. As in any emerging discipline, scholars have tried to achieve credibility in their work as they pursued the opportunity to add to the body of literature. And, as in any new endeavour with little foundation, it is full of exploration, self-questioning and doubt. This has been driven in part by the need to serve two very powerful masters. On the one hand, reseachers have had to measure up to the demands of scholars in general who, in many cases, had decades, even centuries, of prior research experience. On the other, the users of this research are very practical people who demand relevance and immediacy to the solutions of their problems.

These dual demands have had enormous influence on how scholars are developed and the work that they pursue. As we enter this new millennium, scholars and practitioners are beginning to realise that forthcoming research will be needed and is important to all stakeholders in the industry. It is even safe to say that there is emerging a common view or set of expectations about what research is important and relevant. It is indeed, a new dawn for a maturing field of endeavour.

The objective of this chapter is to provide a generalist view of the evolution of hospitality research, the researchers and the value of their work, the status and future of the body of knowledge, research methods and the future of scholarly work. It is not an attempt to provide a comprehensive review of the research over the 20th century because that has been amply done in such works as Brotherton (1999), *VNR's Encyclopedia of Hospitality and Tourism* (Khan *et al.*, 1993) or in recent special editions of journals, including *the International Journal of Hospitality Management* Vol. 17, No. 2. It is instead a commentary on where we started from in the early part of the 20th century and where we may be going now. It is also meant to be provocative and challenging.

**Getting Under Way – A Chronology**

Webster's *New World Dictionary* (of the American Language) defines epistemology as 'the study or theory of the origin, nature, methods, and limits of knowledge'. Figure 5.1 helps to convey this graphically as it summarizes the nature of hospitality research from its earliest stages to the present. In looking at the origins of hospitality research, one can go back to the 1940s, when early interest in research in the hospitality industry was complemented with the development of formal education in the field. At that time, research was very contextual. It was designed around the basic and applied needs of the industry. The focus was simply trying to describe practices and procedures that would assist in improving the performance of hospitality enterprises. This early work may be best characterised as descriptive with attempts to capture the best practices at the time.

In these early stages, numbers drove the core research agenda. The numbers were accounting-related and thus research was somewhat influenced by the work undertaken in the accounting profession. Additionally, food and its quality preparation represented the other area where scholars and practitioners attempted to develop a body of knowledge. Great chefs endeavoured to share their secrets of how best to do things, although somewhat reluctantly. In general, all this work could best be described as *'how to'*.

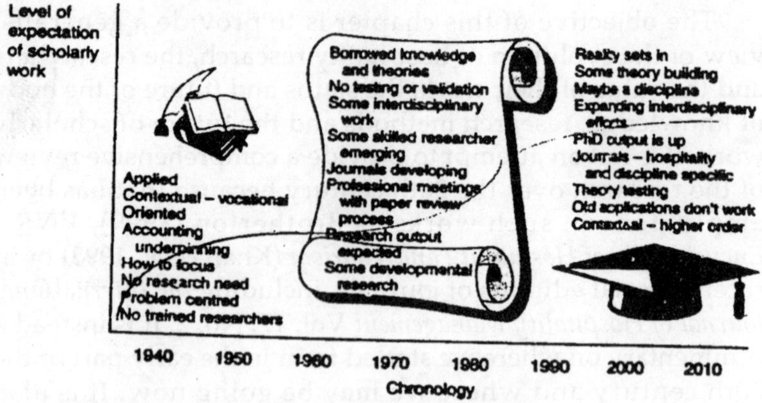


**Figures 5.1:** The evolution of hospitality research.

This inauspicious origin of hospitality research, with a focus on practicality and 'how to', provided the underpinnings for the next phase of work. While no clear threshold marked the beginnings of a more ambitious phase, nevertheless, attempts began to emerge that would move away from the earlier pragmatic efforts. Still, it appeared that no attempt had been made at this time to address the question of whether or not there was a need to follow a more scientific approach to building a body of literature. Research appeared to be driven more by serendipity than by strategy. It may be that the prevailing view was 'anything was better than nothing at all'.

Perhaps this next phase can best be characterised as imitation and borrowing. With only a haphazard array of information to build on, hospitality researchers looked to other fields for foundation and literature. Work that was occurring in the fields of business, engineering and the social sciences served as points of reference and departure for a newly emerging group of hospitality researchers clustered mainly in colleges and universities that offered curricula in hospitality management. This wholesale borrowing often did not really include any serious attempt to validate the application of these theories in the context of the hospitality industry.

During the period from the early 1950s to the late 1960s, scholarly journals began to develop. While they did not come close to approximating the quality of the scientific journals in other disciplines, an organised method of sharing information beyond the typical trade journal had begun. Little effort was given to disciplined scholarly review processes with editorial content being determined by a relatively few academics. Actual manuscript submissions to journals were few as faculty were not encouraged to do much research in this period and emphasis was placed more on knowledge exchange and sharing.

The textbooks that were developed had matured from the pure best practice orientation to attempts to include theoretical underpinnings, although borrowed and applied without serious validation of this application. Writers began to reference scholarly works from a wider array of other fields. It was also during this time that research expectations began to be recognised as important to academics. Professional societies developed which gave scholars opportunities to share their thinking and work. In this case however, what was shared was primarily introspective looks at how educators where doing things.

Reality began to set in in the 1970s and beyond. Academics were begin pressured into publishing and the work was beginning to be looked upon more carefully to see if real contributions to knowledge were occurring. The number of journals in the field began to grow alongwith quality. Serious review procedures were emerging. Scholars were required to develop a research focus and produce a stream of research that actually did contribute new knowledge. While at present this is still sparse, the expectations have been set.

During the contemporary period output of PhDs began to occur, which suggested that hospitality was becoming a more serious endeavour, may be even becoming a discipline. However, according to some, the hospitality field of study had stili not matured in the eyes of those that must sit in judgement of the quality of research effort under way.

Hospitality academics often talk to each other and do not benchmark the standard measures of research effort and quality outside of their own field. The work and evaluation remains insular. This dangerous approach has left research in still a rather primitive state. While new young scholars who have come from outside the field are now beginning to change the ethos, they are fighting an uphill battle as those who now sit in judgement of their work developed their scholarly habits in the free-wheeling days just referred to above. This tends to suppress the quest for excellence in research, which is badly needed if the field of hospitality is to mature to the next level.

**Researchers and the Value of their Work**

Looking back over the past 100 years, researchers can be grouped into four categories of professionals based upon their employment affiliations of academics, consultants, government and trade organisations. Any discussion that I may put forward as to the perceived value of their work is likely to draw controversy from those who will be compelled to defend their efforts. Nonetheless, a discussion of the value of the research should be undertaken, if for no other reason than to stimulate discussion and substantive evaluation of quality and relevancy. The main problem is how to conduct such an evaluation and what metrics to use? In this chapter I will try to present a two-dimensional view of hospitality research and its value. Figure 5.2 contains the graphic designed for this purpose.

The first metric chosen focuses on the complexity of the industry problem or research question at hand. Since hospitality is a complex social phenomenon, it does not lend itself to simple research questions, designs, methods and generalisability. However, given the epistemology just outlined, researchers have tried to simplify this complexity. Nevertheless, we must recognise that there are so many cause and effect relationships affecting the success of hospitality enterprises that trying to offer simple solutions to these challenges is perhaps not possible. Therefore, complexity in this case refers to the number of constructs shaping the relationships, which affect the success of hospitality enterprises.

The value of research is of course a relative issue. Thus, it cannot properly be defined, measured, or judged by any single set of criteria or individuals. Given this dilemma and at the risk of significant and welcomed challenge, I try to use the criterion of relevancy as the second metric. By this I mean, is this research actually read and used by anybody? For academics, this can be measured using a standard citation analysis to see how often a work is quoted or used. The danger in relying on this measure alone is the aforementioned insular nature of the field. The better measure is how are those for whom it was intended using the work. In the hospitality field that would be the industry itself. Thus, relevancy is expanded to mean how much of the scholars' research has penetrated and benefited the industry. This is more difficult to measure but may be put simply as the question is this research and the researcher in demand by the industry?

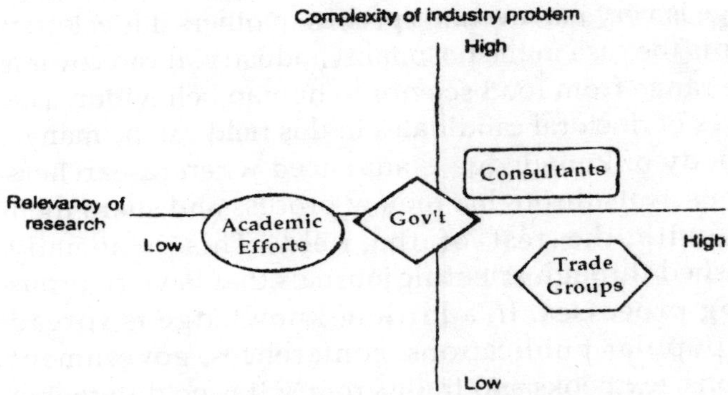


**Figure 5.2:** The researchers and the value of their work.

Using these assumptions, the reader is now given the opportunity to argue for or against the placement of the research of the four categories of scholars in Figure 5.2. As can be seen, scholarly work has not been viewed very highly in this framework. This is not to say that it is of no value, it perhaps is just not perceived by the end user to be or has not been communicated in such a way as to convince others of its value.

Given the current status of the hospitality industry it is not surprising that the research of consultants and trade groups is perceived to have greater value. Perhaps it has to do with the fact that the end user pays for this work which suggests that they need and want it and therefore will value it higher if they had to pay large sums for it. Or perhaps, it is just more relevant to today's needs. Government work is valued but generally the industry is suspicious of anything government does. This work also tends to be more quantitative and underpinned in economic theory.

**Sharing the Body of Knowledge**

Scientific advancement is based upon research that contributes to a body of knowledge in a specific discipline. Any doctoral student preparing for a preliminary examination knows the pressure related to being responsible for knowing that body of knowledge. In some areas the body of knowledge is very narrow and specific, in others it is eclectic. The latter is the case in the hospitality industry. It can cover a complete range from food science to human behaviour. The nightmares of doctoral candidates in this field can be many.

The body of knowledge is advanced when researchers pass manuscripts through a review process and share their findings with the rest of the field. This is usually accomplished through scientific journals that have rigorous refereeing processes. In addition, knowledge is spread through popular publications, conferences, government publications, textbooks and trade groups. It is no different in the hospitality industry. There are four main sources of academic/scholarly journals including textbooks, consultants' reports government reports, and trade and industry publications, including conferences, seminars etc.

One way to judge if a body of knowledge is advancing is to review the media by which this knowledge is shared to determine whether it is being built upon prior knowledge or just repackaging what is already there. From a very personal perspective, I would have to say that the hospitality industry does a lot of repackaging. A casual meta-analysis of the body of knowledge across specific subject-matter areas reveals a tremendous amount of contextual and replicative work. This is especially so in research regarding pedagogy.

There are perhaps several possibilities that exist for this phenomenon. First, possibly scholars have not explored the body of knowledge so as to build upon it rather than repackage it. Secondly, those who referee work may themselves not be familiar with or value the prior body of knowledge. Thirdly, it may be that those who are seeking it do not value the traditional sources of new knowledge such as scientitic journals. Fourthly, there may be a limited number of researchers who are engaged in serious theory building across the multi-disciplinary field of hospitality. Fifthly, a well-developed research agenda from a community of leading industrialists and scholars has yet to be developed to provide direction and need. There are no doubt other reasons behind this observation.

Figure 5.3 attempts to capture the relationships among the media by which the body of knowledge is shared, the extent

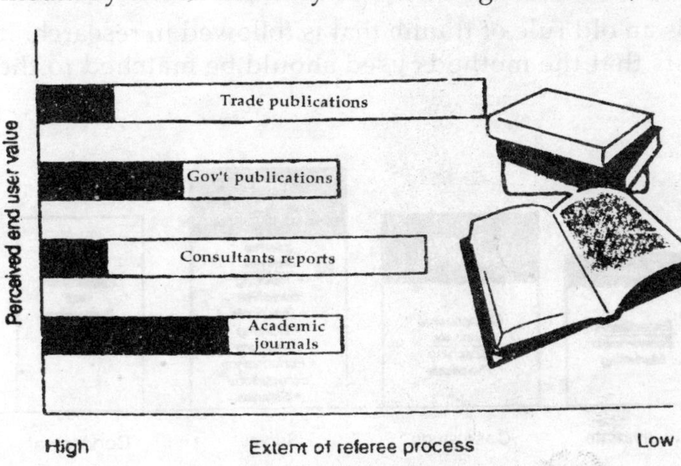


**Figures 5.3:** Sharing the body of knowledge.

to which the information in these channels is refereed and the perceived value of each to the end user. Using this framework it can be seen that trade and industry publications are the primary means of spreading knowledge. The collective readership in the public domain of this source of information is the largest. However, the extent to which this material is reviewed in a scholarly refereed sense is minimum compared to the other medias.

The next most valued source of information in the public domain is government publications and here he review process is more extensive. Consultants' reports are not usually part of the public domain, except for the generic reports that serve as marketing pieces for many firms. It is assumed that these reports are refereed internally but this is not always guaranteed. Academic journals, while probably having the most extensive review process appear to be the least valued source among all four. As stated earlier, the approach taken in this analysis of research is to use the standard of relevancy to industry needs. As Figure 5.3 indicates, the scholarly research in this field has not yet been perceived as having met this subjective standard.

## Methods Used

There is an old rule of thumb that is followed in research. It suggests that the methods used should be matched to the

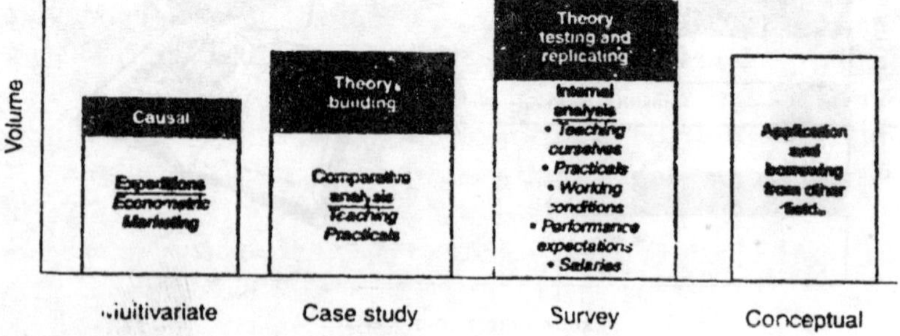


**Figures 5.4:** Research methods.

problem under investigation. This presumes that the problem defines the methods and not vice versa. In reviewing research over the past 100 years, the methods have generally fallen into four categories: case study techniques, multivariate techniques, conceptual and survey tools. Figure 5.4 contains a graphic look at the specific methods employed within each category and provides a rough assessment of the volume of published work in each. Additionally, it points out the relative proportion of work that has focused upon theory testing, building and causal relationship analysis. As can be seen, most of the work is descriptive as indicated by the light grey in the bar charts.

The majority of work has relied upon survey research methods. In this case, a relatively small proportion of the work has been in the area of theory testing which includes replication studies. This makes sense in the context of the earlier discussion, suggesting that scholars have borrowed theory from other disciplines and applied it directly to the hospitality context. Therefore, their work has been focused primarily upon testing theories of others or trying to replicate earlier work in this industry context. The largest proportion of the survey research work has been highly focused upon inclusive types of studies. We have tended to look a lot at ourselves, assessing teaching methods and techniques. Additionally, we have investigated how hospitality programmes have handled the practicals or field experiences. Researchers have also looked into working conditions, and performance expectations within the industry. And hospitality educators have always been concerned about salaries, so efforts have been made to capture this type of information on a regular basis.

Case study research has been employed but less so than survey methods. In this category of research method, a small amount of effort has gone towards theory building. The probable reasons for this are many. Chief among them may be the reliance upon theory from other disciplines, the contemporary ethos of the hospitality researcher, the lack of interest in developing theory, the apparent lack of need for this by practitioners and perhaps a lack of competency in this area. The bulk of case work has been focused upon comparative analysis and also has been inclusive to the hospitality field. Much of the comparative work has been among educators and educational institutions comparing and looking at each other and how they do things.

In the multivariate methods category, the bulk of work has been in the econometric area alongwith marketing investigations into consumer-related problems. In a few instances, causal analysis has occurred where researchers have recently begun to tackle large multivariate problems in the hopes of building theory. This is encouraging work but for the most part is still in the replicative and theory testing arena. However, the collective ability of newly trained researchers suggests that this is a positive sign.

The conceptual approach has supported research development in the field and probably served as important underpinnings for the other methods. This type of work is important but it cannot be confused with what I call the Sunday afternoon manuscript, which characterised much of the early published work. The allusion is that many authors went to the library on Friday afternoon, checked out a lot of books on a topic, reviewed the material and then sat down to write an article on Sunday. This is reminiscent of term paper writing. There were many instances no doubt when a conceptual piece was not researched or validated in the industry context.

**Tomorrow**

I have tried here to share my perception of the epistemology of hospitality research. In trying to step back and take a broad look I have come to some personal disappointing conclusions. For a field that has been a viable academic pursuit for almost a complete century, the body of knowledge is nowhere near defined. There appears to be no common understanding of what should be in this body of knowledge and almost no work that has addressed this problem. Scholars seem to be content in replicating the work of others or continually looking inwardly.

The journals, which now include more than 30 titles, seem to have very mixed review processes. The reviews are often handled within institutions, seriously inhibiting the need to broaden the scope of work and diversity of view. Many reviewers appear to approach the process in a casual fashion. Authors appears reluctant to make changes recommended by reviewers or even fail to see the problems identified in their work. The quality of work, from basic writing and simple methodological flaws to large-scale mismatches of methods and problems suggests we have much work to do. In many instances authors have tried to brow-beat editors into publishing their work despite serious concerns. This assessment is not meant to ignore those who attempt to achieve high standards here. They are, however, in the minority at this time.

Similarly conference programmes that have an official call for papers have refereeing processes that fall short of the rigours one would find in other fields. In many cases papers are sent to reviewers who have absolutely no competency in the body of knowledge in the area. In fact, many efforts in this regard are quite cavalier, with presenters not even beginning to do the research until they have heard whether or not their paper has been accepted. Here again the standards seem to be very low for a field trying to establish itself as more than just another vocational enterprise.

At the start of this new millennium, it is now time to reassess this current state and address the most pressing needs going forward. The first is actually to begin the massive effort to define a body of knowledge, or more appropriately, all the bodies of knowledge that contribute to this diverse and complex field of endeavour. Educational, research and trade associations and societies must accept this as the first step in moving the field forward. This will no doubt be a decade-long effort that will involve hundreds if not thousands of scholars. If future researchers are to contribute in a significant way to the entire spectrum of knowledge, they must know from where to begin.

Secondly, a new ethos of researcher must enter the scene. If we are to become a field with our own bodies of knowledge, then we must limit the theory testing and replicative work in favour of substantive attempts to build theories that are relevant. The key word here is relevance. Recently, after completing an analysis of the abstracts of more than 400 doctoral dissertations, it became quite clear that many failed to answer a very simple 'so what' question. The relevance issue will haunt scholars unless they make serious attempts at determining the long-term research needs of an industry, which is longing for applications of new knowledge. This must become the second most important objective for the new millennium. If we don't achieve relevance, we will simply exist in an esoteric setting that will grow to have less value for all concerned.

Leadership is the third issue. It must begin with the objective of identifying industry needs, not just at present but also well into the future. Once this is accomplished, leadership is required to establish and push a research agenda forward. Leadership is also needed in raising the standards for the research itself, the review and refereeing process associated with publication, and with the journals and other mediums of dissemination. There is some evidence today that suggests that there is a realisation of the need for higher standards across the academic and industry worlds but it will be necessary for research oriented institutions to take up the leadership challenge.

As with any developing field, it must pass through phases of growth and development. Hospitality is no different. However, because it is so diverse and applied, it will demand visionaries from across the spectrum of industry and academic stakeholders who are capable of taking it to the next level. All scholars must address and question their comfort levels with the current state of research and begin to shape theories that are relevant to this heterogeneous hospitality community going forward into the future.

As we move to a knowledge-based world where educational institutions have lost their monopoly on knowledge, it must be accepted that scholars will no longer come from the traditional institutions of higher learning. New knowledge will be created by whoever is in a position to do so and wherever it is needed and valued. If current researchers do not recognise this important trend they will find themselves forever wondering why no one seems interested in their work. Let the new millennium serve as the catalyst for the metamophosis of hospitality into a serious scholarly pursuit.

# 6

# HOSPITALITY AND FUTURE TOURISM FLOWS

## Introduction

Accurate forecasts of tourism demand are essential for efficient planning by the various sectors of the tourism industry. Forecast accuracy is particularly important in the tourism context, as the tourism product is perishable. Empty airline, ferry, bus and restaurant seats, and unused hire cars, hotel rooms, rental apartments, cruise ship rooms, holiday tour packages and tourist entertainment facilities cannot be stockpiled – once the potential sale is lost it is lost forever.

The purpose of this chapter is to review and evaluate the existing empirical literature on tourism demand forecasting in order to draw out any principles that appear to have been established, where principles are defined as empirically supported guidelines.

With regard to tourism demand forecasting, various time horizons are relevant to decision-making; for example, short-term forecasts are required for scheduling and staffing, medium-term forecasts for planning tour operator brochures, and long-term forecasts for investment in aircraft, hotels and infrastructure. However, the bulk of published forecasting studies on tourism demand concentrates on the short to medium term, and hence the principles also relate to these forecast horizons.

Various levels of aggregation are also relevant to decision-making; for example, governments are interested in total international inbound and outbound tourist expenditure at a country level, hotels in tourism demand by city or region, and airlines in tourism demand by route. However, the great majority of published studies on tourism demand focus on highly aggregated (i.e. country to country) forecasts. The principles therefore also relate to this level of aggregation.

International tourism demand is usually measured in terms of the number of tourist visits from an origin country to a foreign destination country. Less frequently it is measured in terms of tourist expenditure by visitors from the origin country in the destination country; and considerably less frequently by the number of tourist nights spent by visitors from the origin country in the destination country.

**Tourism Forecasting Techniques**

A comprehensive review of the tourism forecasting literature indicates that the majority of tourism demand forecasting papers involve econometric studies. Although it is often pointed out in such studies that the econometric models developed may be used for forecasting purposes, the models are often *not* used to generate outside sample forecasts that are then evaluated. Other quantitative forecasting techniques that have been used in tourism situations include spatial models (particularly gravity models) and time series models. Empirical research on qualitative forecasting in tourism has centred on Delphi studies and scenarios.

As the purpose of this study is to investigate whether any forecasting principles have been established, attention will centre on those techniques for which forecast evaluations exist. Therefore, spatial models, Delphi studies and scenarios are not included in our discussion. The focus is on econometric forecasting (in which the factors that influence tourism demand are taken into account in order to generate the forecasts) and time series forecasting (in which past history on tourism demand is extrapolated without reference to the influencing factors).

## Econometric Forecasting

### *Explanatory Variables*

The determinants of tourism demand depend on the purpose of visit. Approximately 70% of international tourist trips take place for holiday purposes, 15% for business purposes, 10% in order to visit friends and relatives and 5% for other purposes (where 'other' includes pilgrimages, and sports and health reasons). The emphasis in empirical research on tourism demand modelling has therefore been very much on holiday tourism, with only a few studies being concerned with business tourism. We shall therefore also concentrate on the demand for foreign holidays. Substantial agreement exists about the explanatory variables that are important in the case of international holiday tourism (Witt and Witt, 1992, 1995).

*Population* – The level of foreign tourism from a given origin is expected to depend upon the origin population, an increase in population resulting in an increase in demand. Sometimes population features as a separate explanatory variable, but generally modifying the dependent variable to become international tourism demand per capita accommodates the effect of population.

*Income* – The appropriate income variable is personal disposable income or private consumption expenditure in the origin country (in constant price terms), and is expected to have a positive influence on tourism demand. Income commonly enters the demand function in per capita form, corresponding to the specification of demand in per capita terms.

*Own price* – There are two price components – the cost of travel to the destination, and the cost of living for tourists in the destination (both in constant price terms) – and these are expected to have negative influences on demand. The cost of travel is often measured by the economy airfare. Usually the consumer price index in a destination country is taken to be a proxy for the cost of tourism in that country on account of lack of more suitable data, and Martin and Witt (1987) have shown this to be a reasonable approximation. The consumer price index is then adjusted by the exchange rate between the origin and destination currencies. If data relating to the price of the tourist's basket of goods services are available these would be more appropriate, but usually such data do not exist.

Exchange rates are also sometimes used separately to represent tourists' living costs, possibly in addition to the exchange-rate-adjusted consumer price index. The justification is that consumers are more aware of exchange rates than destination costs of living for tourists, and hence are driven to use exchange rate as a proxy variable. Clearly, however, the use of exchange rate alone can be misleading because even though the exchange rate in a destination may become more favourable, this could be counterbalanced by a relatively high inflation rate.

*Substitute prices* – The prices of substitutes may be important determinants of tourism demand and are expected to have a positive influence. For example, an increase in holiday prices to Spain is likely to increase the demand for holidays to Portugal. The impact of competing destinations may be allowed for by specifying the tourists' cost of living variable as destination cost relative to a weighted average value, calculated for a set of alternative destinations, and by specifying the travel cost variable as travel cost from origin to destination relative to a weighted average value calculated for travel from the origin to competing destinations. The weights are generally based on previous market shares and are often allowed to vary over time.

*Marketing* – National tourist organisations engage in sales-promotion activities specifically to attempt to persuade potential tourists to visit the country, and these activities may take various forms including media advertising and public relations. Hence, promotional expenditure (in constant price terms) is expected to play a positive role in determining the level of international tourism demand. Much tourism-related marketing activity is not, however, specific to a particular destination (e.g. general travel agent and tour operator advertising) and therefore is likely to have little impact on the demand for tourism to that destination. The promotional activities of national tourist organisations are destination-specific and are therefore more likely to influence tourist flows to the destination concerned.

*Lagged dependent variable* – A lagged dependent variable, that is an autoregressive term, can be justified on the grounds of habit persistence. Once people have been on holiday to a particular country and liked it, they tend to return to that destination. There is much less uncertainty associated with holidaying again in that country compared with travelling to a previously unvisited foreign country. Furthermore, knowledge about the destination spreads as people talk about their holidays and show photographs, thereby reducing uncertainty for potential visitors to that country. In fact, this 'word of mouth' recommendation may well play a more important role in destination selection than does commercial advertising. A type of learning process is in operation and as people are, in general, risk-averse, the number of people choosing a given alternative in any year depends (positively) on the numbers who chose it in previous years.

A second justification for the inclusion of a lagged dependent variable in tourism demand functions comes from the supply side. Supply constraints may take the form of shortages of hotel accommodation, passenger transportation capacity and trained staff, and these often cannot be increased rapidly. Time is also required to build up contacts among tour operators, hotels, airlines and travel agencies. Similarly, once the tourist industry in a country has become highly developed it is unlikely to dwindle rapidly. If a partial adjustment mechanism is postulated to allow for rigidities in supply, this results in the presence of a lagged dependent variable in the tourism demand function, with the parameter lying between zero and unity (Witt, 1980).

*Qualitative effects* – Dummy variables are often included in international tourism demand functions to allow for the impact of 'one-off' events. For example, the imposition by governments of foreign currency restrictions on their residents is likely to reduce the level of international tourism, as are threats of terrorism (for example, after the United

States bombing of Libya in 1986), and threats of war or wars (for example, the threat after the Iraqi invasion of Kuwait in 1990, followed by the Gulf War in 1991). Similarly, various events are likely to stimulate international tourism, such as hosting the Olympic Games and other major attractions. Witt and Martin (1987) discuss a range of one-off events, which have been accommodated in international tourism demand functions by dummy variables.

## Problems with Traditional Econometric Demand Models

Most of the published studies on causal tourism demand models before the 1990s were classical regressions with ordinary least squares (OLS) as the main estimation procedure. The functional form of most of these models was single-equation in either linear or power form. Normally, the simple-to-general modelling approach was followed. This approach starts by constructing a simple model that is consistent with demand theory, and the model is then estimated and tested for statistical significance. The estimated model is expected to have a high explanatory power ($R^2$), and the coefficients are expected to be both 'correctly' signed and statistically significant. In addition, the residuals from the estimated model are assumed to be a white noise process. However, if the estimated model is unsatisfactory, the model is then re-estimated by either introducing new explanatory variables, and/or using a different functional form, and/or selecting a different estimation method. This procedure is repeated until the final model is both statistically and theoretically acceptable. The specific-to-general modelling approach is often criticised for its excessive data mining, since researchers normally only publish their final models, with the intermediate modelling process omitted. Different researchers equipped with the same data set and statistical tools can end up with totally different models.

In addition, the data used in estimating tourism demand models based on the simple-to-general approach are mainly time series, and most of these time series, such as tourist expenditure, tourist arrivals, income, tourists' living costs and transport prices are trended (non-stationary). The estimated tourism demand models have tended to have high $R^2$ values due to these common trends in the data. Statistical tests based on regression models with non-stationary variables are unreliable and misleading, and therefore any inferences drawn from these models are suspect. Moreover, tourism demand models with non-stationary variables tend to cause the estimated residuals to be autocorrelated, and this invalidates OLS. The problem of autocorrelation in tourism demand models has normally been dealt with by employing the Cochrane-Orcutt iterative estimation procedure. However, this diverts attention from searching for the correctly specified model (autocorrelation is normally indicative of model mis-specification).

**General-to-specific Modelling Approach**

Recent advances in econometrics, specifically the use of general-to-specific approaches to modelling, enable us to overcome the problems associated with the traditional modelling procedure discussed above. The general-to-specific modelling methodology was initiated by Sargan (1964), and subsequently developed by Davidson *et al.* (1978). Hendry and von Ungern-Sternberg (1981), and Mizon and Richard (1986). In contrast to the specific-to-general modelling procedure, the general-to-specific approach starts with a general model, which contains as many variables as possible suggested by economic theory. According to this framework, if a dependent variable is determined by $k$ explanatory variables, the data generating process (DGP) may be written as an autoregressive distributed lag model (ADLM) of the form:

$$y_t = \alpha + \sum_{j=1}^{k} \sum_{i=0}^{p} \beta_{ji} x_{jt-i} + \sum_{i=1}^{p} \phi_i \, y_{t-t} + \varepsilon_t \tag{1}$$

where $p$ is the lag length, which is determined by the type of data used, as a general guide, $p = 1$ for annual data, $p = 4$ for quarterly data, $p = 6$ for bimonthly data and $p = 12$ for monthly data. However, the lag lengths of the time series may vary, and they are normally decided by experimentation. In Equation (1) $\varepsilon_t$ is the error term which is assumed to be normally distributed with zero mean and constant variance, $\sigma^2$ i.e., $\varepsilon_t \sim N(0, \sigma^2)$. With certain restrictions imposed on the parameters in Equation (1), a number of econometric models, such as the static, growth rate, leading indicator, finite distributed lag, partial adjustment and error correction models, may be derived. A detailed explanation is given in Song and Witt (2000), but here we only briefly describe the steps and criteria used.

The general-to-specific modelling approach involves the following steps. First, a general demand model that has a large number of explanatory variables, including the lagged dependent and lagged explanatory variables, is constructed in the form of Equation (1). Economic theory suggests the possible variables to be included, and the nature of the data suggests the lag length. Secondly, the *t*, *F* and Wald (or *LR* or *LM* as appropriate) statistics are used to test various restrictions in order to achieve a simple but statistically significant specification. Thirdly, the normal diagnostic tests, such as those for autocorrelation, heteroscedasticity, functional form and structural instability, are carried out to examine whether or not the final model is statistically acceptable. Fourthly, the final model can be used for policy evaluation or forecasting.

Thomas (1997) has summarized the various criteria for model selection within the framework of general-to-specific modelling. These criteria include consistency with economic theory, data coherency, parsimony, encompassing parameter constancy and exogeneity. The first criterion for model selection is that the final model should be consistent with economic theory. This is very important; for example, in general we cannot use a demand model for policy evaluation and forecasting if the model has negative income elasticity. Although such a model may be acceptable according to the diagnostic statistics, it should still be rejected because it invalidates a law of economics. The data coherency criterion ensures that economic data also have a role to play in the determination of the structure of the final model. It implies that the preferred model should have been subject to rigorous diagnostic checking for mis-specification. The parsimony criterion states that simple specifications are preferred to complex ones. In the case of modelling tourism demand, if two equations have similar powers in terms of explaining the variation in the dependent variable, but one has six explanatory variables while the other has only two, the latter should be chosen as the final model. This is because we gain very little by including more variables in the model, and moreover large numbers of explanatory variables tend to result in inadequate degrees of freedom and imprecise estimation. The encompassing principle (Mizon and Richard, 1986) requires that the preferred model should be able to encompass all, or at least most, of the models developed by previous researchers in the same field. The encompassing criterion does not necessarily conflict with that of parsimony; the preferred model may be structurally simpler than other models, but still encompass them. The parameter constancy criterion is particularly important when we use econometric models to forecast. In order to generate accurate forecasts, the parameters of the model should be constant over time. The final criterion for selecting a model is that the explanatory variables should be exogenous, that is they should not be contemporaneously correlated with the error term in the regression.

In modelling tourism demand, the final preferred model should ideally satisfy all of the above criteria. However, this can sometimes be very difficult on account of various reasons, such as data limitations, errors in variables and insufficient knowledge of the demand system. Any of these may result in the above criteria not being satisfied. Even if we find a demand model that satisfies all the criteria, it should be borne in mind that the model can still only serve as an approximation to the complex behaviour of tourists, and it is possible that the decision-making process of tourists will change due to changes in expectations, tastes and economic regimes. Therefore, we should be always prepared to revise our model to take account of such changes.

**Time Varying Parameter Approach**

One of the recurrent features of causal tourism demand forecasting models when compared with simple time series models, such as the no change model, has been predictive failure. Predictive failure is normally associated with model structure instability, i.e. the parameters of the demand model vary over time, and structural instability is mainly related to important social, political and economic policy changes. The appropriate way of dealing with the problem is to choose an alternative approach, e.g. the time varying parameter (TVP) regression, to model structural changes. The tourism industry has evolved from a supply-led industry to a demand-driven one since the 1970s. Political, economic and social shocks such as the two 'oil crises' in the 1970s, terrorism attacks in the 1980s and the Gulf War in the early 1990s have also had sustained impacts on the demand for international tourism. Although the dummy variable approach could be used to attempt to capture structural changes due to the above-mentioned shocks, the use of the TVP methodology is probably a more realistic alternative. The TVP approach is capable of simulating different types of shocks that may influence the relationship between the dependent and explanatory variables, and the model is also unique in incorporating structural changes into the forecasting process.

**Vector Autoregressive (VAR) Modelling Approach**

The above models are single-equation tourism demand models in which an endogenous tourism demand variable is related to a number of exogenous variables. The single-equation approach depends heavily on the assumption that the explanatory variables are exogenous. If this assumption is invalid, the estimated parameters of the single-equation demand model are likely to be biased and inconsistent. Sims (1980) argues that the exogeneity assumption imposed by the single-equation approach is unlikely to be credible, and that the VAR specification is more appropriate when we are not sure about the exogeneity of the explanatory variables. For example, Equation (1) specifies that tourism demand is influenced by the price of the tourism product, but the converse could be true also.

The VAR model is a system equation in which all variables are treated as endogenous. The VAR specification suggests that the current values of the variables should be regressed against lagged values of all the variables in the system. Each equation in the system is individually estimated by OLS.

**Principles**

What does the empirical evidence suggest about the accuracy of different forecasting methods in the tourism context: econometrics versus time series; different econometric models; and different time serious models?

Various principles appear to have been established, but with varying levels of evidence – strong, medium and weak – based on the number of studies and the number of cases examined in the studies. Only those principles for which at least medium evidence exists are reported. In the following, 'short-term' forecasts denote a forecast horizon of up to one year ahead and 'medium-term' forecasts denote a forecast horizon greater than one year and up to two years ahead.

***Causal Modelling***

1. It is not possible to build a single model that is appropriate for all origin-destination pairs. Certain explanatory variables appear to influence international tourism demand for some origin-destination pairs but not others. Furthermore, the estimated coefficients, as expected, vary widely across tourist flows. (*strong*)

*Examples of evidence* – Martin and Witt (1989); Song and Witt (2000); Kulendran and Witt (2001).

***Forecasting***

*General*

1. No single forecasting method performs consistently best across different situations (origin-destination country pairs, forecasting horizons, accuracy measures). (*strong*)

*Examples of evidence* – Martin and Witt (1989); Witt and Witt (1991); Song and Witt (2000).

2. The relative performance of different tourism forecasting techniques is highly dependent on the choice of accuracy measure, so the tourism forecasting requirement must be considered carefully before deciding on a forecasting method. (*strong*)

For example, for some decisions it may be more important to minimise the size of forecast error while for others it may be more important to forecast correctly the direction of movement of tourism demand.

*Examples of evidence* – Witt and Witt (1989); Witt and Witt (1991).

*When forecasting accuracy is measured in terms of error magnitude*

1. The no change model generates more accurate short-term tourism forecasts than simple univariate time series and traditional econometric models. (*strong*)

*Examples of evidence* – Martin and Witt (1989); Sheldon (1993).

2. The autoregressive model generates more accurate medium-term tourism forecasts than the no change, other simple univariate time series and traditional econometric models. (*strong*)

*Examples of evidence* – Martin and Witt (1989); Witt, Witt and Wilson (1994).

3. The TVP model often generates the most accurate short-term tourism forecasts, outperforming both univariate time series models and other causal models (including the ECM). (*medium*)

*Examples of evidence* – Song, Witt and Jensen (1999); Song and Witt (2000).

4. The univariate ARIMA model generates more accurate short-term tourism forecasts than the ECM. (*medium*)

*Examples of evidence* – González and Moral (1995); Kulendran and King (1997).

5. The neural network model generates more accurate short-term tourism forecasts than simple univariate time series models. (*medium*)

*Examples of evidence* – Pattie and Snyder (1996); Law and Au (1999).

6. The no change model generates more accurate short- and medium-term forecasts than the VAR model. (*medium*)

*Examples of evidence* – Song, Witt and Jensen (1999); Song and Witt (2000).

*When forecasting accuracy is measured in terms of direction of change error*

1. Traditional econometric models generate more accurate short-term tourism forecasts than the no change and simple univariate time series models. (*medium*)

*Examples of evidence* – Witt and Witt (1989); Witt and Witt (1991).

Some of the evidence regarding the accuracy of recent forecasting approaches is mixed. For example, González and Moral (1996) found that the basic structural model outperforms the ARIMA model, whereas Kulendran and King (1997) discovered the converse to be true. Song, Witt and Jensen (1999) and Kulendran and Witt (2001) found that the error correction model is outperformed by the no change model, while Kim and Song (1998) and Song. Romilly and Liu (2000) found that the error correction model generates more accurate tourism forecasts than the no change model. Clearly further research is required to establish the relative accuracy of some of the more recent forecasting approaches in the context of international tourism demand.

# 7

# HOSPITALITY IN AFRICAN TOURISM

## Introduction

With its land mass of about 11.7 million square miles and comprised of more than 50 countries, the continent of Africa has an enormous potential for tourism development. This potential is based on an assembly of divers physical and cultural resources that have been well-documented (Teye, 1987; Ankomah and Crompton, 1990). Despite this potential, a viable tourism industry has not emerged in the majority of the countries in Africa.

Africa has made a number of concerted efforts to diversify its economies in order to provide sustainable economic opportunities to improve the quality of life for its citizens. Within this context, tourism development has been highlighted but has actually played a marginal role in the continent's overall economic development. One such concerted effort at regional economic development began in 1980 when the Organisation of African Unity (OAU) adopted the Lagos Plan Action (LPA) which eventually became the bedrock of Africa's economic development strategy (OAU, 1981: UN, 1986). The economic reasons included the urgent need to reverse the economic decline that has characterised the continent since the early 1970s, leading to the label 'the lost decade'. The political arguments for a new strategy for economic development were traced to the consequences of the 'Scramble for Africa' and the 'Partitioning of Africa' which occurred in the latter half of the 19th century. It has been argued that the consequent economic and political realities presented Africa with immense challenges, including fragile national borders, limited effective domestic markets, narrow resource base, and susceptibility to external market shocks (Dieke, 1998). Regrettably, these conditions exist today and pose even greater challenges to African development than they did when the LPA was first adopted. One main reason is that Africa's population has almost doubled to about 700 million during the period, thereby placing tremendous stress on all aspects of economic, social, cultural, environmental, as well as political development. In this context, it is important to note the elevated status of tourism by the United Nations (UN) Economic Commission for Africa (ECA) which clearly recognised the potential role of tourism in the economic and social development of Africa (ECA/WTO, 1984, Sako, 1990).

The discussion in this chapter is limited to sub-Saharan Africa (Africa south of the Sahara), and the term 'tourism' is used to include travel, tourism, hospitality and directly related industries. The focus of the discussion will be on international tourism since data on domestic tourism in Africa are almost non-existent. In general, domestic tourism tends to account for as much as 90% of the total for the industry (both domestic and international) in industrialised countries. As such, it should play a significant role in Africa's economic development as living standards improve, disposable incomes expand, the industry is developed, and residents are encouraged to participate in domestic tourism activities.

A review of the global and regional dimensions of the international tourism industry indicates that while Africa experienced a modest annual growth rate of 6.3% in international tourist arrivals between 1989 and 1999, the region on the whole accounted for a mere 4.0% of world arrivals and an even smaller 2.2% of receipts. Furthermore, the industry is concentrated in a handful of countries, while the majority of the countries on the continent have marginal tourism industries, well below their potential. A question arising from this review is this: What were some of the main obstacles to tourism development in the past, and how can they be overcome in the future? Implicit in this question is the fact that most African countries have, to differing extents, made attempts during the recent past to develop a tourism industry. During this period, the debate over the role of tourism development in developing countries in general was also played out on the African continent. Given the fact that the issues centred on the debate are even more relevant today, it is important to examine them, particularly, since they will have to be addressed in the future.

**Table 7.1**
**Top 20 tourism destinations in Africa, 1998 (international tourist arrivals)**

| *Rank* | *Country* | *No. arrivals (000)* | *% of total* |
|---|---|---|---|
| 1. | South Africa | 5898 | 23.6 |
| 2. | Tunisia | 4718 | 18.9 |
| 3. | Morocco | 3242 | 13.0 |
| 4. | Zimbabwe | 2090 | 8.4 |
| 5. | Kenya | 857 | 3.4 |
| 6. | Botswana | 740 | 3.0 |
| 7. | Nigeria | 739 | 3.0 |
| 8. | Algeria | 678 | 2.7 |
| 9. | Namibia | 560 | 2.2 |
| 10. | Mauritius | 558 | 2.2 |
| 11. | Tanzania | 450 | 1.8 |
| 12. | Reunion | 391 | 1.6 |
| 13. | Zambia | 362 | 1.4 |
| 14. | Senegal | 352 | 1.4 |
| 15. | Ghana | 335 | 1.3 |
| 16. | Swaziland | 319 | 1.3 |
| 17. | Cote D'Ivoire | 301 | 1.2 |
| 18. | Uganda | 238 | 1.0 |
| 19. | Eritrea | 188 | 0.8 |
| 20. | Malawi | 178 | 0.7 |
| | Total | 23194 | 92.7 |
| | Total Africa | 25023 | 100.0 |

*Source:* World Tourism Organisation.

## The Tourism Development Debate

This section of the discussion begins to introduce the challenges facing tourism development in Africa in the future within the context of the post-independence period. It attempts to synthesise some of the main arguments advanced in the 1970s and 1980s in support of tourism development on the continent. For the most part, these were the same arguments, mostly economic in nature, that were advanced for developing countries in general (de Kadt, 1979; Lea, 1988). However, some of the arguments took into consideration specific African conditions and concerns.

**Table 7.2**
**Top 20 tourism earners in Africa, 1998 (international tourist receipts, excluding transport)**

| *Rank* | *Country* | *US$ mn* | *% of total* |
|---|---|---|---|
| 1. | South Africa | 2738 | 27.3 |
| 2. | Morocco | 1675 | 16.7 |
| 3. | Tunisia | 1557 | 15.6 |
| 4. | Tanzania | 570 | 5.7 |
| 5. | Mauritius | 503 | 5.0 |
| 6. | Namibia | 288 | 2.9 |
| 7. | Ghana | 274 | 2.7 |
| 8. | Reunion | 265 | 2.6 |
| 9. | Kenya | 233 | 2.3 |
| 10. | Senegal | 178 | 1.8 |
| 11. | Zimbabwe | 177 | 1.8 |
| 12. | Botswana | 175 | 1.7 |
| 13. | Nigeria | 142 | 1.4 |
| 14. | Uganda | 142 | 1.4 |
| 15. | Seychelles | 111 | 1.1 |
| 16. | Cote D'Ivoire | 108 | 1.1 |
| 17. | Madagascar | 91 | 0.9 |
| 18. | Eritrea | 75 | 0.7 |
| 19. | Zambia | 75 | 0.7 |
| 20. | Sierra Leone | 57 | 0.6 |
| | Total | 9434 | 94.0 |
| | Total Africa | 10011 | 100.0 |

*Source:* WTO, 1999.

First, it was argued that most African governments see their responsibility as including the provision of an adequate supply of foreign exchange for the payment of imports of capital and consumer products. Tourism was seen as a means to diversify Africa's mono-cultural economies, since the economic fortunes of most countries were highly dependent upon the export of a few unprocessed agricultural and mineral products. For example, by the mid-1980s, 25 out of 46 sub-Saharan African countries were totally dependent on agricultural exports, and 17 countries derived over 80% of their export earnings from less than four commodities.

Second, and closely related to the foreign exchange arguments, was assertion that tourism could assist in preventing and alleviating widespread and persistent unemployment in African countries. This argument was even more appealing to development experts since it identified tourism as being labour-intensive, requiring a significant proportion of unskilled labour, and stressed the existence of a hospitable African population to deliver hospitality-based services. Those who held traditional views that pointed to the fact that the service sector (including tourism) is the third phase in the process of economic development, progressing from agriculture and industrialisation, were strongly met with research and statistical evidence to the contrary. For example, Lee (1987) referred to studies carried out by the United Nations Conference on Trade and Development (UNCTAD) and concluded that: 'the development of a whole range of services is a necessary precondition to stimulate growth in other sectors and the services industry finds itself in a key position at the heart of the national economic fabric' (Lee, 1987: 87). Summary (1987) provided further evidence from Kenya, where a 70% increase in tourist expenditure between 1971 and 1976 was estimated to have increased output in the agricultural sector by as much as 262% and enhanced productivity in the food preparation sector by 720%. For the proponents of tourism development, this was further evidence that the industry can promote inter-sectoral linkages.

Third, it was argued that tourism supports policies that pursue spatially comprehensive regional development activities. In this regard, a Zimbabwe minister for tourism stated that the tourism industry 'provides jobs and economic growth points in areas that would remain undeveloped because they are not fit for either agriculture or resettlement purposes. The gains of tourism are ploughed back to the development areas where they are generated' (Novicki, 1983: 53).

In addition to the economic arguments in favour of tourism development, environmental and social benefits were also cited. According to Bell (1987), by the mid-1980s the number of national parks and reserves had more than doubled since the early 1960s, thereby facilitating the conservation of ecological systems that provide the basis for ecotourism in general, and wildlife tourism in particular. The social and cultural benefits that were articulated in support of tourism development in Africa are illustrated by the following statement made by the late President Nyerere of Tanzania: 'To have visitors is a special honour, and to treat a visitor well and hospitably is an act of good manners. A visitor [who] comes to Tanzania, stays for a while, and leaves praising this country, is a good ambassador of us abroad, and he is an ambassador who costs us nothing' (Adelson, 1976: 45). Besides the facilitation of international understanding, goodwill and contributing to peace, the educational benefits to both residents and visitors provided claims of additional benefits. For example, the Zimbabwe Tourist Board attempted to establish cultural centres close to major tourist attractions so that visitors could meet with locals and be afforded the opportunity to learn the history and culture of the area (Novicki, 1983).

It must be emphasised that African countries were presented with not only the positive side of the tourism development debate, but the negative arguments as well. While the issues that emerged from the debate are too diverse and complex to be adequately examined here; suffice it to say that they have been extensively covered elsewhere with respect to developing countries (de Kadt, 1979; Britton, 1982; Erbes, 1973; Lea, 1988; Go and Jenkins, 1997) and about Africa (ECA, 1986; Teye, 1991, Dieke, 1993). Briefly, the counter-arguments against tourism development include the possibility of enclave development, leakage of foreign exchange; state subsidised development for the benefit of foreign investors; seasonal unemployment; exacerbating rural to urban migration; destruction of social patterns; reinforcement of neo-colonialist relationships of exploitation, dependency and servitude; inflationary pressure and land speculation; commercialisation of cultural assets; westernisation of society, particularly Africa's youth; increase in crime; and threats to the moral fibre of society. After considering both sides of the argument, Tanzania, for example, denounced tourism development in the late 1960s as inconsistent with the country's political philosophy. Despite his initial more positive stance on tourism, the late President Nyerere went on to label tourism as a 'necessary evil' and suggested that tourists must be isolated from the general population (Nyerere, 1969). There are other examples of concerns about the potential adverse impact of tourism development in Africa. In the early 1970s, a national debate that involved the head of state focused on the impact of foreigners on Ghanaian culture through the social demonstration effect. One contribution to the debate pointed out that: 'Without mincing words, the youth of Ghana today have come to accept anything British, American, and for that matter foreign as the all-in-all. Anything African and Ghanaian is second rate. . . No decent society will sit down aloof to see its youth copy useless foreign cultures at the detriment of the nation . . . Africans nations cannot allow the nation-wrecking Western permissive society to corrode our society' (Ayi, 1974: 5). Cultural activities such as festivals and special events also generated concerns such as: 'The Americans brought out the curse of traditional ceremonies in West Africa – the European or Black American with a camera. Possession of this device, may appear to thing, entitles them to roam the area at will, obstructing the view of other people and generally reducing the whole sacred ceremony to a second class circus. . . . The rule had better be firmly established before all the German tourists arrive' (Williams, 1974: 10-11). The Gambia, with its small population of less than half a million, also had its share of social problems back in the 1970s whereby: 'Swedes have sometimes offended Gambian morals by appearing naked on the beaches or scantily clad in the towns. As a result, the authorities have insisted on proper dress . . . and have been known to expel overland tourists who do not conform to the Gambian concept of well-dressed Westerners' (Uweche, 1975: 73).

**Critical Issues**

The economic, social and environmental issues embedded in tourism development constitute greater challenges for the African region in the future for a number of reasons. First, the majority of African countries are economically worse off than they were at or shortly after independence in the 1960s. The World Bank (1990) estimated that sub-Saharan Africa's gross domestic product (GDP) grew by only 1.45% during the period 1991 to 1994. The Bank went on to say that: 'In most of the continent, growth is not nearly sufficient to make a dent in poverty reduction, and despite recent improvements, Africa's GDP and export growth rates, savings and investment levels, and social indicators remain below those of other regions' (World Bank, 1996: 71). Even countries such as Botswana, Ghana and Uganda, which were recently regarded as economic success stories by the World Bank and its affiliate institutions, are currently experiencing serious problems. The situation in Ghana illustrates the nature and persistence of old economic problems at the close of this century; specifically, foreign exchange constraints due to dependence on a few mineral and agricultural exports. The price of cocoa, the country's leading agricultural export, which was $1711 per tonne during the 1997/98 season, had declined to $1040 by September 1999. Similarly, the country's principal export, gold, which was $288 on ounce in December 1998 had declined to $260 per ounce. To complicate the economic situation – and placing enormous pressure on foreign exchange reserves – the price of imported crude oil was \$10.21 in December 1998 but had more than doubled to about \$23 at the end of September 1999. While the short-term solution appears to lie in the implementation of several austerity measures, the long-term economic diversification strategy includes the comprehensive development of the tourism sector. For example, Ghana established a Ministry of Tourism in 1993 and has a 15-year tourism Master Plan for the period 1996 to 2010. This appears to be the trend in several African countries which are pursuing planned tourism development projects, with the assistance of such agencies as the United Nations Development Programme (UNDP). WTO and regional organisations such as the Southern Africa Development Community (SADC).

Second, the environmental challenges in Africa are even more diverse, complex and critical today, mainly due to such factors as the rapid population growth, expanded land-use and congested urban areas. While many African countries have established environmental protection agencies and ministries for the environment, several are turning to tourism-related activities in order to protest the ecosystem. For example, the Upper Guinea Forest Ecosystem in West Africa which extends from Ghana through the Ivory Coast, Liberia, Guinea and Sierra Leone, originally occupied about 728000 square kilometres but currently all that remains is only about 13% (92797km$^2$). This reduction has been attributed to human activity over a long period of time but most intensely in the past 20 years. Classified as one of the world's priority conservation areas because of what is regarded as its high endemism, Conservation International (CI) has been working with the governments of Ghana and the Ivory Coast to establish National Parks and reserves with tourism components such as attractions and visitors centres. Similar projects directed at conserving the environment and its habitat with potential for ecotourism development can be found in such countries as Madagascar and Botswana (the Okavango Delta).

Finally, cultural tourism and in particular, the ethnic tourism component has provided several African countries with the opportunity to begin to preserve and restore cultural attractions, including several World Heritage Sites. However, in addition to the old issues that were discussed earlier in this chapter, new challenges are beginning to emerge. For example, the restoration of the slave forts and castles in Senegal (Gore Island) and Ghana (Elmina and Cape Coast) have evoked emotional responses from Africans in the diaspora, mostly from the United States and the Caribbean (Bruner, 1996). The Slave Route Project currently being proposed by the United Nations Educational, Scientific and Cultural Organisation (UNESCO) in partnership with the WTO is bound to add tremendous resources to Africa's cultural tourism inventory, but will certainly raise many complex issues. The diverse economic, social, cultural and environmental issues related to tourism development will have to be addressed at country, region and local levels as well at the intra-African regional level. In the broader context, however, several factors constitute impediments to tourism development. These will have to be addressed by African countries if they are to succeed individually or collectively in their tourism development efforts.

## Obstacles to Tourism Development

A myriad of obstacles has been identified in the literature as hindering tourism development in Africa (Ankomah and Crompton, 1990). A few of them are summarised below.

### *Political Instability*

These include civil wars, *coups d'état*, dictatorships, terrorist activities and other forms of political unrest. These can adversely affect the flow of visitors as well as investment into Africa, and impact the delivery of existing tourism goods and services (Teye, 1986, 1988). Events associated with political instability usually include human misery and tragedy which, when relayed through the print and electronic media, reinforce the negative images that are incompatible with the safe and relaxing destinations desired by the majority of leisure visitors. Some studies published in the tourism literature have documented the fact that international leisure and business travellers use beliefs and ideas about Africa to construct it socially as 'dangerous and to be avoided' (Carter, 1998: 349). There are still many areas of political conflicts such as Angola, the Democratic Republic of Congo, Rwanda, Sierra Leone, Somalia and the Sudan. Even countries that appear to be relatively stable have fragile political conditions, which threaten safety and security of visitors as well as residents. Recent examples from Egypt, Nigeria, Kenya, South Africa, Tanzania and Uganda illustrate this point. Furthermore, there is a tendency on the part of potential visitors from the long-haul points of origin to perceive local events in Africa on a more continental scale.

### *Economic Restructuring*

Most African countries inherited large government bureaucracies from the colonial period. After independence, they expanded these institutions and added layers of activities in the primary and manufacturing sectors; such as state farms, mining companies and industrial holdings. A feature of the African economy since the mid-1980s has been the Structural Adjustment Policies (SAPs), aimed at implementing economic reforms including privatisation of public enterprises, deregulation of prices, interest rates and overall financial liberalisation. It was also aimed at attracting foreign investment and to improve efficiency of resource utilisation. SAPs have direct impact on tourism by attracting investment in the tourism sector as well as increasing the inflow of the business market segment (Dieke, 1995). While the results of SAPs are debatable and even controversial, it appears that it will become a feature of the economic landscape of Africa in the next century, with its attendant impact on tourism.

### *Human Resource Constraints*

Tourism requires a variety of inter-disciplinary competencies at various phases of its planning, development, marketing and management (ECA, 1992). Investment in the training activities that build local capacity in the tourism sector should ensure that Africans obtain maximum economic benefits through better-paying jobs, while reducing economic leakage that arises from hiring foreigners such as hotel managers. Ultimately, it also ensures development of indigenous tourism products as well as the delivery of quality services with staff who are knowledgeable about their own country and its attractions.

### *Regional Cooperation*

Regional political and economic unions that promote regional growth through easy movement of capital, goods, services and people have become a common feature of global interdependence. Africa has been rather unsuccessful at establishing lasting and viable economic sub-regional groups, even though such a large number of these organisations are scattered throughout the continent. Unfortunately, some, such as the East African Economic Community, which appeared to be the most viable regional organisation in Africa, became a casualty of political differences between the member states (Kenya, Tanzania and Uganda) and broke up in 1977 (Delupes, 1969). Others, such as the Economic Community of West African States (ECOWAS), which was established in 1975, is ineffectual and has not delivered most of the programmes it set out to implement. The benefits that accrue to the tourism industry from regional cooperation cover almost every aspect of the sector's development. They include joint marketing programmes, human resource training, common transportation services, immigration, customs and health policies, standardisation of research activities and classification of tourism plant (Teye, 1991; see also Dieke, 1998). Currently, the Southern Africa Economic Community (SADC) appears to be the regional organisation with the greatest assets and potential in facilitating tourism development on the continent.

### *Other Constraints*

There are a number of other obstacles that would have to be overcome in order to develop a viable tourism industry in Africa. These include provision of adequate and basic infrastructure, including lodges, telecommunication and transportation services; overcoming health and medical challenges; strengthening weak institutional frameworks for tourism planning; encouraging effective community participation in tourism; promoting domestic tourism; effective utilisation of the information technology, and minimising the adverse economic, social and environmental impact of tourism. Ultimately, this means that what constitutes an appropriate form of tourism (Brown, 1998) at the country and local levels needs to be determined and then comprehensively planned in a sustainable manner.

## Conclusion

This chapter examined the main issues that African countries will face in developing viable tourism industries in the new millennium. It began with a review of the international tourism industry in Africa within a global context. This was followed by a discussion of the reasons for and against tourism development in Africa during the post-independence period. It was concluded that these issues are even more relevant today and will present challenges in the future. Finally, a number of obstacles restricting tourism development were summarized as a basis for further discussion. An extensive list of sources follows this brief overview.

# 8

# HOSPITALITY IN ASIA PACIFIC TOURISM

## The Financial Crisis

In 1996 visitor arrivals in the area grew by 9.6%. Confidence about the future of Asia Pacific tourism was at its height. Yet, in less than a year, the area dived from being the fastest growing region to bottom place.

What happened? It all started on 2nd July, 1997 when the Bank of Thailand floated the baht. From there the dominoes began to fall with great rapidity. Currency values and stock markets dropped dramatically. Korea is a case in point. The won fell from around 900 to the US$ to 1960. The stock market index fell from almost 1000 to 300. Unemployment rose from 2.3% of the labour force to 8.4% and the consumer price index rose from 3.2% to 13.5%.

Korea, Thailand, Indonesia and Malaysia were hit the most. It was also felt strongly in Singapore, Hong Kong and even the South Pacific. China and South Asia felt it the least. Tourism was, needless to say, badly impacted. In Japan, outbound travel fell for 14 consecutive months. Business travel between Asia's capital cities fell by up to 30%. The focus of industry was on survival. Short-term needs created an environment of rate cutting. Yield was sacrificed for cash flow.

Overcapacity increased the impact on the hotel sector. Occupancy rates plunged by as much as 48% in some places.

Hundreds of hotels have closed or become technically bankrupt. Among the airlines, all the performance indicators fell. Philippine Airlines closed altogether for a while. Hundreds of travel agents were reported to be in trouble. In Korea, the forecast was that only about half of the outbound travel agents would survive.

Why did all this happen? Contributing factors included the withdrawal of foreign short-term capital investments, bank loans and portfolio investments plus overvalued exchange rates and excessive credit expansion for speculation in land and real estate. In addition, there was declining relative competitiveness, a severe asset bubble and an insufficiently regulated and weak financial system. Export growth slowed. Current account deficits grew. The bubble was ready to burst. And, it did.

In many of the Asia Pacific countries a turn around began in the second half of 1998 and there was continued improvement in 1999. As the millennium closed Thailand and Korea were the real success stories. In Korea, the won rate rose 40% and its stock market by 123%. In Thailand, interest rates came down from the ugly 22% to 9%.

Visitor arrivals have risen in virtually all Asia Pacific countries and, by the end of 2000, totals were expected to have climbed back to where they were before the crisis, almost everywhere. This has been achieved at the expense of prices. In 12 out of the 16 Asian countries surveyed, hotel occupancy was up but room rates were way down. Low prices attracted more long haul visitors, especially Europeans and restimulated demand within the Asia Pacific region. Among airlines, flights are being added back and loads improved.

In summation, the Asia Pacific industry is now moving in the right direction all across the region. The weak have fallen by the wayside. The strong have a low cost environment in which to regroup and expand. Confidence is returning. One worry is that the recovery may be happening too fast and that renewed growth may lead to the underlying structural problems that contributed to crisis being forgotten in the rush to chase new business and short-term gain.

**Future Trends**

***Globalisation and Liberalisation***

Most of us in the West see globalisation and liberalisation in a very positive light. If you speak to business people in Asia, you will find they see things from a quite different perspective. The 1999 UNCTAD report states:

> The humbling of the Asian tigers since 1997 has revealed the vulnerability of even the strongest developing economies to the powerful forces unleashed by globalisation. While the developed world suffered little from the Asian crisis and even derived some benefit from it, the impact on the rest of the world has been dramatic. Growth in the developing world slowed from almost 6% in 1996 to under 2% in 1998.

Developing countries are being pushed towards greater liberalisation and integration, to relax foreign investment rules, and to be more transparent. But, many Asians see that the countries in the region which were hurt the most by the crisis were the ones who pursued these policies and those hurt the least were the ones who did not. They see the process as being lopsided and feel that it is widening the gap between the developed and the developing worlds. A major problem is that it is moving too fast, faster than the structure and rules needed to manage it. In developing countries, the institutions, the systems and, for that matter, the mind set are often not ready for what is happening.

In tourism, power is increasingly being concentrated and there is concern that foreign multinational companies will take advantage of distressed situations and the low cost environment to gain a bigger share of the Asia Pacific tourism industry.

Greater understanding of the impacts on developing countries is needed. Without this, it is not hard to envisage conflicts and possibly renewed protection lying ahead, all of which could pose problems for tourism development in the region.

### *Consolidation*

Perhaps the most significant development has been the creation of four major global airline alliances. Some Asia Pacific airlines, hit by the financial crisis, are signing up with one or other of them. More will no doubt do so. These alliances can use technology and their advantages of scale and reach to be a very powerful force in the Asia Pacific travel scene. Everyone in every sector of tourism is going to have to deal with that reality.

There is also consolidation going on in the Asia Pacific hotel and tour operator sectors. The financial crisis exposed the weak; the strong are buying the weak and others are looking for alliance partners so as to create a collective organisation that is stronger, to build new regional distribution networks.

The message for the future, learned from the crisis, seems to have been 'do not get left out on your own'.

### *The Internet*

Now the worst of the financial crisis is hopefully over, the Internet is the hottest topic in Asia Pacific tourism. Communication by e-mail is becoming standard practice. The proportion of travel companies with their own website or pages in a collective one is high. In part, this is a response to what is happening in the key generating markets. If one in every four German homes is online, they need to be online also. Internet sales are still small in percentage terms but are growing every month. In the future, the Asia Pacific travel industry will continue to develop its capacity to use the Internet and other information technology to advantage and will be a match for any region in these respects.

### *Distribution*

It has been said that 'vertigo is caused by looking down from a great height or, in the case of travel agents, when faced by the prospect of zero commissions'. Impacted by the financial crisis, airlines operating in the region had to reduce costs and the floodgates are now open, releasing an onslaught on agents' commissions.

Agents are realising that they have to make a fundamental change in the way they do business. Singapore's National Association of Travel Agents led the way in Asia when it resolved that it 'must prepare agents for a service fee environment'. It must convince them that their focus should be on serving their customers and charging for the services they provide. By eliminating so many of the weaker agents, the financial crisis helped to prepare the ground for this transition to be made.

*Markets*

Attracted by the low prices available as a result of the financial crisis, European tour operators are expanding their programmes and the North American market is once again on the wish list. Above all, however, there are three markets that will influence Asia Pacific tourism the most in the 21st century.

The first is Japan. It has been the dominant market for every Asia Pacific country. If you ask any of the region's tourism leaders about how the recovery will go, the answer is likely to be 'it all depends on Japan'. The view in Japan is that the economy has bottomed out, public confidence is recovering and travel remains on top of the wish list. The recovery remains slow but once confidence fully returns, the volume of Japanese travelling abroad will return to a pattern of sustained growth.

Then there is China and India. Each has a number of people in the middle class able to afford overseas travel that is already estimated to be bigger than the total population of all but a handful of countries and it is growing. No other region has potential markets on this scale. Both will inevitably impact the area's tourism in a big way in the coming century. A recent Kuoni study predicted that outbound travel from India will increase by 20% per year for the next five years. The World Tourism Organisation (WTO) estimates there will be 100 million Chinese overseas trips in 2020. And most will be to other destinations in the Asia Pacific region.

### *Asia Pacific Travellers*

Australians and New Zealanders are experienced travellers, but the Asian outbound markets, on the other hand, are all new, most of them very new.

Japan started as a modern travel market in 1964 when exchange controls were lifted and it is now a relatively mature market. Travel is within reach of most people. The courier with the flag has largely gone; people are travelling with family members or a few friends. Growth is in independent travel with customised itineraries, and special interest travel is well established. Itineraries are not so crammed and even shopping is lower on the scale of preferences. These trends will continue.

The rest are really young markets. Restrictions on Taiwanese and Koreans travelling abroad, for instance, were lifted in 1988 and 1989 and it was only in 1992 that China relaxed its rules. In the early 1990s, the characteristics of their travellers were similar to those of the early Japanese tourists. Now these markets are maturing rapidly and catching up to where Japan is today. There is a growing amount of independent travel and an increasing number of people who expect to travel abroad at least once a year. One thing that is unlikely to change very much, however, is the length of their holidays, which will remain short.

### *National Tourism Organisations (NTOs)*

Many governments are looking to reduce public expenditure on tourism and would like to see more private sector money in the tourism pot. For its part, the private sector is not particularly interested in putting in its money unless it has say in how that money is spent. In this situation, Nepal decided to close its Department of Tourism and establish an autonomous public/private sector tourism board. The Maldives set up a Tourism Promotion Board recently and Sri Lanka is on the same track.

One Asian Minister recently said: 'The government firmly believes that it should move out from conducting business and the private sector should do what it is good at, so that we can maximise the use of scarce resources (*The Island*, October 1999). With globalisation, intensified competition and the impacts of information technology, it seems likely that this is the direction in which more Asia Pacific NTOs will be heading.

### *Cruising*

Cruising has been around a long time in the South Pacific. The big new development is the recent growth of cruising in Asia. Cruising by Asians began to take off in earnest in 1990 and grew rapidly in 1993 when Star Cruises arrived on the scene. In 1998, the Port of Singapore handled over one million passengers. Most cruises are of three to four days' duration, which suits the urban Asian very well.

Star Cruises now operates cruise programmes based in Singapore, Hong Kong, Bangkok, Taipei and Osaka and has become the fourth largest cruise line in the world. Japan also has its cruise ships and in Korea, Hyundai Merchant Marine is filling two ships with a third on order. The potential of the Asian market is enormous and the future for cruising looks very bright.

## Future Growth

### *Forecasts*

In the final part of this chapter, I would like to refer to the WTO *Tourism* 2020 *Vision* report. WTO says that, despite the financial crisis, the Asia Pacific region will grow faster than the others do and will pass the Americas to be second only to Europe in the number of visitor arrivals. I have my doubts, though, about the region receiving five times as many visitors in 2020 as it did in 1998. I question the forecast of 59.3 million visitors arriving in Hong Kong in 2020: that is 162500 per day with perhaps 250000 on a peak day, and if they all stayed an average of four days, that would mean there could be 800000, perhaps even one million visitors in Hong Kong at one time. All I can say is that I would not want to be there or to have to go through Hong Kong airport!

Similarly, I worry about 141.5 million Japanese overseas trips at that time, not only from the demand viewpoint but also from the logistics of the situation. That figure breaks down to almost 400000 leaving per day and over half a million on a peak day. Including arriving, departing and transit passengers, airports would be called upon to handle well over 1000,000 passengers per day. And this in a country where, after many years of trying, Narita still does not have a second runway in operation.

With Asia's population and the growth of its middle class, there could well be the potential demand for international travel to create five times as many arrivals. But only if there were not five times as many people everywhere they went.

### *Restraints on Growth*

This is one restraint on growth that must be taken into consideration. Others are:

- Market pressure on governments to protect the environment and develop in a sustainable manner.
- Environmental and consumer protection legislation.
- The physical limits of the places every tourist wants to see and the impacts on them.
- Congestion at airports and in city centres. It might not be possible to move at all in some Asian cities.
- Destination opposition – the 'Not in my back yard' syndrome.
- Visitor expectations: surveys indicate that people are looking for customisation, time efficiency, personal service and a unique experience plus the ability to relax and to get away from it all. These are not attributes that fit well with a five-times increase in visitor numbers.
- Quality – the more crowds, hassles and overdevelopment the more the quality of the visitor experience will be reduced.
- Prices – prices will rise if demand exceeds supply where space is restricted.
- Safety – aircraft disasters, air space congestion, civil disturbance, terrorism, health and natural disasters could all affect the desire to travel.

### *Domestic Tourism*

And then there is domestic tourism, a much-neglected aspect of the industry. It has been rising rapidly in the Asia Pacific region with the growth of the middle class and of car ownership. WTO has estimated that the ratio of domestic to international tourists may be as high as ten to one. In Thailand, for example, WTO forecasts there will be 37 million visitor arrivals in 2020 and, on a ten to one basis, that could mean 370 million domestic trips. Even if the ratio is only five to one, that is still 185 million. How much breathing room is that going to leave for the 37 million international visitors looking for a unique experience?

I feel that, at some point, a rising visitor quantity line on the graph will cross with a declining experience quality line and, together with the other factors mentioned, will restrain tourism from reaching the levels predicted by WTO.

### *The Development Matrix*

Tourism has always been much better at building on strengths and taking opportunities than it has at correcting weaknesses. Its response to a problem has too often been to throw more promotion at it. In the 21st century, if quality is to be sustained and the optimum number of visitors sent home happy, tourism must be better at managing the framework within which the industry grows.

The restraints on growth that I have mentioned are all part of that framework. They are parts of a tourism development matrix which, in an ideal world, should all move together in the same direction and at the same pace. To begin to make that happen, we need to have decided where we want to go and how to get there or, in other words, to plan strategically. Whether or not such planning is both undertaken and implemented will have a significant bearing on the future growth of Asia Pacific tourism.

### *A Responsible Industry?*

The WTO report comments on the degree to which markets are unsaturated and says: 'International tourism can be seen to be an industry truly in its infancy'. As my earlier comments suggest, I disagree with that. I believe that the time has come for tourism, as one of the biggest industries in the world, to recognise that it has acquired responsibilities. This is going to be especially difficult in the Asia Pacific area since this is where there will be the greatest demand pressure. It is also where money talks and where return on investment talks the loudest. How the Asia Pacific region handles these responsibilities will say a lot about the future of its tourism industry.

But, whatever happens, the impact of Asia Pacific markets, destinations and its tourism industry on the world's tourism scene will be greater in the 21st century than it has been. As John Naisbitt has said, 'the West may come to need the East more than the East will need the West'.

# 9

# HOSPITALITY IN CARIBBEAN TOURISM

## Introduction

The Caribbean is one of the most tourism-dependent economies in the world. It is estimated that tourism generates 560000 jobs (directly and indirectly). Visitor expenditure contributed an estimated US$ 17.5 billion in revenues in 1998. The tourism sector represents about one-third of all regional exports. For islands such as Antigua and Barbuda and the Bahamas, tourism contributes most of the GDP.

It is imperative that Caribbean islands develop the strategies and take the necessary steps to ensure the sustainability and competitiveness of the tourism sector. The need to make the tourism sector work for the region is even more acute today in the light of key developments at the global level, namely the banana crisis and the deterioration of the manufacturing sector. In addition, many other developing countries (South Africa, Thailand) as well as developed market economies (UK and USA) and former Eastern-bloc countries (Hungary, China) are intensifying competition in the tourism market. Increased economic challenges in many tourist-destination countries is also pressuring outbound travel resulting in stark competition for the tourist dollar. Changes brought on by the rapid adoption of information technologies also pose a number of new challenges and opportunities.

There are many excellent initiatives taking place in the Caribbean that poise the region for further growth and competitiveness of the tourism sector:

- The Caribbean tourism industry is very competitive. The sector has not been weaned on protectionism as has sugar, bananas and import substituting manufacturing. Yet, the industry continues to hold its own in the international marketplace – countries such as the Dominican Republic, with superior price competitiveness, has been able to grow its industry by leaps and bounds.
- The highly innovative and dynamic all-inclusive hotel sector, led by Sandals and SuperClubs continues to post consistently superior performance. They are a driving force in the growth and expansion of the tourism industry.
- The cruise tourism sector is growing rapidly and the Caribbean continues to be the number one destination globally.
- There is growing concern and interest in sustainable development on the part of the public and private sectors. The Caribbean Action for Sustainable Tourism (CAST) led by the Caribbean Hotel Association (CHA) and initiatives such as the Caribbean Tourism Organisation (CTO) regional annual conference on sustainable tourism are examples. In addition, many individual resorts and non-governmental organisations (NGOs) have won ecotourism awards.
- Progress has been made toward greater public and private sector cooperation, although much more work remains.
- The region is now marketed under one umbrella in Europe, with the assistance of the European Union.
- There have been several initiatives in the area of human resource development, although these initiatives are as yet inadequate to meet the needs of the region. One of these is CTO's initiative to establish a Caribbean Tourism Human Resource Council.

**Importance of Tourism and Recent Performance**

Although the Caribbean region accounts for only 3% of international tourist arrivals, tourism plays a significant role in many Caribbean economies. The Caribbean (excluding Cancun and Cozumel) recorded 16.5 million tourist arrivals and 12.3 million cruise ship passenger visits in 1998. In 1997 gross visitor expenditure by all visitors to the Caribbean reached an estimated US$ 14.45 billion.

The total number of persons employed in accommodation establishments in the Caribbean in 1997 was estimated at 146000. Available data suggest that total employment (direct and indirect) generated by tourism is about three times the employment in accommodation establishments (*Caribbean Tourism Organisation*, 1997).

Despite temporary hiccups in 1973/74 (oil crisis), 1980/81 (second oil crisis), 1988 (Hurricane Hugo), 1991 (Gulf War) and 1995 (Hurricane Iris), stayover arrivals to the Caribbean continue to increase. However, while the trend in Caribbean tourism arrivals has generally been upward, this growth trend has not been the same for all islands. Different islands have experienced different levels of growth and have different levels of resilience to the global environment. An examination of the comparative rates of growth of Jamaica and Barbados, for example, shows that Jamaica has been far more resilient than Barbados and indeed the rest of the Caribbean during the 1980/1981 recession. A superior level of innovation in Jamaica (the development of all-inclusive hotels, for example), was certainly a contributing factor to Jamaica's superior performance.

As can be seen from Table 9.1 the cruise industry in the Caribbean has grown very rapidly and the rate of growth of cruise arrivals exceeded that of stayover arrivals in many years.

The rapid growth and development of the cruise tourism industry opens key opportunities and poses a number of threats to the Caribbean destinations in which they operate. The environmental and economic impacts of cruise tourism are

**Table 9.1**
**Comparative growth of stayover and cruise arrivals, 1986 – 1996**

| *Year* | *Stayover ('000)* | *Growth %* | *Cruise ('000)* | *Growth %* |
|---|---|---|---|---|
| 1986 | 8460 | 6 | 5000 | 20 |
| 1987 | 9590 | 13 | 5600 | 12 |
| 1988 | 10400 | 8 | 6340 | 13 |
| 1989 | 11170 | 7 | 6710 | 6 |
| 1990 | 11850 | 6 | 7450 | 11 |
| 1991 | 11650 | –2 | 8700 | 17 |
| 1992 | 12344 | 6 | 9400 | 8 |
| 1993 | 13368 | 8 | 9615 | 2 |
| 1994 | 14270 | 7 | 9790 | 2 |
| 1995 | 14490 | 2 | 9710 | –1 |
| 1996 | 14838 | 2 | 10696 | 10 |

increasingly in question. Moreover, with its pace and magnitude of development, the cruise industry has almost appeared as a 'thief in the night', directly competing with land-based tourism.

The Caribbean is the most important geographic market for the cruise industry, accounting for over one-half of all cruises taken world-wide. According to informed observers the Caribbean is expected to retain its position as the dominant region for cruising for a number of reasons, including the region's proximity to the US market, its tremendous physical attraction and image of relative stability, and constraints to growth in some of the competing regions.

## Strategic Issues Facing Caribbean Tourism

### *Competitiveness*

One of the key strategic issues facing the Caribbean tourism sector is that of ensuring the continued competitiveness of the sector in global markets. A number of factors will reinforce the competitiveness of the Caribbean tourism sector.

*Human resource development* – One of the keys to quality is the human resources that deliver quality services. The development of the human resource base of the Caribbean tourism sector is a key priority. There is an urgent need to invest in the training and development of human resources that would manage the tourism industry in an efficient, profitable and sustainable manner and also provide quality services to an increasingly demanding international clientele.

It is in the critically important field of human resource development that the accommodation sector faces its toughest challenge. In the increasingly competitive world of international tourism, the days of enthusiastic amateurs are over. Technical efficiency and professional service are the distinguishing marks of success.

*Quality standard* – It is also important that appropriate standards that meet global customer requirements are implemented. The problem of small hotels is the key concern. The Caribbean hotel sector, for a number of reasons, prefers to avoid any discussions or actions aimed at classifying its properties. More emphasis has been placed on developing and meeting certain minimum standards. However, much more work needs to be done in developing regional standards and re-developing and re-positioning the region as a destination of quality.

Ancillary services sector also needs attention. The ancillary tourism sector (which comprises a wide variety of services provided outside the hotel sector, including restaurants, ground tour operations, taxis, duty free shops, handicrafts, water sports operations, etc.) is generally not accepted as a mainstream component of the tourism product but operations within these services generally reflect the need for a closer examination of financial support systems, improved training and certification programmes, and improved marketing skills.

*Safety and security* – Increasingly, lack of adequate security for visitors is becoming a major deterrent to the growth of healthy tourism in many destinations. The increasing trend towards harassment of visitors on the beaches and on the streets, the rise in crimes directed at tourists, and the open peddling of drugs is a growing concern for policy-makers.

*Research and market intelligence* – Another key pillar of competitiveness is research, information and market intelligence. The Caribbean needs to strengthen its information/intelligence base with which to monitor the tourism industry, anticipate change and identify policy instruments to address/control any adverse impacts anticipated. More research is needed to understand the dynamics of competition within the tourism industry – why some islands perform better than others; why do some sectors perform better than others (e.g. cruises and all-inclusive hotels compared with standard hotels); and what policy measures need to be put in place to ensure competitiveness of the industry. There is also need to focus research and efforts on the environment; monitor the impacts of tourism on the environment as well as the negative environmental impacts of other sectors (agriculture, manufacturing) which could have negative impacts on the tourism industry.

*Use of technology* – The Caribbean region will need to adopt strategies and the actions to put it in the forefront of technological change. It is in the marketing and distribution areas that the use of technology is most critical. Natural advantages (sun, sand and sea) are no longer sufficient to give the Caribbean the competitive edge in global markets. New technologies are driving the new tourism from the supply side. New technologies are making it possible to supply individual tailor-made holidays that are *cost-competitive* with mass standardised and rigidly packaged options. Technology is driving the new tourism. It is creating the basis for flexibility and individuality of the travel experience without necessarily increasing costs. The key differences in the old and new technologies are identified below:

- new technology is well developed;
- it is not simply the internet or a video brochure that is being used, but the whole *system* of information technologies;
- it is not only travel agents or tour operators or hotels that use the technology, but all suppliers and even consumers;

- the pace of adoption of the technology is rapid;
- technology creates new rules of the game for competitors and creates wealth.

***Sustainability***

It is a well-known fact that the tourism industry in the Caribbean is very dependent upon its environment. Tourism is a major user of the region's environmental resources (sun, sand, sea, nature, wild life, flora, fauna, reefs, nature reserves and national parks, etc.) Ensuring sustainability and protection of the environment is one of the key strategic issues facing the Caribbean region, and especially its tourism sector.

*Environment aspects* – With rapid growth of uncontrolled tourism development in the Caribbean, the fragile eco-systems of the region are exposed to an ever-increasing risk of environmental degradation which could destroy the very raison d'être of the Caribbean's appeal. A number of factors increasingly threaten the environmental quality of the Caribbean and hence the sustainability of the tourism industry. These include: poor sewage disposal; growing quantities of ship/boat-generated waste; beach erosion; destruction of reefs; water quality; overfishing; destruction of wildlife habitat; overcrowding; carrying capacity limits; treatment of solid waste.

*Finding the balance with cruise tourism* – The issue of sustainability is also at the heart of the debate on cruise tourism vs. stayover arrivals. Issues that need to be addressed in the cruise tourism industry are as follows:

- maximising the economic contribution of cruise tourism through –
  (a) increasing cruise ship purchase of Caribbean suppliers (an initiative already started by Caribbean Expert Development Project of CARICOM);
  (b) increasing absolute expenditure of cruise passengers (expansion of the range and quality of local crafts, activities, tours, duty free shopping and other items of interest for cruise passengers);

(c) converting cruise passengers into long-stay arrivals;
(d) increasing head taxes paid by cruise passengers;

- determining the environmental impacts of cruise tourism and developing measures to minimise negative impacts. Areas to be addressed include; cruise ship dumping; identifying optimal carrying capacity for each destination, taking examples from the Bermuda model;
- the need to understand the relative economic impacts of cruise and stayover tourism.

*Local involvement* – A critical aspect of the sustainability of the Caribbean tourism sector is the meaningful involvement of the indigenous population in the production of and the benefits from the tourism sector.

Successful tourism destinations are those in which visitors feel a total sense of welcome – the locals that smile are not only those who are paid to smile (workers in the industry). Yet, so little effort and energy is spent on creating the reasons for locals to smile. Much of the effort of tourism authorities is spent on tourism awareness and 'smile training' – teaching locals about tourism and why they should smile at tourists. They fail to realise that unless locals feel tourism in their pockets and on their tables (food to eat), all the smile training will not help. According to an observer in the industry 'you do not teach people to eat, just give them the food'. Similarly, you do not teach locals to smile at tourists, just give them the reason.

It is believed that the responsibility for involving local communities in the tourism sector is the job of the government. Many private sector establishments operate in communities (many tourist attractions are located in communities where people live) and do not even think about the relationship that they build with their communities. Yet, they expect that their tourists will be safe and everyone will be smiling to them. The evidence suggests that it is those far-sighted entrepreneurs who build relationships with their local communities that are the most successful. Curtin Bluff Hotel in Antigua is a shining example of such involvement.

Unexploited and unexplored ways in which the established private sector can support community involvement in tourism include:

- advertising local products and services;
- sourcing goods and services from the community (e.g. eggs, bread);
- providing training and mentoring for small business that supply the hotel;
- out-sourcing certain services (laundry, gardening, water sports);
- employing persons (e.g. nannies) as free agents to build entrepreneurship;
- ensuring that community services are employed in building and construction;
- training and skills upgrading;
- employment from surrounding communities;
- identifying key opportunities for communities (e.g. production of fresh herbs; organically grown vegetables);
- introducing new services to guests (e.g. cooking classes in preparation of local food and local language training; story telling; traditional games, catch and release fishing and entertainment);
- featuring local cuisine on the hotel menu;
- identifying career opportunities for locals;
- encouraging staff and local schools to experience being tourists at the hotel.

The key approach to local community involvement in tourism is not aid, but private sector development in partnership with the local communities. As the saying goes, do not give people fish, teach them to fish.

### *Marketing and Promotion*

Effective marketing, promotion and product distribution is also key to the success of the Caribbean tourism sector. Here the issue is lack of adequate resources effectively to market and promote the region, effectively to distribute products in the marketplace and to adopt the necessary technologies for competitiveness.

### Air Access

Adequate, reliable and efficient air access is of paramount importance to the development and continued survival of Caribbean tourism. Caribbean destinations can fail or succeed depending on the actions of a single airline. Pan Am, for example, carried about 14% of passengers to Barbados; 17% of all seats to the Bahamas and 60% of all seats to the Turks and Caicos in 1991. When the airline shut down in 1991. Pan Am left many islands without access to a large part of their market.

The transportation challenge facing the region can be summarized as follows: how to guarantee air access with adequate capacity at competitive prices to all Caribbean destinations. Adequate air access is critical to the long-term survival of the Caribbean tourism industry.

### Facilitation

There is need to facilitate the free movement of tourists and remove any barriers to the movement. Common issues need to be implemented as well as standardised immigration forms. The legal, policy and legislative framework for the development of the tourism sector needs to be put in place.

### Economic Impact

The tourism sector offers a number of opportunities for linkages, which have not been fully exploited. From organic food production and cut flowers, to health services, high fashion for the tropics and environmental services, the potentials are enormous. These potentials must be analysed on a sector by sector basis using new strategies of development based on the principles of product focus and production flexibility.

There is need to create more linkages between tourism and other sectors of the economy, particularly services of developing the axial potential of the tourism sector: using the presence of a tourism sector to develop other exports, e.g. sports, ecotourism, high fashion, environment services, health tourism.

Three key issues of economic impact have also been identified: the high leakage of the tourism sector and the low levels of linkages developed between tourism and the other sectors of the economy; the need for more research and analysis; and the need to develop strategies and actions to maximise the economic impacts of tourism.

**Investment**

Governments should seek to maintain an interest rate regime that is supportive to the tourism sector and, through fiscal incentives, encourage the banking sector to offer longer-term loans to the tourism sector. Consideration needs to be given to implementation of a taxation policy that seeks to minimise the tax burden placed on the tourism industry, given its competitive nature. Governments must ensure that careful consideration is always given to the potential impact of new tax measures on the tourism sector.

While there has been a large increase in investment in new hotel plant in the Caribbean in recent years, much of this has been restricted to relatively few countries. There is evidence from the previous studies that high tax regimes, bureaucratic delays and other factors inhibit the attraction of foreign investors to some countries in the region. Steps must be taken to eliminate as far as possible these barriers to investment and to attract new tourism investment to the region.

Lack of matching investment in essential infrastructure (such as roads, airports, seaports, electricity, water supply and telecommunications) has inhibited the development of tourism in some Caribbean countries. There is a continuing need for investment in the improvement of the region's tourism infrastructure, which also serves and benefits the local populations, if growth targets for tourism are to be realised. At the same time, greater attention needs to be paid to the preservation and development of the region's rich heritage of historic buildings as an important, but presently neglected, component of the region's tourism product. Expanded use also needs to be made of indigenous architecture, designs and handicrafts in the tourism sector.

**Future Prospects**

In 1950, a mere 25 million persons crossed international borders world-wide; by 1990, 425 million persons travelled abroad; this figure is expected to reach 661 million in 2000 and 937 million (or double the number of tourists in 1990) by 2010. Consider that in Britain, Germany, Japan and the USA, more adults already travel during any particular year than visit a library, attend a sporting event or have gone to see a play or concert.

That the industry will continue to grow is not in question. However, it is increasingly evident that:

- the *rate* of growth will vary from country to country;
- the *distribution* of growth will shift;
- the *direction* of growth will change;
- the *capacity* to absorb growth will be limited for some countries.

The Caribbean Tourism Organisation predicts a positive future for tourism arrivals where the Caribbean will receive 22.5 million tourists by the year 2000 and 37.9 million tourist arrivals by 2010. Tourist arrivals to the Caribbean in 2010 will be double those who came to the Caribbean in 1997.

The expected growth to the Caribbean by the year 2000 raises important questions. Will this growth impose limits to growth in some Caribbean islands? Do islands have the capacity to absorb more visitors? What are the environmental, social and other related limits to growth? Are there adequate skilled workers managers and long-term capital at reasonable rates of interest to fuel this expected growth? Are the infrastructure (ports, airports) adequate to facilitate this expansion? Are locals adequately involved in the industry?

# 10

# HOSPITALITY IN EUROPEAN TOURISM

## Introduction

In product life cycle terms, Europe as a tourism destination has passed from the strong growth to the mature stage. Having led the expansion of tourism in the second half of the 20th century and been the principal tourist-receiving region. Europe has below-average growth prospects over the first two decades of the 21st century. However, while competition is eroding Europe's market share with virtually every country (and territory) in the world now embracing tourism as a key strategic economic sector, Europe will still record substantive growth. The reasons are as diverse as the forecast strong expansion over the first quarter of the century in outbound Asian tourism and growing tourism product diversification in European countries, catering for newly emergent market segments.

## Forecasts of European Tourism

The World Tourism Organisation's *Tourism 2020 Vision* study has been finalised to be published in a series of volumes during 2000. Drawing on the volume dedicated to Europe (*Intraregional and Long Haul Flows: Europe*), the following key factors and forecasts are identified:

- Forecasts of international tourist flows to Europe show that there will be 717 million arrivals in 2020. This represents an average annual growth rate of just under 3.1%, compared with the rate of expansion world-wide of approaching 4.2%, for a global total of 1.56 billion arrivals by 2020. Europe will retain its regional leadership of international arrivals but with a declining share from 59% in 1995 to 47% in 2020.

- Within Europe, the largest sub-region of Western Europe will show the lowest rate of growth between 1995 and 2020, at 1.9% a year. The Central/Eastern Europe sub-region will record the strongest rate of growth, at 4.4% a year. Southern Europe will see below regional average growth, at 2.6% a year, while the two remaining sub-regions will record better than average rates of expansion, i.e. Northern Europe 3.8% a year, East Mediterranean Europe 4.2% a year.
- Long-haul travel to Europe will grow, at just over 4% a year between 1995 and 2020 as against 2.9% for intraregional travel. None the less, there will still be a 6:1 ratio between intra-European and interregional tourists to Europe in 2020.
- Almost 200 million arrivals a year are recorded in the 22 countries bordering the Mediterranean Sea (including non-European countries with a Mediterranean coastline). Average annual growth of below 3% is forecast for the first two decades of the century, producing a volume of 346 million arrivals in 2020 for a global market share of 22%, as compared with almost 32% in 1995.
- The top three Medierranean destinations in 2020 will remain the same, i.e. France, Spain, Italy. However, the strongest rates of growth among the Mediterranean countries will be achieved by two groups of countries: those in the rapid growth phase of development, e.g. Turkey and Eygpt; and those rebuilding their tourism sectors from one form or another of disruption in recent years, e.g. the new countries of the former Yugoslavia, Lebanon, Libya.

**Trends in the Pattern of Europe's Tourism**

A number of researchers have presented information on likely future trends in Europe's tourism. A distillation of these is made from the following sources: the European Travel Commission's *Megatrends of Tourism in Europe (to the year 2005 and beyond)* (1999); the World Tourism Organisation's *Tourism 2020 Vision* study volume *Intraregional and Long Haul Flows: Europe* (2000); that same body's *Strategic Issues for Europe*, arising from the June 1998 Leadership Forum of Advisers of the WTO Business Council; the European Travel and Tourism Action Group/European Travel Commission/British Tourist Authority August 1998 conference report *Marketing Intelligence for Planning the Future: Europe in the Global Context* (ETAG, 1998); and the issue of the *Tourism Trendspotter* bi-monthly service which identified eight trends for Europe's tourism (Tourism Trendspotter, 1999).

***Increased Competition***

Stronger competition will come both from inside and outside the region. More Europeans will switch their holidays to destinations outside Europe. This trend is likely to outpace the rise in interregional tourists (where the biggest rate of increase will be provided by Asians) coming to Europe. Also, the increased range of goods and services competing for the prospective tourist's discretionary spend will be manifested in one respect through a growing number of leisure offers within a few hours' travel from many peoples' homes, such as theme parks, health and sporting clubs, cultural events, entertainment complexes etc. leading to more shorter-duration, closer-to-home trips. Demand will be diverted from longer trips further afield.

***Changes in Lifestyle***

The fragmentation of household type and composition (i.e. less traditional family groups and more singles, single parents, couples without children), alongwith ageing of the population, is leading to a greater range of differentiated market segments and niches (and the need for tourist products to be developed for them).

The insecurity of tenure of employment is resulting in growing rather than lessening workplace pressure. The computer is proving not to be a liberating force reducing work but a facility which, because it can be accessed at all times, results in a blurring of work and leisure time. In consequence, there is occurring a rise of combined work and pleasure trips. The Scottish Tourist Board reports that more business travellers to Scotland are being accompanied by their families – not just partners but children too (Hay, 2000). This may reflect *inter alia* the increasing difficulty of scheduling a traditional summer holiday break given both partners in a household working, school term time-tables, etc.

Another manifestation of the flexibility but 'tie' of the computer is likely to be the growth of holidays where the laptop and modem are taken along to enable daily contact to be maintained with the office, client, etc.

The growth of that group of consumers who are 'money-rich but time-poor' has spurred the expansion of the all-inclusive market segment – initially in the Caribbean, but now increasingly (though with a somewhat broader market segment focus) in Europe too. Of course, it is the 'money- and time-rich' consumers (the early retirees and others with protected pension incomes) who constitute the most potentially rewarding segments for the travel trade – particularly intra-European, and from North America and Japan into Europe. However, with the economies of the industrialised nations finding it difficult to finance the state pensions of the growing proportions of the older age groups, a consequence much discussed is the raising of the retirement age to 70 or over. This will dampen down demand from the most promising travel market segment.

***Short Breaks***

From the first product and market developments in the 1980s, short break holidays have grown rapidly in popularity, and the signs are that this growth will continue. Short breaks now cover a wide range of types, i.e. from out-of-season promotions, to 'sampler' visits (a strategy used by many Eastern European countries), to luxury breaks, to thematic stays, to shopping trips, to concert/event visits. The pattern of a main holiday with a number of short break trips is a norm for increasing numbers of Europeans. In less strong economic times, the main holiday may be replaced by the short breaks.

It is this short breaks component which will be largely responsible for the growth rate in intraregional European tourist arrivals over the period to 2020 being as high as the 2.9% a year forecast by the WTO. This clearly demonstrates the difficulty of using 'arrivals' as the unit of measurement for forecasting tourism, but it is the only realistic option as the data availability for alternative (more useful) indicators such as nights or spending is much poorer across the countries of the world.

### *Growth Segments*

The European Travel Commission's *Megatrends* include the following market segments earmarked for especially strong growth senior citizen travel, business travel especially in the MICE (Meeting, Incentive Travel, Conventions and Exhibitions) categories, visiting friends and relatives (VFR), city visits (especially for sporting and cultural events), winter sunshine and cruise holidays (which are expected to rise faster than either winter sports or summer holidays), day trips for varied purposes, adventure holidays and trips to 'off the beaten track' places (e.g. to the jungle in comfort and safety), society/association etc. group visits, and rural tourism.

Within the VFR segment the relative importance of visits to friends is reported by at least one destination to be rising faster than to family (Hay, 2000). This may be attributable at least in part to the expanding geographic boundaries of each individual's community of business and personal connections facilitated through the electronic communications age and the ease of travel. The spread of the impact of European air deregulation, noted below, could be a further positive influence. Given the key role of the 'friend' in the destination in influencing the potential traveller's decision to visit, destination marketing activities may in future include some undertaken in the destination itself targeted at residents with friends outside the area, e.g. money-off purchase or entry if accompanied by someone with a provable place of residence overseas or in some other part of the country.

***Accommodation and Catering***

Again drawing on the European Travel Commission's *Megatrends,* it is anticipated that demand for three-star and budget accommodation will continue to rise, as it will for less formal types of accommodation (e.g. bed and breakfast, university facilities out-of-term). Hotel accommodation will be increasingly packaged, especially for short break pleasure trips. More hotel-created packages combining a variety of features will be offered through direct sell methods. More provision of in-house accommodation and catering at major leisure and sporting venues will be developed, e.g. theme parks, sporting, cultural, health centres and holiday villages. Second homes and timeshare will both continue to expand, resulting in increased homes for holiday rental.

Demand for catering is likely to polarise: with good quality, individualised small restaurants and inns maintaining strong demand despite the growth of chain and themed restaurants.

***Technology***

One-third of Europeans presently have access to the Internet, whether at home or at work. Between 1998 and 2000 e-commerce is estimated to have quadrupled, while marketing use of the World Wide Web increased from 44% of firms to 75%. Organisations like hotels (noted above) are increasingly developing their own marketing and sales packages communicated to individual market segments and niches. This is made possible by the large amounts of information which the current generation of electronic database systems can hold on individual customers. Electronic communications networks simultaneously support two important marketing strategies: segmentation and globalisation. A supplier can contact the whole world, while creating specific products for very different market segments. Traditional marketing techniques are turned on their head: the supplier defines its own interface with the world (its web-site), stating what they have to offer, and the potential customer accesses it if it is of interest. The medium is also attracting new suppliers, e.g. the Microsoft Expedia site sells a wide range of travel and tourism services. While the threat to the traditional high street travel agent from this technology is real, there are also opportunities for agents to develop on-line product and service offerings since they can represent a variety of suppliers and give choice to the consumer.

***The Euro***

The January 2002 introduction of the Euro in 11 European Union member states seems less likely to have the wholesale impact on the region's travel and tourism than was widely assumed to be the case when the dates were finalised and the 11 committed to it in 1999. Generally speaking, the main benefit to tourism will come from increased intra-European travel, with the following main impacts arising from the Europe's introduction: holidaymakers saving on converting cash and credit card bills; greater predictability of costs for travel companies booking overseas; more transnational tour operating businesses resulting in better deals for consumers; the loss of fee and commission income from foreign exchange business; greater price transparency leading to more harmonising of air fares. The single currency could provide a strong marketing tool for incoming tour operators offering multi-country Euro zone holidays to travellers from interregional markets.

***Airline Deregulation***

European air deregulation has produced a number of new, no frills airlines, some independent, others as subsidiaries of the major carriers in response to the upsurge in consumer interest (including from business travellers) to cheaper air travel. Though the low cost airlines operate between secondary airports they have been successful in fuelling the growth of the short breaks market segment in particular. Despite the demise in late 1999 of one of the original entrants. Debonair, the prevailing high level of standard European air fares (which are set to ensure that the business traveller pays a high premium through the condition that a Saturday night should be spent away from point of origin for any concessional fare to apply) offers scope for the continued incursion in the European air travel market by the low cost carriers. Whether this will be a strand of the big carriers' business or whether genuine competition will continue through the success of the independents remains to be seen. The dice are loaded against the independents if the US deregulation experience is replicated.

The dilemma for destinations is that while they wish to encourage the new market segments able to visit their attractions through the low fares, they do not want to risk alienating their existing (by and large higher spending) clientele. Selective market segmentation is needed to realise the optimal potential across the whole range of opportunity segments.

The consequence of the increased power of the major airline groupings (e.g. Star Alliance, Oneworld partnership, North Atlantic Excellence alliance, North-west-Continental alliance, all of which have European airline involvement) is that Europe's regional airlines are joining up with the alliances because they are finding themselves squeezed between the premium and low cost carriers.

### *Sustainable Tourism*

As tourism in Europe continues to expand and tourists become more aware of socio-environmental aspects of their activity, there will be rejection of certain operator practices as well as of destinations that do not pursue sustainable strategies. The issue was a focus of the WTO Business Council's Leadership Forum of Advisers which in its

*Conclusions: Strategic Issues for Europe* warned that those European cities and regions which are totally built and developed will need to look at measures like the decommissioning of existing bed stocks, replacing sub-standard hotels or, at the very least, regenerating bed stocks or resorts, if they are to satisfy the more demanding tourist of the future. New partnerships and models will be needed in order to create sustainable tourism.

The evidence to date as to the degree of commitment of either the industry or the consumer to sustainable practices in travel and tourism is not conclusive. Despite initiatives like Green Globe, there is one line of argument that states that consumers are able to afford to be concerned about the environment presently because economic performance in the industrialised countries is solid (Willmott, 2000). From the industry standpoint, it is perhaps telling that only 200 out of 16000 tourism businesses in Scotland have signed up for a Green Business scheme operated by the authorities (Hay, 2000).

### Taxation

The European Travel Commission's *Megatrends* document, while optimistic about Europe's prospects, warns that external conditions and government attitudes are uncertain and growth can no longer be taken for granted, especially since increasing tax and regulation are eroding Europe's competitive edge.

The ETC particularly bemoans the fact that the European Union has no coordinated tourism policy or strategy, and that the weak voice which tourism has in putting forward its case holds back the creation of favourable conditions for profitable and sustainable development. It argues that this vacuum in the policy area at a time of great change needs to be filled with a strong and collective presentation on agreed key issues by all the main sector organisations consulting and cooperating together.

### *Congestion and Capacity*

The capacity of airports and all traffic control systems, along-with road congestion at peak times and in popular tourist destinations, will lead to both delays in travel and abandoned plans to travel with a nearer-to-home activity or a non-travel alternative being chosen in preference (Todd, 2000). Combined with approaching ceilings in travel time availability in several Western European countries like Switzerland, the challenge to the industry will be to find ways to achieve growth despite the squeeze on capacity growth and congestion. It is in respect of an area such as this that a European-wide strategic approach may prove most valuable.

# 11

# HOSPITALITY IN MIDDLE EAST

## The Middle Eastern Travel Market

Key trends in international tourism show that tourist arrivals across state boundaries reached about 625 million in 1998 worldwide. International tourism receipts (excluding international transport) increased by just 2% in 1998 over 1997 to US$ 445 billion, which was mainly due, perhaps, to Asia's financial crisis. The Middle East was the second fastest growing region in 1997 after Africa, registering an increase of 6.1% in arrivals and 10.5% in tourism receipts over 1996. In 1998, tourism in the Middle East grew much faster than the world average – by 5.3% in terms of arrivals and 6.4% in terms of receipts.

The Middle East region enjoys a competitive advantage in its attractions, consisting of unparalleled cultural and religious wealth, its still unpolluted and unspoiled beaches and the well-known warmth and generosity of its people. The WTO 'Vision 2020' forecast 19 million tourist arrivals in the Middle East in the year 2000, 37 million tourist arrivals for 2010 and 69 million for the year 2020. This represents an average rate of growth of 6.7% compared with a world average rate of increase of 4.3% (WTO, 2000).

The Arab Middle Eastern travel market was a predominantly business market. Gulf travellers, for instance, were mostly business-oriented and did not give much attention to leisure travel, at least in the Arab world. However, other Arabs such as Egyptians, Tunisians, Syrians and Lebanese, have been travelling for leisure for a relatively long time. As an illustration, well-off Egyptians were accustomed to spend their summer holidays in Lebanon and Syria in addition to Europe since the dawn of the 20th century. The Gulf people started their leisure travel to Lebanon, Syria and Egypt in addition to European countries perhaps in the 1960s. They used to buy villas and flats as second homes to visit in urban centres and in resorts. More recently the Arab leisure market has become large enough to justify dealing with it as an important market, particularly after some Arab investors became interested in new resorts in certain Arab countries such as Egypt, Lebanon, Syria and Tunisia.

The Arab travel market has its own peculiarities, depending upon the character and temperament of the Arab traveller/tourist in various Arab countries. Irrespective of the many links and common features that tie Arabs together, their motivations and behavioural patterns differ. The combination of business and leisure is perhaps the most striking purpose of travel besides visiting relatives and friends. The Arab market segments, whether economic, social, cultural educational or geographic, dictate variations in attitudes and travel patterns. Urban settlers would have different motivations and attitudes than rural people, which is a distinction that is common to most nations of the world; the distinction may be more prominent with Arabs.

## Factors Influencing the Tourist Traffic in the Arab Middle East

### *Positive Factors*

- Worldwide economic recovery with the countries of the region contributing to resumed economic growth.
- Growing interest of the populations in developed countries in the culture and ways of life of people of developing countries.
- Scale and variety of natural and cultural tourist attractions and development in the Arab world.

- Growth in tourist-generating markets which results in the increase in the number of consumers with sufficient discretionary income to travel outside their own country.
- Expansion of international airline connections between tourist-generating countries and main Arab destinations.
- As a result of the up-swing in Middle East traffic, charter flight traffic is expanding.
- Easement of currency and travel regulations affecting foreign tourists.
- Growing impact of computer technology on distribution systems.

*Negative Factors*

- The negative image that used to exist about some countries in the Middle East region characterised by low hygiene standards, tourist harassment, moderate safety records in air, sea and land transport, standing tensions and political upheavals.
- Lack of sufficient infrastructure and major tourist development projects in some destinations.
- Insufficient numbers of skilled personnel and ineffectiveness of education and training programmes.
- Risk of conflict between tourist developers and local communities concerning sustainable tourist development projects.
- Low level of environmental conditions in some towns and localities.
- Ineffective marketing and promotional efforts exerted by some countries of the region.

**Trends in the Expanded Middle East in 1997**

The Expanded Middle East (EME) covers the following three sub-regions: Middle East; Northern Africa and Europe – Mediterranean region. Many of the countries of the EME have experienced unrest and tensions. In some countries, the security of foreign tourists was seriously threatened while in others tourists were the target of terrorist movements and attacks. Many destinations in the region would therefore benefit significantly from Middle East peace agreements.

Some traditional destinations of the region have already invested heavily in tourism and they are reaping benefits of such investment. Other countries, particularly those of the Gulf, are realising the importance of investing in tourism as a tool for development and are adopting progressively measures to create a better climate for potential investors, both within and outside the region.

All three regions taken together registered almost 36 million tourist arrivals in 1997, generating an estimated US$ 22.8 billion in tourism receipts, or an average of US$ 633 per tourist arrival. This average conceals significant differences between one sub-region and another. The average receipts per tourist arrival in Northern Africa were US$ 343 against US$ 871 for the East-Mediterranean Europe and US$ 582 for the Middle East region (WTO, 1998). The share of the EME in world tourist arrivals was 5.9% and in world tourism receipts 5.1%. This share has fluctuated only marginally on a year-to-year basis. Compared to 1996, this share has increased in terms of tourist arrivals (5.6% in 1996), and tourism receipts (4.9%).

In 1997, countries most visited by European tourists were Tunisia (2.1 million), Egypt (nearly 1.9 million), Syria (286000), Dubai in the United Arab Emirates (183000 in 1995) and Jordan (171000). Growth in European tourism to the region since the late 1980s is attributable in large measure to the tourism development promotion of Egypt. Lower real air fares make the countries of the region more 'price accessible' to European holidaymakers. The continued significance of the region in international trade has generated substantial extra business tourist volumes from Europe. The principal tourist-generating market to the Middle East is Saudi Arabia (intraregional traffic). As to inter-regional travel, Germany, the UK, United States, France, Italy and the Netherlands constitute about one-third of the tourist traffic to the region.

Insofar as outbound travel from the region is concerned, Middle Eastern residents have increased the volume of their overseas travel noticeably. The most favoured destinations for Middle Eastern tourists are tourist destinations in the region (intraregional), such as the Gulf states, Egypt, Lebanon, Syria, Jordan and Tunisia. The next favoured destination regions are Europe, North America and East Asia. Data on outbound tourism by the residents of Middle Eastern countries are inadequate to conduct any detailed analysis. Such data are not recorded by separate country of origin for Arab travellers between many states. Moreover, some governments regard these data as politically sensitive. Likewise data on expenditures overseas by country are not reliable and are not even available in most countries of the region.

A new regional tourism association, called the Middle East Mediterranean Travel and Tourism Association (MEMTTA), was created in October 1995 at an international economic conference in Amman, Jordan. Its goal is to pave the way for increased tourism development in the region and at the same time, forge bonds between private sector tourism interests that will help ease some of the political tensions in the region. Cyprus, Egypt, Israel, Jordan, Morocco, Palestine, Tunisia and Turkey signed its charter.

In March 1996, a 'conference of peacemakers' was convened in Sharmel-sheikh, Egypt, and was attended by leaders of 27 nations, including a broad swath of the Arab World. They joined in a sweeping condemnation of bombings and vowed to cooperate in cracking down on terrorist attacks and in promoting peace throughout the Middle East.

The private sector should become more active, experienced and more participative in achieving economic growth. Middle Eastern tourism will continue to benefit from moves towards more free-market economies and the search for alternative growth sectors in the economies. Many Middle Eastern countries see tourism as an excellent developmental tool, which can fulfil balanced and sustainable growth.

## Changing Market Segments, Product Development and Marketing Strategies

### *Growth of Tourist Outbound Travel and Purpose of Visit*

The tourist demand for outbound travel is growing due to the enhanced discretionary incomes and increase in the reasons for travel. Visiting friends and relatives (VFR) still occupies a large portion of the tourist market in the Middle East. Continuing advances in computer technology and the even more rapid growth in the use of these developments for business applications is likely to restrict the expansion of business travel. Companies are now applying technology more and more as a substitute for a business trip where possible.

### *Patterns of Holiday Travel*

The Middle East region has developed its tourism not on the basis of beach resort holidays as so many long-haul destinations from Europe and North America have done, but on the basis of the rich cultural and religious heritage of the countries of the region. It is the birthplace of three major world religions: Christianity, Islam and Judaism. The archaeological sites in Egypt, Jordan, Lebanon and Syria have constituted the attractions for foreign tourism for decades. However, these sites clearly have finite carrying capacities. The tourist authorities in Jordan strictly limit new hotel development expansion in the ancient hidden city of Petra because of concerns that consequent large increases in tourist numbers will cause irreparable damage to the antiquities. The same concern prevails now in Egypt, particularly in the Valley of the Kings in Luxor's West Bank, where studies to limit the numbers of visitors are in process.

Many of the countries of the region now embrace tourism as part of their economic development strategies. There is consequently a need to develop more natural and archaeological sites for tourist use and or to diversify the types of tourism catered for, including beach tourism. The region possesses a wide array of natural as well as cultural and historical resources, including the Mediterranean, Red

Sea, Arabian Gulf and Indian Ocean coastlines. These offer considerable potential for beach resort development. The Middle East is the first logical interregional tourist destination for the European tourist market because of its geographical proximity, but the unsettled political climate of the region over recent decades has prevented both interest and the flow of investment in coastal tourism. The expansion of European beach resort tourism has been to the west (e.g. to the Caribbean and North America) and to south and south-east Asia (e.g. Goa in India, Sri Lanka and Thailand). The governments of the region, including Egypt, recognise that the Middle East tourism product should not be developed solely as an extension to the Mediterranean resorts of Spain, France and Italy. It should be manifested through facilities and attractions, which are an expression of the cultural heritage and intrinsic features of the Arab people of the Middle East. The recent growth in European interregional tourism has been based on long-haul beach resorts reflecting the 'trend-setters' move away from the closer to home destination areas towards far flung destinations which are perceived as 'exciting and unspoilt'. Marketing activities by many of these destinations and improved air transport access, including through charter operations, have ensured that the momentum of trend has been maintained. The North American and Asian origin markets (principally the United States, Canada and Japan) are geographically more distant form the Middle East region than is Europe. The lure of the region for the tourists from these markets will remain predominantly its culture and heritage, with beach resorts constituting relatively limited appeal until late in the forecast period.

In volume terms, Europe will remain the largest potential interregional market for the Middle East. Yet Europe is a mature tourist-generating region and overall could be approaching its ceiling (both in terms of free time and personal income) for tourism growth potential. The Middle East region will continue to attract for some years before ceiling limitations come into effect. None the less, ceiling constraint on the European market in the mid- to long-term will be of increasing concern to tourism planners in the region.

***Quality and Quantity***

An important question for the Middle Fast is how tourist traffic in general and intraregional tourist movement in particular could be economically, socially and environmentally viable.

As Middle Eastern tourist products are mostly quality products, they should be addressed to quality markets. While quantity (number of tourist arrival and tourist nights) count in placing the tourist destination among the leading places to visit, quality is becoming more and more a decisive criterion in the economic viability of tourism as a productive industry. How quality tourist flows could be marketed is a technical and professional question that requires expertise and know-how that cannot be explained in the present chapter. On the other hand, service quality in tourism is a cornerstone in the competition between destinations.

The full range of elements, features and characteristics that go to make up any tourist experience is quite wide and varies from one customer to another, but good field research in tourist motivations would help in diagnoing those desired components of the tourist experience. Among these would be quality of attractions, facilities, safety, superservices, good general atmosphere, comfort, warmth friendliness, care, immediate corrective action for any default, etc.

**Tourism and Sustainability**

International tourist markets are becoming increasingly conscious of the need for sustainable tourism development, which meets the needs of present tourist and host regions while protecting and enhancing opportunity for the future. Tourists are more knowledgeable about their possible contribution to the degradation of nature and culture and are increasingly scrutinising tourism development occurring in a country or region before making their choice. Knowledge leads directly to interest in the intrinsic features of countries and regions.

In practice few tourists undertake a holiday solely related to nature or a country's culture. Despite the upsurge in awareness and interest noted, the avid ecotourist will remain a small market segment. However, an increasing proportion of tourists will include a nature or culture component in their holiday (as a day trip for example). Even more will select a destination, which has an environment-friendly approach to its tourism development. Marketing strategies (supported, of course, by appropriate product development) should stress this sustainable approach to tourism development. This can influence the destination decisions not only of special interest culture or nature-oriented tourists, but also of tourists wishing to pursue conventional general interest pursuits such as beach or touring holidays.

Tourist product development in the region could fall under four categories namely:

- Full development of tourist resorts, e.g. in Egypt, the Gulf of Aquaba, the Red Sea coast, the North West coast and North Sinai, Mutrah/Muscat, and Salala, in Oman, Aquaba in Jordan, Jumeira Beach in Dubai, Lattakia in Syria.
- Creating new and re-establishing tourist destinations of Oman, Yemen and eventually Iraq. Libya, once freed from the economic blockade, could be developed as a potential tourist destination provided that tourist awareness of the population and efficient tourist training could be conducted.
- Reconstruction of secondary existing tourist-oriented cities in Jordan (Jarash) and Syria (Aleppo and Homs).
- Restoration and improvement of prime historical attractions and archaeological sites, such as the Giza pyramids area, Valley of the Kings and Fayoum in Egypt, Petra in Jordan.

**Future Prospects**

Although 'growth sustains growth', which means that tourism in the Middle East would continue to grow, this does not necessarily apply at continuous high rates of expansion. Some air transport studies show that the Middle East will match the world's average for all scheduled air traffic growth but will lag behind slightly in the expansion of international route traffic. The *Economist* study 'International Tourism Forecasts to 2005' shows that tourism expansion prospect in the Middle East would average 4.3% a year.

WTO forecasts to the year 2000 and beyond suggest more than 4.5% annual growth. This average rate of increase is low when compared with the rates of growth achieved and/or anticipated by a number of countries in the Middle East region for their inbound tourist traffic. Some of these forecasts are close to or in excess of 10% a year. Egypt is one of these countries while some important European tourist-generating markets such as Germany, the UK, France and Italy, responding to the good resort developments in Egypt, are expected to achieve faster rates of growth. This would be contingent upon continued stability in Egypt and in the whole Middle East region.

The development potential of tourism in the Middle East looks good but the question is how much would its average growth rate be? Accurate scientific forecasting is difficult as almost all base years are exceptional years because of the repetitive negative events that occur in the Middle East, i.e. conflicts, wars and terrorist acts. If real sustainable peace and stability prevail, the Middle East would become a tourist heaven. Beside peace, perhaps the three most pressing needs for action both by individual countries and on a collective basis, are:

- Encouragement and generation of investments in and resource commitments to the region's main tourism sectors including air transport, accommodation and recreation.
- Image improvement: substantially increased and well-planned focused aggressive marketing and promotional activities are necessary to win the conviction and confidence of potential tourists of the major tourist generating markets that the Middle East

region has a competitive advantage in offering a wide range of bona fide holiday destinations that cater for almost all forms of tourism.

- Developing more effective safety and security measures to guarantee a more stable tourist climate that contributes to longer-term tourism development programmes in the face of international competition.

Moreover, a revival of the consciousness of Arab solidarity and realisation of exogenous risks and dangers that threaten Arab identity in the age of globalisation should result in more solid and substantial efforts to constitute Arab economic and tourism integration. These would lead to a brighter future through complementary productive endeavours, among which Arab intraregional tourist traffic would be one effective operational tool.

# 12

# HOSPITALITY IN NORTH AMERICAN TOURISM

## Introduction

This chapter examines North America – specifically the United States, Canada and Mexico – as origin and destination markets for international tourism. It provides statistics on the size and scope of international tourism, how North America fits into the whole, and analyses international tourism performance in the United States, Canada and Mexico in the 1990s. The chapter also reviews some major factors likely to affect international tourism to and form North America in the future, and includes official forecasts where available.

## The Americas

The Americas (including North, South, Central America and the Caribbean), home to nearly 800 million people, 14% of the world's population, is second as a regional destination for international travel, after Europe. The Americas received nearly 123 million international visitors in 1998, up 41% since 1989 and comprising 19% of all international tourist arrivals. International tourist receipts (excluding international fares) have increased more than twice as fast as arrivals. The Americas received 27% of international tourism receipts or US$ 120 billion. Receipts in the Americas rose 99% over 1989. South Asia (117%), Africa (114%) and the East Asia/Pacific region (101%), however, enjoyed larger gains.

These differential growth rates have resulted in a loss of share of arrivals for the Americas, falling from nearly 26% of the total in 1970 to 19% in 1998. The region, however, has seen a small increase in its share of international tourism receipts, rising from 26.8% in 1970 to 27.3% in 1998, due primarily to the changing composition of visitors to the region.

**North America**

The remainder of this chapter deals with North America alone, including the countries of the United States, Canada and Mexico. In 1998, the US was placed third as an international visitor destination, losing its second place ranking of the year before to Spain. The US hosted over 46 million international arrivals, 7.3% of the world total, in 1998.

Mexico and Canada are considerably smaller inbound markets, receiving 19.8 million (3.1%) and 18.8 million (3.0%) international arrivals, respectively. In total, then, North America hosted over 85 million international visitors in 1998, 69% of the Americas' regional total and 13% of all international arrivals.

North-America, however, accounted for a significantly greater share of international receipts, 20%, due largely to the influence of the United States. In 1998, international tourism receipts in North America totalled US$ 88 billion. The US garnered 81% of this, or over US$ 71 billion, making it the largest international destination in the world in terms of receipts. The US, while hosting only 7.3% of arrivals, received 16.2% of receipts, due to the longer stays and higher spending patterns evident among many of its visitors.

Canada came in ninth in tourism receipts in 1998, capturing US$ 9.1 billion (2.1% of the total), while Mexico received US$ 7.9 billion (1.8%). In both cases, their shares of receipts were smaller than their shares of arrivals, the reverse of the pattern evident for the United States.

**United States**

According to Tourism Industries International Trade Administration in the US Department of Commerce, the US has benefited greatly from this international tourism boom. International arrivals in the US increased 28% since 1989 to total 46.4 million in 1998. In 1998, however, international travel to the US declined nearly 3% from its record high level of 47.8 million international visitors in 1997.

This decline in arrivals also generated a similar decline in international travel receipts in the US in 1998. Receiving a total of US$ 71.1 billion in international tourism receipts, however, the US remained the top international tourism receipts earner in the world, well ahead of second place Italy, with US$ 30 billion in receipts.

As an origin, the US is the second largest outbound market in the world, following Germany. Since 1989, the United States' outbound international tourism market has increased more than its inbound market, rising 37% over the 1990s to total 56.3 million in 1998. Over the period, international departures from the US have shown a rather steady increase year after year, with the exception of 1991. In response to the Persian Gulf War and an economic recession at home, US residents reduced their outbound travel by nearly 7% that year.

International payments by outbound US travellers increased nearly twice as much as did departures – 61% during the past decade to reach US$ 53.7 billion in 1998.

To summarize, the United States experienced slower growth as an international tourism destination than as an international tourism origin of international travellers. But, because of the changing country composition and nature of its visitors, the US actually enjoyed a much greater increase in receipts than in payments during the same period. As a result, it increased significantly its international travel trade balance from a surplus of US$ 5.2 billion (including international passenger fares) in 1989 to US$ 18.7 billion in 1998.

**US Markets**

The US is quite dependent on its two neighbours, Canada and Mexico, for many of its international visitors. In 1998, these two countries accounted for nearly half of the total, while overseas origins generated the remaining 51%.

This represents a major shift, however, from 1989, when Canada produced 42% of all international visitors to the US, as compared to only 29% in 1998. Ten years earlier, Mexico generated 19%, about the same share as today, while overseas countries generated only 38% of all international arrivals in the Us, compared to 51% in 1998.

The real growth in international travel to the US, therefore, has been from overseas markets. While all international travel to the US increased 28% between 1989 and 1998, arrivals from overseas origins grew more than twice as fast, 69%, to total 23.7 million in 1998.

The year 1998, however, was not a particularly good one for international travel to the US, reflecting a continuing slide in arrivals from Canada, which first started in 1992 in the wake of a weakening Canadian dollar. Travel from Canada declined a significant 11% in 1998 to total 13.4 million arrivals as the Canadian dollar sunk to historic lows. This decrease was almost completely offset by the gain in the United States' second largest country market, Mexico, with a 10% increase to top the 9 million mark in 1998.

Both these markets are extremely sensitive to exchange rates between themselves and the United States. Economic problems in Asia, volatility in South America and a sluggish economy in Europe all contributed to the 2% drop in overseas visitors to the US in 1998. Overall, inbound international travel to the US declined 3% in 1998.

Europe is the United States' top regional origin, from which 45% of its overseas visitors embark. Asia/Oceania accounted for 31% of all overseas visitors to the US in 1998, followed by South America (12%), the Caribbean/Central America (8%) and Africa/Middle East (4%).

Three of the United States' top overseas country markets are in Europe – the UK, Germany and France. The UK is the United States' leading European market, with nearly 4 million arrivals in 1998. Germany produced 1.9 million visitors to the US in 1998. Japan, however, is the largest overseas country market for travel to the US, generating 4.9 million arrivals in 1998. Since 1989, travel from Japan has increased rather significantly (+59%), although it was down 9% in 1998, less than might have been expected given the Asian financial crisis. Other Asian countries, however, posted even more significant declines, such as South Korea (–51%) and Taiwan (–13%), as origins of international travel to the US in 1998.

Brazil stands out as the real star in terms of growth over the past decade, increasing its production of visitors to the US by 172%. Today, Brazil is the United States' fifth largest overseas market.

**International Travel from the US**

Outbound international travel from the United States has shown strong growth throughout the 1990s, increasing 37% overall. In 1998, the US experienced a record year for outbound tourism with departures totalling 56.3 million, up 6% over 1997. Growth was particularly strong in travel to Canada (+11%), as the same exchange rates that kept many Canadians away from the US stimulated US travel to Canada. Travel to overseas destinations was also strong, up 7% over 1997 and a well-above-average 56% over 1989.

Among US travellers visiting overseas destinations. Europe is the most popular, garnering 45% of the total in 1998. Asia/Oceania received 21% of US overseas departures; while Central America and the Caribbean receive a combined total of 19%.

With approximately 11 million US visitors. Europe is more than twice as large as a regional destination for overseas travel from the US than the second most popular, Asia/Oceania. In 1998, US travel to Europe grew 14% but even more so to South America (17%), the fourth largest overseas destination for US departures.

By country, the UK benefits most from outbound US travel, receiving 3.6 million US visitors in 1998, a gain of 2% over the prior year. France was the second most popular destination of overseas US travellers, followed by Italy and Germany. Over the past decade, Italy has seen the greatest growth in US visitors (+60%), receiving almost 1.9 million in 1998.

**Travellers to and from the US**

So, who are these people behind these impressive numbers? We know that the worldwide international travel community consists of a relatively very small number of people. The WTO estimates that today only about 3.5% of the world's population are international travellers. That translates to about 200 million people out of a global population of 6 billion.

- This small group of people take lots of trips; they tend to be repeat visitors to their destinations and, therefore, over time they have become very experienced, sophisticated and demanding travellers.
- Most international travellers, like a growing percentage of the population in many of the developed nations of the world, are middle-aged.
- Not surprisingly, international travellers tend to be quite affluent, especially US outbound travellers to overseas destinations.
- Leisure purposes dominate international travel to and from the US.
- International travellers tend to take substantially longer trips than do domestic travellers: overseas travellers to and from the US average more than 15 nights.

**Canada**

Let us look now at another North American travel market – Canada. Canada's inbound international visitor market is less than half the size of the United States' and has been on a slightly slower growth curve. Since 1989, international arrivals in Canada increased 25% to reach 18.8 million in 1998. Growth came primarily from overseas and less so from the US. Because of this, Canada has enjoyed a dramatic increase in tourism receipts which more than doubled from US$ 6.7 billion in 1989 to US$ 13.9 billion in 1998. This surpasses the United States' growth in receipts of 99%.

The big difference between Canada and the US is Canada's declining outbound market. This is due exclusively, however, to the big drop-off in overnight visits to the US as mentioned before. Canadian departures to the US were 12% fewer in 1998 than in 1989. On the other hand, departures to overseas destinations grew 41% among Canadians, as compared to the 56% growth in US travel to overseas countries during that period.

Again, reflecting the fact that overseas destinations now capture a much larger share of Canadian outbound travel – where travellers spend more time and money than they do in the US – payments of outbound Canadian travellers soared 62%, despite the decline in departures.

To summarize, unlike the US, in the 1990s Canada showed greater growth as a tourism destination than as an origin. But like the US, because of the changing country composition and nature of its visitors. Canada enjoyed a much greater increase in receipts than in payments during the same period. As a result, Canada's travel deficit fell to US$ 2 billion in 1998, down 45% over 1987 and its lowest level in 12 years.

Despite the significant increase in overseas arrivals in Canada, the US remains its number one source market, with nearly 80% of its total inbound market coming from its southern neighbour in 1998. The share coming from overseas origins, however, rose from not quite 18% in 1989 to 21% in 1998.

Europeans made up 56% of Canada's overseas market in 1998, increasing their visits to Canada by 37%. Three of Canada's top four country markets are in Europe. Growth has been particularly strong from France and Germany over this period. Travel from Asia grew 25% between 1989 and 1998, but was down a dramatic 19% in 1998.

**Mexico**

In Mexico, the Americas dominate international travel. In 1997, nearly all international tourist arrivals in Mexico (18.9 million) came from this region. Travel from Europe to Mexico totalled 347000 arrivals that year.

In 1998, there were nearly 10 million Mexican international tourist departures. The vast majority of these (9.3 million) were destined to the United States. After the US, the next most popular destination for Mexican international travellers are Italy, Spain and Canada, with around 100000 visitors each.

**Forecasts**

Forecasting international travel in total and between countries can be a difficult task in that there are so many factors that can affect it. There are currently several trends favourable to the growth in international tourism.

Population growth, immigration and an ageing population in many developed nations of the world will continue to have profound impacts on the travel industry in North America. For example, the ageing of Baby Boomers (those born between 1946 and 1964) in the US, and similar trends in other leading developed nations in Europe and Asia, have produced and will continue to produce significant gains in the numbers of people in the middle-aged and older categories, those groups most likely to travel internationally.

Where the economy goes, so goes the travel industry. The travel industry in North America is also likely to prosper over the next several years thanks to steady growth in the economies of the US and Canada, and renewed growth in Europe and Asia. DRI/McGraw-Hill, the econometric forecasting firm used by the Travel Industry Association of America, projects that real GDP will increase in the 2.5 – 3.5% annual range for each of the major world regions between the late 1990s and the early 2000s.

These positive factors are reflected in the bullish outlook for international tourism presented by the World Tourism

Organisation (WTO). According to WTO, total international arrivals are predicted to rise to 668 million in 2000, top 1 billion in 2010 and reach nearly 1.6 billion in 2020. This represents a growth rate of about 4.1% a year. Spending by these travellers is expected to increase even more, so that spending in the year 2010 is expected to be US$ 1.6 billion – nearly four times more than in 1998.

Prospects are also improving in the United States. According to Tourism Industries, short-term growth in arrivals may be slow but expected recoveries will spur the US into a record breaking international visitation level in 2003 when international arrivals will top out at nearly 55 million.

Growth between 1998 and 2003 is expected to be 18%. Arrivals in the US from Canada should total over 15 million by 2003, as the recent strength of the Canadian economy is expected to reverse the decline in travel to the US in the 1990s.

In Mexico, stability of the economy is also expected due to the US$ 24 billion financial agreement reached with the International Monetary Fund, World Bank and Inter-American Development Bank. Assuming sustained growth in its NAFTA partners which would also help support Mexico's upward GDP trend, arrivals from Mexico to the US should grow steadily by over 3% a year to reach 10.6 million by 2003.

And, overseas arrivals in the US are expected to continue to grow the fastest, 22% over the next five years to total 28.9 million arrivals in 2003. Growth should be strongest from Venezuela (+38%), the UK (+27%), Argentina (+25%) and Germany (+23%).

Growth is expected to be even stronger in international travel to Canada, up 20% between 1998 and 2003. Travel inbound to Canada from the US is projected to reach 18.3 million arrivals in 2003. This long-term forecast assumes continued growth in the US economy and benefits of the Open Skies agreement.

The outlook for France is decidedly upbeat, due to pent-up demand for travel to Canada among the French and a resilient economy. The outlook for Germany is less favourable and it will take some time for the German economy to rebound. The forecast for Japanese travel to Canada is negative as well Canada expects to start to see small increases from the Japanese market.

Looking even further ahead, the WTO predicts that the East Asia/Pacific region will continue to be the world's fastest growing tourism regional destination in the upcoming decades, overtaking the Americas as the world's number two receiving region, holding a 26% share in 2020 as against 15% by the Americas.

The top ten receiving countries will change significantly with China (currently not even in the top ten) becoming the leading destination in 2020, with a predicted 130 million arrivals. France, the US and Spain will be in second, third and fourth place. Hong Kong, if treated as a separate entity, will also become one of the main destinations. Also entering the top ten will be the Russian Federation.

In terms of generating countries, Germany will remain number one as it is today. The next largest will be Japan and the United States, followed by China in fourth place. The Russian Federation will also become a major outbound tourism country by the year 2020.

# 13

# HOSPITALITY IN SOUTH AMERICAN TOURISM

## Introduction

South American countries have realised that tourism is an excellent way to diversify their economies. Every day more and more capital is being invested in infrastructure and at the same time there are a number of initiatives to attract foreign capital, especially geared to financing hotels and other kinds of accommodation for tourists. In addition to the traditional options of 'sun and sand' holidays, as well as ecotourism and cultural tourism, it is now possible to witness the rise of cruise tourism, with cruises towards the Antarctic becoming increasingly popular.

South America benefits from 14.9% of the total of arrivals of international tourism to the Americas and its proportion of income stands at 12.6% (WTO, 1999). According to data from the World Tourism Organisation (WTO, 1999) arrivals of foreign tourists reached 18,247,000 in 1998, amounting to a growth of 15% compared to the year before. This growth is reflected in receipts, which during this period amounted to US$ 15,075 million, that is an increase of 11% over 1997. During the period between 1989 and 1998 arrivals grew at an average rate of 9.1% and income at 12.2%. The principal market for South America is regional; Europe and the United States are the principal long-distance markets.

The most important countries in terms of attracting international tourism to South America are Argentina, Brazil and Uruguay (Figure 13.1), although Uruguay finds itself only in eighth position as regards tourist income, preceded by Argentina, Brazil, Venezuela, Chile, Colombia, Peru and Paraguay in that order (Figure 13.2).

Brazil (14.7%), Peru (10.4%), Chile (9.2%) and Colombia (9.1%) are the countries with the greatest growth in arrivals during the period 1989 – 98. Surinam (21.2%) and Paraguay (21.1%) demonstrate the greatest percentage of income in US$ during the same period (WTO, 1999: 211).

The Tourism Survey Panorama 2020 (WTO, 1998) predicts that in this new millennium the annual growth in tourism in South America will be 4.9% compared to North America where there will be a decrease of 3.6% a year.

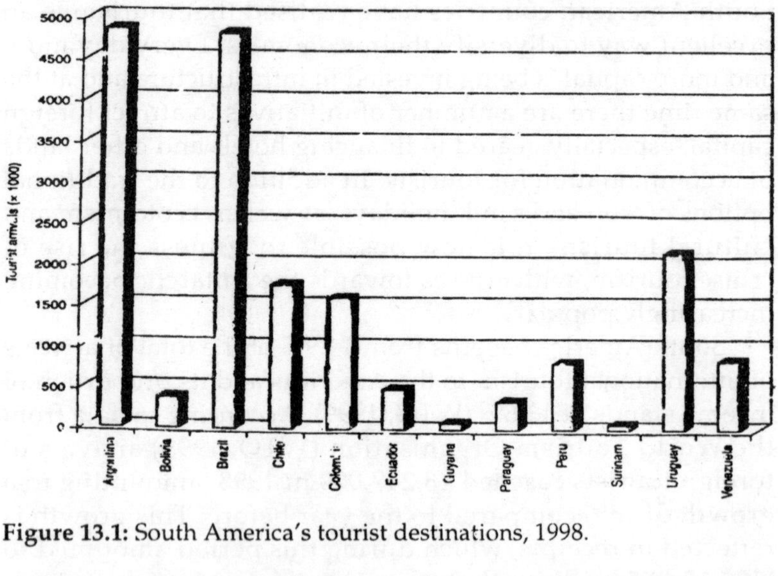


**Figure 13.1:** South America's tourist destinations, 1998.

It is generally considered that ecotourism allows for a greater participation by the local population in its development. This is due to the fact that it is practised on a small scale, thus achieving a less conflicting relationship between visitors and those visited. Income gained by those

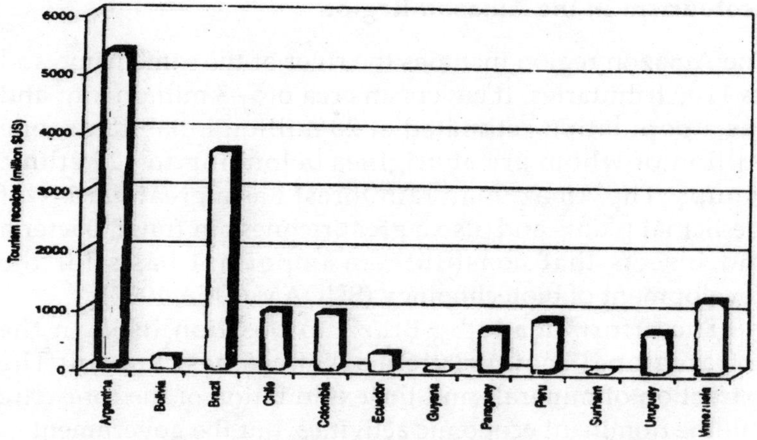


**Figure 13.2:** South Ameria's tourist receipts, 1998.

offering services complements traditional sources of income. The growth in participation on the part of the local population has added to a commitment towards the environment and led to ecotourism being regarded as one of the most popular expressions of the sustainable development of tourism. There is every reason to hope that this will continue. In many South American countries rural tourism is another form of tourism that is considered sustainable.

## Ecotourism and Rural Tourism as Forms of Sustainable Tourism

The 1970s witnessed a growing concern for the deterioration of the environment and this led to this creation of what became popularly known as ecotourism. In South America the Galapagos National Park (Ecuador) was an important ecotouristic destination well before the term 'ecotourism' was coined. On the threshold of the new millennium two parks of the subcontinent are growing in popularity: the Amazon and Patagonia, Bolivia is looking for a strategy of sustainable development within the parameters of 'eco-ethno' tourism while Peru can count on an alternative in adventure tourism.

**Ecotourism in the Amazon Region**

The Amazon region includes the river of the same name and its 1100 tributaries. It covers an area of 7–8 million km$^2$ and has a population estimated at 20 million inhabitants, one million of whom are aborigines belonging to 420 ethnic groups. The Amazonian rain forest has a great variety of medicinal plants and also a great richness in fungi, bacteria and insects that constitute an important basis for the development of biotechnology (SUDAM/OEA 1997).

The efforts made by Brazil to position itself in the extraregional ecotouristic market are best known. The extraction of minerals and the exploitation of the forest are still the dominant economic activities, but the government as well as the private sector are trying to develop ecotourism, which is growing rapidly and has a conservationist nature as well as permitting a sustainable way of life for the local population and the generation of income for companies in the area (Chua, 1995). The region has a great capacity to develop ecotourism and thus attract considerable international tourism. Other attractions are of a historic and cultural character, as well as scientific interest, technical activity and programmed events (SUDAM/OEA, 1997).

While there is evidence that in the 1960s there were already travel agencies specialising in ecotourism, the boom took place between the end of the 1980s and the beginning of the 1990s. An ethical code of the practice of ecotourism was established in 1996 (Pires, 1999).

The Pantanal is another region of Brazil being developed for ecotourism. Its system extends to the neighbouring countries of Bolivia and Paraguay and it is considered one of the greatest concentrations of fauna on the planet as well as being one of the most important natural nurseries in the world (SUDAM/OEA, 1994b). While the region started to receive sporadic visitors from the 1960s it was not until the 1990s that the area witnessed an accelerated influx. The arrival of visitors brought economic benefits to the region and cattle-estate farmers saw in tourism an excellent opportunity to increase their earning power. However, given the considerable fragility of the eco-system, conservationist groups are afraid of the negative impact that might be generated. With the objective of minimising this negative impact, a number of programmes which aim to preserve the environment and educate the local population have been implemented. The objective is to transform the Pantanal into an important destination within the context of international ecotourism, which allows for a sustainable development for the whole area in the new millennium. With this in mind, a convention will be signed between the Inter-American Development Bank (IDB) and the Brazilian government to develop a programme that will improve the existing infrastructure.

## Penguins, Whales and Elephant Seals on the Atlantic Coast of Southern Argentina

Tourism in Argentina has always been closely linked to the National Parks and the network of provincial reserves. As a result of the success of the tourism-protected area formula a system of fauna reserves was established in Patagonia along the southern Atlantic coast with the objective of favouring economic growth by attracting the market segment interested in contact with nature. At the present time, the system of fauna reserves protects whales, penguins, sea elephants and seals and a great variety of birds. It extends from the Southern 41° parallel to the extreme south of the continental coast of Argentina.

The creation of this system of protected areas positively influenced the reproduction of coastal fauna and allowed for the consolidation of growth of tourism in the area. The area which most benefited from this was the city of Puerto Madryn given its proximity to the Valdes Peninsula Reserve, which was added to UNESCO's World Heritage List in 1999.

## From the Andes to the Pacific: The Search for Sustainable Development in Argentinian and Chilean Patagonia

In the Andean-Patagonian mountain range of Argentina, National Parks are the principal attraction for tourism. They consist of a number of settlements and their surrounding areas and allow for the growth of non-conventional economic activities such as the cultivation of berries and aromatic plants (Schlüter, 1999). Away from the protected areas farmhouses constitute an accommodation option for visitors which leads to additional income for those families that make their living from sheepfarming. At the same time, in areas of considerable interest to tourists, small enterprises have sprung up as 'ecolodges' administered by people who live in the area and who apply a conservational approach both to the management and practice of recreational activities.

In Chilean Patagonia rural tourism is benefiting from important development. It started almost two decades ago in the surrounding area of Puerto Montt, in the south of the country. Szmulewiez (1995: 204) points out that the area was colonised by Germans who transplanted their distinctive architectural style to Chile, which, added to the extensive availability of wood, led to large houses being built. The houses were of a very high standard in terms of construction. In the 1980s, when young people moved to the cities in order to find work, most of these houses became unoccupied. At the same time the south of Chile was becoming a popular tourist destination, not only for Chileans but also for foreign tourism (mainly Argentineans). The houses were refurbished and converted into tourist accommodation with or without breakfast.

## Ethnoecotourism in Bolivia

Bolivia is known as 'The country of the High Plateau', given that Lake Titicaca, its most representative site, is to be found there. It can count, at the same time, on traces of a rich pre-colonial past and a very considerable jungle. As Bolivia is unable to offer the 'sun and sand' option, the government looked for a way, from 1994, to base a strategy for sustainable development on a product called 'Ethnoecotourism from the Amazon to the Andes' (Vera-Mendia, 1999). This concent aimed to integrate the physical, biological and cultural diversity of Bolivia, emphasising not only the variety but also the quality of the environment. From a practical point of view, ethnoecotourism consists of different kinds of nature tourism in close association with the culture of the place. Vera-Mendia (1999: 364), optimistic about the possibilities for ethnoecotourism in Bolivia in the 21st century, states that:

> It is the instrument for a model of socio-economic development based on sustainable use, this being harmonious, not wasteful of natural resources or the national heritage. It is based on the capacity of the prehispanic population in Bolivia to present itself to the world, expressing its cultural characteristics. At the same time, in order to enhance diversification of tourism in Bolivia, a number of specialised options has been developed, taking into account the nature of national geography. Among these specialisations are to be found pot-holing, mountain climbing, fishing, walking, bird-watching, scientific tourism and archaeological tourism.

## Ecotourism and Adventure Tourism in Peru

While it is the case that ecotourism is different from adventure tourism in that the latter implies activities with a certain degree of risk, in the Andean environment simple contact with nature implies a certain degree of risk in itself. This is the case in Peru, where the most important natural and cultural sites are found at high altitudes which implies physical discomfort for people of advanced age or with precarious health.

Among the most promoted areas of the Peruvian Andes are the Huascaran National Park and the Inca site of Macchu Picchu. The first offers mountain climbing and trekking (Morales-Arnao, 1994), which can also be practised on the four trails that lead from Cuzco towards the Inca fortress of Macchu Picchu. The trails allow for the appreciation of this UNESCO World Heritage site as well as a number of other interesting sites in the Sacred Valley of the Incas.

**Tourism in the South American Caribbean**

The first tourist product for the international market to be developed in South America was sun and sand holidays. Colombia and Venezuela have the great advantage of having coasts on the Caribbean Sea and thus benefit from the flow of tourism to that region. While Colombia is currently associated with social problems deriving from the struggle against drug trafficking, it can still offer tourists, mostly from Europe and the USA, two popular and traditional resorts: Santa Marta and Cartagena de Indias. The San Andrés Islands are also an important destination.

Venezuela also benefits from a considerable flow of tourists heading towards the Island of Margarita in the Caribbean. However, the search for more sustainable forms of tourism has led to the practice of ecotourism in National Parks (M. Ascanio, 1999) and has fostered travel to various areas of the country characterised by considerable natural beauty but at the present time without the necessary infrastructure or equipment for tourism.

With the objective of offering the visitor a way of life similar to that of the native population, and using the natural geography to promote tourism, the idea of tourist camps has been initiated. A. Ascanio (1997: 159) states that:

> The tourist camps in Venezuela are very different to those known as camping in other countries. In Venezuela the tourist camps in the jungle, the plains or even in the mountains offer a habitat designed using the indigenous type of housing. For example, in the plains and the jungle can be found a kind of accommodation known as *churuta* and this adapts well to the environment and the climate. In the mountain area, old country houses are being remodelled and cabins are being built while, in the open countryside, a shelter is being built from which to hang a number of hammocks.

A programme of inns for tourists has recently been implemented in Venezuela. This has enabled all those who own an attractive dwelling in a rural setting to offer accommodation to tourists. The inns, combined with the organisation of walks and excursions, have led to the development of new routes which are attracting more and more tourists to the area. (A. Ascanio, 1997)

**Beach Tourism in Brazil**

Brazil was among the first South American countries to compete in the inter-regional market with its 'sun and sea' product. In the early 1970s a chain of seaside resorts along the Atlantic coast, from Rio de Janeiro to Santos, was developed for both domestic and international tourism. These resorts attracted mainly tourists from Argentina, who also visited the beaches that stretched from Santos to Porto Alegre (Schlüter, 1998). Later, Brazil started exploiting a number of tourist developments in the northwest of the country, with the objective of capturing an important international market. Another important element is the creation of a number of nature reserves.

**Culture as a Tourist Resource**

South America counts on important traces of its pre-colonial culture, among which are the outstanding archaeological heritage of Inca civilisation, the most important example being Macchu Picchu in Peru. There are also a number of colonial cities, most of which are included in the World Heritage List of UNESCO. Among them are Lima (Peru), (Quito) (Ecuador), Colonia del Sacramento (Uruguay), Olinda (Brazil) and Cartagena de Indias (Colombia).

South America also offers a wealth of socio-cultural expression in which pre-Columbian rituals are mixed with elements introduced by the former colonial powers and influenced by the African slavery system. However, the Rio Carnival is the only socio-cultural product that is highly competitive in the international market (Schlüter, 1998).

Facing the challenges of the 21st century, communities located at a short distance from popular coastal tourist destinations have also sought to benefit from this flow of visitors, developing products based on popular festivals or gastronomy. This is the case of Blumenau (Brazil) and Gaiman (Argentina). Blumenau, in the state of Santa Catarina, is a community whose inhabitants descend mostly from Germans. It is located next to Camboriu, Florianopolis and

Laguna, important sun and sand destinations in the South of Brazil. From the early 1980s a 'Beer Festival' or 'Oktoberfest' was organised which has its roots in an important event held annually (actually in the month of September) in Munich, Germany (Machado, 1996). In the coastal region of Argentinian Patagonia, the small town of Gaiman has sought to develop its economy by offering the classic 'five o'clock tea', which has become known as 'Welsh tea' (Schlüter, 1998: 186).

**Concluding Comments**

South American countries can count on excellent natural resources to attract international tourism, both from neighbouring and distant countries. Efforts are centred on achieving the sustainable development of tourism in the subcontinent. However, it is still the case that there are not sufficient studies to determine whether development within the concept of sustainability can realise, in the long-term, the necessary benefits to achieve the desired profitability of companies, the improvement of the quality of life of the resident population, tourist satisfaction of care of the physical environment.

There are already signs that sustainability is not an easy road to follow and is likely to be beset by many problems in this new millennium. Small undertakings can count on the benefits offered by the Internet but they will have problems in making themselves known to potential tourists. Longedfor community participation in the future could easily degenerate into apathy (Romero-Mayo, 1997; Masri de Achar and Robles-Ponce, 1997) if the inhabitants do not feel sufficiently involved in decision-making and in the sharing of benefits. There is the danger that as the new millennium advances, the environment will be increasingly exposed to pollution with the result that the tourist market could be damaged.

# 14

# WHAT ARE TOURIST ATTRACTIONS?

### What are we Talking About?

As we contemplate the trends in the new millennium, it is curious that tourist attractions in the UK and elsewhere are still broadly defined and assessed from a traditional 1960s resource-based definition of sites or places 'where it is feasible to charge admission for the sole purpose of sightseeing (and where) the primary purpose is to allow public access for entertainment, interest or education, rather than being primarily a retail outlet or a venue for sporting, theatrical or film performances'. The UK definition further notes that attractions 'must be open to the public without prior booking . . .' (*Sightseeing in the UK*, 1998).

Primarily heritage-orientated, this definition includes:

- Historic properties
- Museums, galleries and science centres
- Wildlife/aquarium attractions
- Botanical and other gardens
- Country parks
- Heritage and other visitor centres
- Leisure/theme parks
- Cathedrals and some churches
- Other attractions, such as industrial archaeology sites, steam railways and farm-based attractions

Within this definition, the UK had an estimated 6164 attractions in 1998, drawing around 400 million recorded visits per annum. Only 7% of all attractions (428), however, including those that are free, achieved over 200000 visits per annum. Between them they achieved just over 225 million visits or 57% of all recorded visits in 1998. The 428 comprised 111 country parks, 73 museums or galleries, 60 historic properties, 40 leisure parks, 31 wildlife attractions, 16 gardens, 10 visitors centres and 87 'other'. These attractions draw on an audience of UK and overseas staying tourists but the bulk of all visits are day visits from home in leisure time.

These estimates are based on recorded visits and estimates of visitor volume at known attractions. In other words, they are supply-side estimates of demand and many of them at free attractions are 'guesstimates'. This author believes that, while the available data are indicative of the utilisation of traditional attractions, they tell us nothing about the total demand potential for visitor attractions, especially if the attractions are outwith the traditional tourist board definition.

**Market Demand for Traditional Attractions Falters as Supply Increases**

The UK evidence, based on surveys of known attractions, reveals some clear trends. Table 14.1 shows 20-year trends on an index basis for the volume of visits recorded at four main types of attractions in England. Table 14.2 notes growth in the number of attractions entering the market. Bearing in mind that newer attractions tend to be larger on average than existing attractions, there is no doubt that capacity in the UK increased faster than demand in the last two decades of the 20th century. The UK enters the 21st century with an excess of capacity that has major economic implications for future viability. Reflecting the size characteristics noted in Table 14.3, the majority of visitor attractions are not profitable in a normal industrial sense and their return on capital is inadequate. Five key points help to explain the implications for the future of the three tables.

**Table 14.1**
**Trend in number of visits to attraction in England, 1978 – 98**

| *Year* | *Historic properties* | *Gardens* | *Wildlife sites* | *Museums and galleries* |
|---|---|---|---|---|
| 1978 | 100 | 100 | 100 | 100 |
| 1982 | 85 | 98 | 85 | 91 |
| 1990 | 112 | 139 | 127 | 112 |
| 1994 | 109 | 162 | 111 | 119 |
| 1996 | 116 | 174 | 117 | 121 |
| 1998 | 117 | 170 | 129 | 121 |

1978 = 100. 1978 was chosen as the base year because it was the high level of the 1970s.

**Table 14.2**
**Years in which UK attractions first opened to the public**

| *First opening* | *Historic properties (%)* | *Gardens (%)* | *Museums and galleries (%)* | *Wildlife (%)* | *All (%)* |
|---|---|---|---|---|---|
| 1990 – 98 | 9 | 19 | 16 | 26 | 20 |
| 1980 – 89 | 17 | 26 | 28 | 29 | 27 |
| **Sub-total** | **26** | **45** | **44** | **55** | **47** |
| 1970 – 79 | 15 | 18 | 20 | 19 | 19 |
| 1960 – 69 | 8 | 13 | 10 | 11 | 3 |
| Pre-1969 | 51 | 26 | 26 | 15 | 26 |
| Total | 100 | 100 | 100 | 100 | 100 |
| Number known in 1998 | 1418 | 347 | 1724 | 300 | 5890 |

**Table 14.3**
**The small size of tourist attractions in the UK**

| *Visits per annum* | % |
|---|---|
| Less than 1000 | 10 |
| 1001 to 10,000 | 32 |
| 10,001 to 50,000 | 34 |
| **Sub total** | **76** |
| 50,001 to 200,000 | 17 |
| More than 200,000 | 7 |
| Total | 100 |

- The volume of visits to main attractions has grown over 20 years but at a very low rate. The average growth disguises losses in volume of 20% or more over the period for many established attractions that make a charge for admission.
- Around one-half of all known attractions in the UK opened in the years between 1980 and 1998. The impact of many large new attractions to celebrate the millennium is yet to be felt.
- The average size of tourist attractions in the UK is small – with an average of 46,000 visits per annum to attractions that charge; 76% of all attractions record no more than 50,000 visits a year.

The economics of the sector are confused by the fact that ownership is split between government and its agencies, local government and the private sector (including not-for-profit trusts). Reflecting public sector ownership, 42% of recorded attractions within the official definition do not charge for admission and they receive over 50% of all visits to attractions. An even larger percentage are dependent on one or other form of public sector subsidy for survival Not shown in Table 14.1, available evidence indicates that demand has been rising faster at free attractions than at those that charge. From 1989 to 1995 the private sector attractions achieved total growth of just 3.3% in total visits.

To cope with weak demand, a typical resource-based response is to put up prices ahead of inflation. Between 1989 to 1995, for example notwithstanding the UK's worst economic recession in half a century, prices at charging historic properties rose by 75% against a 29% increase in the UK retail price index. Annual revenue increased but rates of increase of this order for a largely unchanged product are not sustainable in the face of other competition.

In common with other industrialised countries, the 1980s and early 1990s were years of extensive urban decline and dereliction in many parts of the UK. Global economic competition forced the closure of large sectors of traditional manufacturing and extractive industries in areas once dedicated to coal mining, iron and steel making, shipbuilding, textile industries, fishing and the associated trades that supplied them. The European Commission, national governments and local government endeavoured to alleviate the social hardship caused by this decline and to promote other forms of post-industrial economic activity that could generate employment and wealth creation. Leisure and all forms of cultural and heritage activity together with tourism and hospitality have been high on the development list for all sun areas.

In the UK much of this thinking came together in the government funded Garden Festival movement of the 1970s that changed national attitudes to visitor attractions as an engine of redevelopment and created major one-year visitor attractions on reclaimed derelict land in cities such as Liverpool, Glasgow, Gateshead and in the former mining valleys of South Wales. Visitor attractions were identified as one of the government's chosen vehicles for focusing regeneration possibilities and changing attitudes to modern forms of employment. Following much the same philosophy, the UK's Millennium Dome, itself built on previously poisoned land used for gas making, is being used to trigger economic regeneration in the Greenwich/Woolwich area south of the Thames and carry eastward the momentum of the Docklands Development north of the river.

The size of UK tourist attractions shown in Table 14.3 explains why Middleton (1990, 1998) and other authors have noted the extent to which many traditional tourist attractions, especially in the heritage sector, are still operated in effect as cottage industries. Middleton uses the term *management deficit* to summarize what is arguably the principal structural weakness in the traditional attractions sector that frequently inhibits the development of effective responses to its difficulties. For example, in 1998 only 17 charging attractions in the UK achieved at least 1 million visitors and 12 of these were in or near London (including Windsor Castle and Legoland). Within the sector, entering the new millennium, effective, continuous market research is still unusual;

traditional publicity is used but branding and marketing is weak and much of it is provided on an amateur basis or through public sector agencies and committees often lacking commercial visitor management skills.

## The Underlying Consumer Demand for Leisure-based Attractions is Growing Strongly

By evaluating the available research evidence from the consumer side rather than the supply side one gains insights and a new perspective into the demand for and supply of attractions for leisure day visits. It is possible to provide at least a broad estimate of the overall size of the UK market by combining information from surveys of UK domestic tourism (United Kingdom Tourism Survey, UKTS) and overseas tourism to the UK (International Passenger Survey, IPS) with data from the *UK Day Visits Survey* (UKDVS). The latter is a survey commissioned jointly by the Department for Culture, Media and Sport (DCMS, the sponsoring government department for tourism in the UK) and a consortium of the national agencies responsible for recreation and tourism. It measures all leisure trips from home regardless of duration and by agreement between DCMS and tourist boards, a *leisure day visit* is defined as being of more than three but less than 24 hours away from home for any 'non-regular' purpose not connected with the daily routines of work and sustenance.

Leisure visits cover recreation, sport and informal leisure including walking, driving for pleasure as well as visiting traditional attractions. Very importantly in reviewing the market for attractions, it also covers non-regular shopping excursions, non-routine eating and drinking out and all forms of cultural and entertainment choices that are associated with mobile populations in post-industrial societies.

Drawing on a recent report (Middleton, 1999), it is possible at least broadly to quantify the total potential market for leisure attractions in the UK over a year. The UK generates, in rounded terms, some 1500 million potential leisure day visits. This is the total market in which traditional attractions are competing on the threshold of the 21st century.

It is nearly four times larger than the estimated number of 400 million visits to traditional attractions noted earlier. It is not possible to plot this growth statistically over the years because comparable back data on leisure day visits from home are not available. But a combination of rising income per head and greater personal mobility as well as the massive commitment of commercial money to the developments noted in the next section provides all the proof that is needed of recent and anticipated strong consumer interest and market growth. While the traditional attractions market shows only slow growth overall and decline for many, the new leisure market is booming and prosperous.

**A New Formula for Leisure Time Destination Attractions – Funded by Massive Private Sector Investment**

Since the economic prosperity years of the 1980s and the economic boom years that followed the 1990/92 recession, large commercial operators in the hospitality industry as well as in retailing have analysed consumer leisure trends generally and noted the rapidly growing demand of a mobile society for eating and drinking out, health and fitness clubs, a range of family focused recreation activities, entertainment, cultural activities and live shows and especially in the UK, multiplex cinemas. These trends have combined with remarkable commercial synergy with another major growth sector of more affluent societies – shopping as a leisure activity.

The development of shopping malls in the United States dates back to the 1960s, of course, but in its more modern form it effectively crossed the Atlantic in the mid-1980s and was remarkably successful in the form of pioneer developments in the UK of large, one-stop, under-cover, multi-component centres, as at Gateshead Metro Centre, Merry Hill (Dudley) and Meadowhall (Sheffield).

In the 1990s, stimulated by the evidence of success of the 1980s centres and the emergence of a buoyant economy combined with the knowledge that the government would impose a halt to all new out-of-town developments after 1997, there was an astonishing scramble to develop sites with the essential motorway access and economic potential in all parts of the UK. There are now around ten major complexes each attracting more than 25 million visits a year and many more at around the five million visits level. All are providing for a remarkably similar combination of retail, leisure, entertainment and catering offered in an integrated 'one-stop' under-cover complex with easy access by car and operated for at least 12 – 18 hours a day. The key concepts or principles in this development are *leisure destination, entertainment, family day out, multiple facilities, dramatic architectural forms and internal ambience, and something for everyone.* With the somewhat smaller-scale development of designer outlet villages since around 1993/4, the leisure destination formula is an internationally powerful formula for profitable development. The new wave of destination attractions has moved through mainland Europe for most of the same consumer-related reasons as in the UK.

The one-stop leisure/retail/entertainment complex development is highly profitable because it fits perfectly with a multiple car owning society that is 'money-rich and time-poor'. It has developed in the 1990s from a retail concept, although retail remains a key element, into quite a new animal – destination leisure centres, often identified as 'parks' or 'villages' to sustain the day out concept. Opened in March 1999 and located in a former chalk quarry between the M25 and M2 in Kent, the largest development in the UK and Europe to date is Bluewater Park. Owned by Lend Lease, an Australian-based developer which has some 40 other centres around the world, it comprises 1.7 million square feet, over 300 shops and car parking for some 13,000 cars. Larger than most town centres and aiming for around 35 million visits a year, Bluewater is truly a 'new resort for the 21st century'. Under its roof it provides an indoor 'tropical rainforest', a 'town square' and a street cafe leisure environment within a spectacular setting more reminiscent of Disney than traditional shopping malls (Middleton, 1999). 'In order to satisfy consumer expectations of a complete day out experience . . . leisure facilities . . . will be centred around three themed "village areas" (South East England Tourist Board, 1998). The size of the new centres is contrasted with the largest traditional attractions in Table 14.4

**Table 14.4**
**A comparison of traditional and new UK attractions (visitor numbers)**

| | | | |
|---|---|---|---|
| Blackpool Pleasure Beach | 7.1m | Bluewater Park | 30–35m |
| Madame Tussauds, London | 2.8m | Trafford Park | 30–35m |
| Alton Towers | 2.8m | Lakeside – Thurrock | 20–25m |
| The Tower of London | 2.5m | Meadowhall | 20–25m |
| The British Museum (free entry) | 5.6m | McArthur Glenn | 5–6m |

### *The New 'Resorts': Business Strengths*

The new leisure destination centres or 'resorts' have the following characteristics and business strengths:

- They are large-scale complexes capable of sustaining between 5 and 35 million visits a year.
- They are open for 15 (and up to 24) hours a day, 363 days a year – under cover – providing for maximum dwell time on site.
- Free at point of entry, often with sheltered walkways from the car parks.
- A safe, graffiti-free, patrolled, clean, air-conditioned and relaxed environment designed and managed around consumer interests – uniformed staff are available as 'hosts' to guide and help visitors.
- Multiple product base – retailing, themed catering and bars, entertainment, recreation, family and health facilities – select your own experience.
- Spectacular surroundings with space for live shows, events and exhibitions and architecture designed to appeal to the imagination.
- Multiple repeat visits and excellent prospects for developing a loyal clientele using databases and relationship marketing.

- Professional management, strong branding and typically linked into international alliances, often making designer label products available at advantageous prices.
- Appreciating capital assets, with profitability ploughed back into refurbishment.
- Attractive to private sector investors such as pension funds and investment trusts seeking profitable growth and attractive to public sector planners for the economic benefit they bring, often to formerly derelict industrial sites.

### *Traditional Attractions: Business Weaknesses*

The contrast with the business weaknesses inherent in many traditional attractions is stark. Most are:

- Stand alone, the majority on a very small-scale basis with less than 50 visits on average per day.
- Short opening hours – short dwell time on site of 2–3 hours, many not open every day.
- Seasonal demand – often weather-dependent.
- Up front, very visible charge for admission – either at a car park or a reception building or kiosk.
- Many with a long-standing public sector management ethos and a single/limited product focus designed and managed around the resource needs rather than consumer interests.
- Mostly once only visitors with few reasons for repeat visit (cost of attracting first time visitors rising).
- Revenue inadequate for the essential refurbishment cycle so that major changes are unusual and visible dilapidations are all too often evident.
- Weak management/management deficit. Often with only weak links to other businesses.
- Unattractive to private investors since very few offer growth prospects in capital asset and revenue growth terms.
- Often unattractive to the public sector as it seeks to limit and withdraw from its revenue funding commitments.

## Concluding Thoughts

The way ahead for visitor attractions is clearly dividing between the traditional and the new. The 1960s supply side definition of traditional tourist attractions has been overtaken by subsequent developments and it now serves to obscure rather than clarify real trends. In answer to the classic business strategy question, 'what business are you really in?' the answer for a growing number of attractions is leisure and entertainment, not tourism.

The new leisure destination attractions are the new resorts for the 21st century. Just as seaside resorts met the needs in Northern Europe of railway excursionists at the end of the 19th century, so modern out of town leisure entertainment destinations meet the needs of modern mobile post-industrial consumers.

Looking ahead, the number and size of the new resorts and the sheer sameness of much of the product offer may carry with it the seeds of decline from fashion. There is a danger that much of the provision will be seen as bland, standardised, synthetic and boring after the first flush of novelty and convenience has worn off. Creativity, originality and individuality do not sit easily with lowest common product denominators often associated with large-scale provision.

**Table 14.5**
**Approximate number of UK attractions opening and closing since 1978/80**

| *Type of attraction* | *Opened 1980 –98* | *Closed 1978 – 98* | *Total[a] in 1998* |
|---|---|---|---|
| Historic properties | 370 | 113 | 1418 |
| Gardens | 156 | 51 | 347 |
| Museums and galleries | 760 | 246 | 1724 |
| Farm attractions | 210 | 49 | 249 |
| Wildlife attractions | 165 | 36 | 300 |
| All attractions | 2770 | 776 | 5890 |

[a]Total reporting on this issue (5890) compares with 6164 known attractions in total for UK in 1998.

In the traditional tourist attraction sector there are uneasy, often unspoken compromises as to what extent they should be judged to be businesses and to what extent they are a core part of public sector provision, publicly funded for the conservation of heritage, the good of the visiting public and quality of life in the areas where they are located.

As for the way ahead for traditional attractions, a war of attrition seems inevitable in which many existing attractions will continue to fail and be closed. This is not a new process as Table 14.5 shows. Survivors will make best use of their unique blend of originality and personality but systematic collaboration will be the hallmark of survivors. The core solutions as identified by Middleton (1998) will include:

- Quality assurance to attract customers and encourage repeat visits.
- Integration wherever possible with other services associated with post-industrial society, such as education for life, speciality retailing, the arts and other cultural provision.
- Networking using modern information and communications technology (ICT) for communication, management training, research, branding, marketing and customer access.
- Association, strategic alliances and sometimes collocation for attractions to achieve the economies of scale essential to efficient and cost-effective management and marketing.

# 15

# HOSPITALITY AND THE TOURIST

## Opening Thoughts

In anticipating the future, the key challenge is to identify emerging patterns from the complex array of information that lies before us. This assumes that leaders of organisations will be in a constant search for ideas that will offer opportunity to lead their competition at every chance. This requires not only the ability to synthesise the patterns emerging from all sources of information, experiences and exchanges; it also requires creativity in order to develop a vision out of what all this means and how it can then be used to develop competitive advantage. In doing so, that leader must avoid what Linden (1998) refers to as 'the tyranny of the near past'.

The meaning of this is for many that they are unable to see the emerging patterns because they are anchored in the comfort level of the present and recent past. And as complex and uncertain as the environment is these days, it is often safer to cling to the tyranny of the near past rather than risk bold new initiatives to capture the customer of tomorrow.

The purpose of this chapter is to attempt to break with the past and offer another view of the future and how the customers of tomorrow will differ from those of our near past. These views have been developed over five years through a series of 'Visioning the Future' workshops and think-tanks, which have been conducted by the International Hotel & Restaurant Association. These sessions have produced ideas, feedback and discourse from more than 5000 industry professionals who have either participated in, or received the messages from, the results of these efforts. The task put forth to participants in each case was to try to answer the questions in Box 15.1. In other words, attempts were made to solicit their foresight regarding the future. As such, their views represent a collective view of emerging patterns from professionals in more than 20 countries across the globe. This chapter is a synthesis of those ideas.

**Box 15.1**
**How will you interact with the guest of the future?**

- How will the guest be travelling in the future?
- How will the guest be communicating in the future?
- How will you distribute your product to the guest in the future?
- What new customer benefits will the guest demand in the future?
- What competencies will be necessary to serve the guest in the future?
- What standards will be accepted in the future?

## Underpinnings Influencing the Customer of Tomorrow

Throughout the last 20 years of the 20th century the distinction between the business traveller and leisure traveller became blurred as people tried to pack into each trip an opportunity to conduct business as well as attempt to take some time for themselves. It can be anticipated that this desire will not change in the future. In fact, it may even be heightened as individuals find themselves in a more complex and uncertain world that no doubt will add stress to their lives. Globalisation and the dawning of an information age have helped to bring on much of this complexity and uncertainty.

Globalisation itself is complex. It is phenomenon that often defies simple understanding using basic concepts familiar to most. The terms like economics and free trade are now blended with ideas like geo-political and ecological sustainability. The complexity of the world today will serve as an underpinning shaping business forces and customer behaviours well into the 21st century. It implies that the simple rules used to try to analyse and describe hospitality customer behaviour will be insufficient in this growing web of local, national and international relationships between businesses and their customers. The task of trying to understand these relationships in order to anticipate customer needs will be daunting indeed, may be even impossible. It is clear that customers will be perceived as more fickle if attempts to describe their future behaviour use dated concepts in simple isolation.

The information age will also create more challenge in terms of trying to understand the customer. This is partly a function of what Tapscott (1995: 58 – 59) refers to as the convergence of computing, telecommunications and content. This union of three industries will bring the customer into closer contact with their world and at a speed and clarity that has yet to be experienced by them. As Davis and Meyer (1998: 6) state:

> Almost instantaneous communication and computation, for example, are shrinking time and focusing us on Speed. Connectivity is putting everybody and everything online in one way or another and has led to the 'the death of distance', a shrinking of space. Intangible value of all kinds, like service and information, is growing explosively, reducing the importance of tangible mass.

Their thesis is that the world is becoming a 'blur' as a result of their conceptualisation of this concept as a formula that states, *Blue = Speed × Connectivity × Intangibles.* It seems clear that speed and connectivity will continue to influence how we live our lives. We will become used to receiving information instantly when we want it as we continue to become more connected to each other. It is also clear that this concurrence will result in a better-informed consumer. For, in addition to speed and connectivity will come increased transparency with regard to each and every purchase decision that this customer will make.

This transparency will be a function of almost perfect information available on all the offerings of products and services that are made by sellers. This near perfect information will exist regarding the physical products that are offered because they are easily described, observed and measured. And because of this, information will be similar to what is often referred to as *word of mouth* commentary but the difference will be that it will now be available for the world to see and even hear.

More challenging will be the management and marketing of the third element of the formula, *intangibles.* Most firms that provide services including hospitality services offer intangibles. However, they are difficult to describe or even measure. They often are characterised by such terms as: *feel, comfort, experience, look, satisfaction.* In each case, these terms are very personal and defined by the customer based upon their perceptions, attitudes and beliefs. It is the intangibles that will drive customer behaviour and motivation in the future as they seek to obtain satisfaction and value from all the experiences related to their purchase. The level of satisfaction anticipated will drive their view of the economic value of the offering of the enterprise. Here again, information will drive how many view the quality of the intangibles and their subsequent value.

When you combine the cumulative effects of globalisation and information most individuals are overwhelmed. Yet, judging by all the emerging patterns identified by participants in the think-tanks and visioning workshops, this will continue to be the ease. Thus, consumers will be in search of ways and means to reduce this confounding environment. While it is difficult to predict how they will accomplish this, it is clear that they will expect those who plan to offer them products and services to help simplify their world. This will no doubt translate into a new set of new standards for making the offering, delivering the products and services, and following-up on it all. The firms that can do this with the greatest amount of integrity, reliability, consistency and honesty will be the long-term winners of tomorrow's hospitality customer.

**The Customer of Tomorrow**

The consumer of tomorrow can be viewed using the metaphor of the historic tribal community. Members of the tribal community lived, defended and often gave their lives protecting the tribe; such was their loyalty. In contrast, tomorrow's consumer, whose attributes are listed in Box 15.2, will have little tribal loyalty at all – or at least not enough for which to sacrifice one's needs. This future consumer feels compelled to remain in search of new tribes, always looking for the best deal or new community. In other words, this new consumer is *fleeting and irreverent* when it comes to remaining loyal to the tribe. The consumer of today, and more so of tomorrow, will be much like a mercenary. She or he will sell out to the highest bidder and the company that offers the best value proposition. In today's terms, this usually translates into competition among travel and hospitality providers to create and manage the best guest loyalty programmes. The future, however, will take this concept much further. Beyond this threshold, the price of loyalty will be superior products and services that add real and significant value to the guest. Determining what that means for each and everyone is no small challenge, especially in the context of the 'blur' environment referred to earlier by Davis and Meyer.

**Box 15.2**
**The Tribal Traveller**

- Fleeting and irreverent – brand loyalty will probably go to the highest bidder unless the brand is unquestionably value positive.
- Seek entry into tribal groups that satisfy specialised needs in discontinuous patterns – the mall of life *via* your favourite chat room
- Acquiring product knowledge through several filters – most likely non-human – the personal agent – Wildfire, the ultimate
- Will sell information about themselves for overall value; money, integrity, authenticity, honesty and reality.

Whereas the historic tribal member was born into and died as a member of the same tribe, tomorrow's member will hold many tribal affiliations. The historic member had little choice in this case, for seldom would she or he be accepted into other tribes, nor experience what membership was like in others. Today, the information highway permits access for the modern day tribal traveller to a number of tribes or communities depending upon his or her needs at the moment – almost like shopping in the *mall of life*. Thus, whether it comes to sports, clothes, music, books, art, travel or hospitality, tomorrow's consumer will enter as many or as few tribes as necessary to satisfy their needs.

This can be experienced today by simply entering into any one-line chat room – a modern-day version of the tribe. It is not uncommon to find that participants enter just to see what the discussion is like, often doing so in both audio and video mediums. If they find it boring or not of interest they move on. If they like it, they enter into the exchange until they grow tired and move on. While many are just shopping for interesting dialogue, others are more specific about what they are seeking. It is difficult to know what they are looking for or how to keep them interested. If one is a hospitality enterprise seeking to attract this type of traveller, it is important to be able to reach them at the time they are looking, capture their interest and make joining your tribe worthwhile. This cannot be done by yield management systems, as we know them today. It will require something different.

That something different may take the form of a *personal agent*. The personal agent is the non-human tribal warrior driven by artificial intelligence software programmes and neural networks. It is programmed initially by the human tribal traveller but then continues to learn by itself what drives this human in terms of desires. It does this by remembering each decision made by that traveller throughout the decision-making process. Once enough of a history has been experienced, this software agent is often free to act on behalf of that person when choosing what products and services *or tribes* to enter. This tireless agent is constantly looking out for the interests of its master. It can shop many tribes, far more than the human wants or has the time to explore. An early example of this form of technology at work can be seen by TheTrip.com's IntelliTrip product. With just a few quick keystrokes, a consumer can quickly and easily shop multiple on-line travel services for the best airfares or hotel rates. In this new model, the consumer never even visits the web-site of the service provider or supplier. Such a model poses a great challenge to the firm trying to each the customer and appeal to his or her desires through the filter of the personal agent.

This new consumer will be more confident in all types of transactions involving the information highway. The personal agent will do most of the information gathering and analysis. This analysis will be objective, based upon previously established criteria set out by the consumer and built upon by the learning capabilities of the software. Armed with better information, the decisions will be more rational, turning basic ones like airline and hotel reservations into more of a commodity exchange process. Price and location will often be the determining factors.

In this context, consumers will actually control more of this exchange process. Therefore, they will determine who will have information about them and how much they will acquire. They will demand to receive value for providing this information. One does not have to look too far to see the frequent flyer points awarded these days for those customers who are willing to fill out the market research forms. In other words, the consumer will be happy to sell information about themselves to the tribal masters who are willing to pay the price so long as the end result is better value in the consumers' eyes. Without question, consumers will continue to become more powerful in this new environment.

What will be essential in this new era of information exchange will be the *integrity of the overall process.* Consumers will not accept the transfer of information about themselves from one tribe to another. They will seek and obtain control of this. The selling of name lists from one company to another will extract a high cost if the consumer does not want this to happen: the cost will be abandonment of the tribe. With so many alternatives available, either through human searches or those done by non-human personal agents, and the lack of loyalty by the consumer, the firm will never be able to maximise the economic lifetime value of that consumer who has felt violated. As consumers becomes more comfortable in this new role, those firms that have been passively trying to hang on to that value will find themselves deserted, often forever. For the hospitality enterprise, there is little that can be done to prevent this.

Of course, many are trying to prevent this growth in consumer buying power. The industry consolidation that is occurring either through strategic alliances or mergers and acquisitions is one example. Although this consolidation is driven by many other factors besides this one, it is one way of balancing the growing power of the tribal traveller. And while this will work temporarily, the inevitable consequence is that these mega corporations will still have to compete for the consumer's loyalty through price and reward systems, bringing about further commoditisation of the industry's products and services.

One alternative to this unpleasant thought is for the hospitality enterprise to expand its domain, to think beyond the present boundaries of food, accomodation and transportation. In the future, these will only be seen as elements of some greater whole. There are many who feel that this greater whole will be the entire travel experience, which will be part of the emerging *experience economy* (Pine and Gilmore, 1998) in the developed world. This suggests that if the hospitality enterprise seeks to compete in the future, it will be required to enter into the desired portfolio of providers that will meet the *experience* requirements of the guest. Figuring out how to do this will be no easy chore.

**Other Drivers of Change**

It is no secret that in the Western world the average age of the population is increasing. The so-called Baby Boomers are turning 50 on a daily basis in large numbers. This demographic shift in the part of the developed world that possesses the greatest spending power will pose one of the more interesting drivers of change in the hospitality industry.

The first major concern of this group of customers will evolve around safety and health. Consider first just the physical aspects of ageing, like the ability physically to get around. If this group is experiencing the normal consequences of ageing, it is not likely that they will want to be climbing mountains, forging streams or crawling through antiquities. Thus, physical limitations will drive destination choice. That future consumer will want ease of access and assurances that they will be able to get around comfortably.

The second consideration regarding the ageing process is the ability to fight disease. Evidence suggests that there is a growing spread of disease occurring as a result of both new and old bacteria and viruses. Further, the globalisation of the food chain has resulted in widespread food-borne illnesses across the globe. This is expected to continue as globalisation envelops the world. This puts at risk those who, either through the natural ageing process or as a result of other disease, have experienced a suppressed immune system function. They will be more concerned about their ability to meet the challenges of these threats when they travel, especially if there is reason to suspect poor medical care at the destination.

This future customer will also avoid those destinations that create risk to safety and well-being brought about by increased crime, nationalism or growing threats from fanatical groups seeking to right wrongs they perceive have been done. As the gap between the *haves* and *have-nots* continues to grow, this can be expected to be more of an influence upon travel than most currently realise.

The uncertainties and complexities of the world appear to be creating a need for the consumer of tomorrow to seek answers as to why this is so. They find it hard to understand the brutalities occurring in the former Soviet Union and the continuation of ethnic groups maintaining old hatreds. Extremist groups and their behaviours are equally as puzzling. There is also a growing guilt regarding the gap between the *haves* and *have-nots*. In response, there is a movement to righting the wrongs that have been done. This again appears to be the collective guilt of those living in developed countries who are now looking back over lifetime and becoming concerned that they, in their rush to accumulate wealth, may have forgotten a few things along the way.

Many refer to this shift as a new spirituality. This does not necessarily mean a movement closer to some God as much as it means a re-evaluation of the values that have guided development over the past century and a half. The consumer is in some ways going to continue to try to right the wrongs of the past. This is very evident in the new social responsiveness observed by many companies. For example, both consumers and investors are rewarding those firms that have aggressively addressed environmental concerns or social injustices. They are doing so with capital, a powerful motivator in today's global economy. The pattern seems clear here: tomorrow's consumer will demand greater social responsibility by all firms and will reward this with their pocket books. This may indeed be the new spirituality.

Lastly, the consumer will demand greater levels of integrity and honesty in their dealings with them, workers and society in general. A higher standard of quality, responsibility and message will be expected. And if they don't find it, they will be able to let the world know immediately. No executive today or tomorrow will want, nor can afford, to let this happen. Everyone will be held more accountable in this new transparent environment.

## Concluding Thoughts

The information age and globalisation will continue to drive changes in the way the consumer of tomorrow will do business with companies in the hospitality industry. This consumer will demand greater assurances of quality, safety and well-being. They will look more for intangible experiences that match their wallets and physical capabilities.

Their loyalty will be easily transferable, making it more difficult to keep them. Their demands will be relentless as they seek to maximise their wishes and economic realities.

The question becomes, is the hospitality industry ready for this new consumer? Many would argue no. They believe that the industry is more concerned about financial engineering as a way of producing wealth as opposed to meeting the challenges of the consumer of tomorrow. If this is true, then it is very unfortunate. It leaves little optimism regarding the ability of firms to compete in the future. As theory has it, firms that are in co-alignment with the forces driving change in their environment and invest in competitive methods to meet the opportunities they present will be successful going forward (Olsen *et al.*, 1999). As this chapter has tried to point out, the forces and patterns are clear as to where the consumer is headed. So, for those firms that follow this principle, the new millennium will be a fun place to be; for those that are guided by *the tyranny of the near past*, they will continue to long for the good old days when the consumer remained with one tribe for life.

# 16

# CRUISING AS TOURISM

## An Introduction to Cruising

The UK cruise industry is young and growing rapidly – 140% in the past five years alone. This is due primarily to the introduction of tour operators entering the UK market and the increase in new ship builds. Cruise lines are investing heavily in the future of the cruise market, with the planned launch of more than 50 new ships over the first five years of the new century. The average age of a British cruise passenger is now 55, but in recent years cruising has attracted younger passengers, with 12% being under 35.

The industry is supply-led, and owing to slower growth in the mature North American domestic market the American-based cruise companies are putting more effort into marketing and sales from the UK and Europe, with a resulting increase in traffic.

Cruising meets with all of the requirements that customers expect from a holiday with exotic destinations, luxury staterooms, exceptionally high standards of service, the opportunity to meet new people, a wide range of gourmet cuisine on offer, and the activities and entertainment onboard all included in the price. Generally, the only items not included are shore excursions, port taxes, gratuities and drinks. However, some of the luxury cruise lines do include these in the holiday price, so apart from the odd massage and bottle of bubbly, there are no hidden extras whatsoever.

Cruising can appeal to everyone, no matter what their budget or interests. Activities onboard range from aerobics to aromatherapy, art auctions to rock climbing! Cruising is attracting more families, with a wide range of children's facilities and childcare on board. There is also a length and type of cruise to suit everyone, whether it is a mini-cruise for three or four nights, a seven or fourteen night fly cruise, a scenic river cruise or a relaxing three week voyage on a working ship.

**The Roles of the PSA and PSARA**

The Passenger Shipping Association (PSA) is the trade association for cruise and ferry companies operating in the UK. The PSA offers its members advice and information on subjects ranging from safety to statistics, acts as a bonding authority for non-licensable activities and runs a conciliation and arbitration service.

One of the main functions of the PSA is to act as a forum for discussion on areas of mutual interest. This is achieved by lobbying the government and the EU and working with other bodies, including the Association of British Travel Agents (ABTA), the Chamber of Shipping and the Council of Travel and Tourism. The PSA also runs a generic PR campaign promoting cruising to the public.

PSARA (Passenger Shipping Association Retail Agent scheme) was formed in 1987 to train and educate travel agents to help increase their cruise sales. The scheme, which is self-funded based on contributions from both the cruise industry and retail agents, provides an extensive programme of nation-wide training seminars, a cruise manual, ship visits, educational materials, newsletters and a freephone helpline to achieve this aim. It is an important factor in the growth of cruising traffic in the UK and is steadily increasing its membership in the travel agency world.

**Current Cruise Statistics**

For the fifth year in a row, the number of British cruisers in 1998 grew by 20%. More than 700,000 British people took a cruise in 1998, 635,000 of those an ocean cruise and 65,000 a river cruise. The most popular destinations continue to be the Mediterranean followed by the Caribbean, Scandinavia and the Baltics, with a third of British cruisers coming from the North of England and a quarter coming from London and the South East.

Cruising has a higher commission than other products and is becoming much more popular with British holidaymakers because cruises give clients greater satisfaction than any other type of holiday and therefore produce a high percentage of repeat business. Cruising only makes up 3.7% of the UK holiday sector and as less than 2% of the people who can afford a cruise actually do so, there is a vast untapped market.

**The Development of Cruise Ship Design**

Since its inception in 1844, when P&O claimed to have invented the first deep-sea cruise, the industry has come a long way. However, it is only in the past 20 or so years of its 155-year history that the industry has been most of its most dramatic increase in ship size. In terms of gross registered tonnes (grt), the early 1970s saw Royal Caribbean order the 22945 grt *Song of Norway*. However, by the mid-1980s ships of about 45000 grt began to emerge on the market. By the early 1990s Carnival's Fantasy class, the largest cruise ship series ever built, had taken the tonnage levels up to the 70000 grt mark. In 1996 the 100,000 grt mark was passed with the launch of *Carnival Destiny*, with dimensions that preclude her from transiting the Panama Canal.

According to a recent study by Ocean Shipping Consultants, the present cruise ship order book is about 60 vessels with a combined capacity of over 93000 berths. The new generation of 'post Panamax' ships will account for 19 ships with 50000 berths or 25% of the current fleet of 217,000 berths.

The 'post Panamax' ships have ushered in a new era of 'floating resorts' offering a wide variety of entertainment and activities including rock climbing, state of the art health clubs, a variety of dining options, spacious cabins with interactive TV and a high proportion of balconies. With 'floating resorts' the itinerary of the ship becomes less important and to increase onboard spend it is in the interest of the cruise line to encourage passengers to stay onboard.

The quay length will curtail the length of future ship designs. Plans for 'Super Wide' cruise ships are beginning to develop on the drawing boards of major shipbuilders. The ship is constructed with a large central atrium accommodating the public areas overlooked by cabins. Therefore cabins can be sold with balconies which can be seafacing or facing inwards.

## Globalisation and Cruise Ship Deployment

The cruise map of the world has been dramatic change since 1960, when most of the world's cruise liners were positioned in the Caribbean and seasonally in the Mediterranean and Alaska. Nowadays the Caribbean is a seasonal destination accommodating 100,000 berths in the winter but only 41000 in July, whereas the Baltic will attract 37000 berths in July 2000.

The US cruise industry is showing some signs of reaching maturity in that growth rates have slowed down and recently faltered, although penetration of the domestic market is four to five times that of the UK market. The leading cruise lines are adopting a more global strategy by positioning their ships in the Mediterranean throughout the summer and even in the Indian Ocean in the winter months.

The main thrust to globalisation of the cruise industry is investment and the growth of the world's cruise fleet. New, bigger ships are cheaper to operate and therefore force smaller ships to operate new itineraries. Additionally, of the 6 million people cruising in 1999 more than 50% are repeat passengers and therefore demand a range of new itineraries to choose from.

Socio-economic trends are influencing the demand for cruising. Emerging middle classes in countries such as Korea and Brazil produce new markets of educated and wealthy potential customers. Similarly political and international events open up new cruise opportunities. The fall of the Berlin Wall saw an increase in both river and ocean cruising in Eastern Europe and the former Soviet Union. Similarly, the Barcelona Olympics produced a sophisticated hotel infrastructure which attracted cruise activity. It is anticipated that the forthcoming 2000 Olympics in Australia will stimulate demand for cruising in Australasia. Indonesia is seen as the sleeping giant of the Far East, with more water than land combined with a rich cultural and historical background it is a potential target for European and Australian markets.

## Distribution Technology – Its Impact on the Cruise Industry

### *Current Agent Distribution Systems*

Around 85% of cruise bookings are presently being sold through travel agents. In the UK the travel agency market is dominated by multiple travel agency groups, which are vertically integrated with ownership of airlines, tour operators and retail outlets. The major multiple groups are Thomas Cook, Carlson World Choice, Lunn Poly and Going Places.

### *Technology*

There has been a generally slow uptake of newer technology due in part to incompatibility with back office functions. 'Viewdata' continues to be widely used, although Royal Caribbean is the only cruise line offering the facility to book *via* Viewdata and GDS. It is estimated that one in ten bookings are presently made *via* Teletext and a recent report estimates that the present £12m spent per annum on holidays bought *via* the TV will grow to £2 billion by £2003.

### *The Internet*

The Internet is cheap, quick, convenient, 24 hour and global and the phenomenal growth in the use of the Internet is forcing suppliers to provide improved information and services. An estimated 18 million European households were on-line in 1998 with a forecasted 80 million by 2002. Virtually all PSA members have a web-site, although Royal Caribbean is the only PSA member to have a real time booking facility on their site. Of UK agents presently 28% have web access (16% in 1996). Considering that 62% of people using the net do so to access travel information, there is a threat that the role and service of the high street travel agent will be threatened, although most on-line travel sales presently include air tickets and hotel room bookings. Although some direct purchasing is inevitable, generally the more complicated and expensive products such as cruises continue to be sold on a face-to-face basis. Additionally, cruising is still an unfamiliar type of holiday to the majority of people and therefore prospective buyers will have a wide range of questions and misconceptions, which are not easily answered through the on-line sales process.

### *Digital Television*

This is the interactive technology of the future. It is estimated that within 10 years all UK TVs will be digital, with free set-top boxes accelerating the transition. Unlike a PC, watching television has the advantage of being a sharwed family activity and therefore offers a more conducive and compatible way to shop for a holiday.

### *The Impact of Technology on Suppliers*

Cruise web-sites are already proving very popular. Technology is bringing ensuing to life in ways previous media failed to do; for example, Princess Cruises' web-site has a live link with the bridge of the *Grand Princess* filming the progress of the ship. Electronic 'word of mouth' recommendations *via* chat forums will become a powerful consumer tool. The Internet and specifically e-mail will offer frequent and cheap relationship management, instant personalised communication and feedback. Large cruise lines are increasingly distributing pre-booking information direct to customers *via* the web and the fastest growing sector of Internet users are females aged 55 – 60, which is the exact profile of the typical cruise purchaser.

*The Impact of Technology on Distributors (Travel Agents)*

Although electronic media cannot replicate the experience of shopping, retail agents do have to have access to the information that their customers can get on line and be fully aware of the available sources of information. Proactive cruise specialist agents will not have to fear the Internet if they become electronic information brokers, offering well-researched advice and third party endorsement. Also, as more commoditised travel products adapt more easily to direct sell, agent reliance on cruising will grow.

**The Future**

The cruise industry is confident that the total number of cruise passengers worldwide will increase to the 12–13 million required to fill the extra berths that will be on sale by 2005. Reflecting the substantial investment required to build these giant ships, typically in the region of $450 – 500 million, ownership is limited to the industry's largest players, namely Carnival, Royal Caribbean and P&O, although other smaller operators have also ordered new builds to serve their markets.

# 17

# TRANSPORT: THE TAIL THAT WAGS THE DOG

As we step into this new millennium, we must ask whether life is going to change. The basic theme of this chapter is that the relationship between the tourism dog and its transport tail is going to change. Unless the tourism industry fully understands, anticipates and influences these changes, the outcome may well be unfavourable in that the tourism dog will in the future be hindered rather than helped by the action of its transport tail.

Without transport there is, by definition, no tourism. This means that, although transport accounts for only a part of the tourism business, without it there is no tourism business. The future of transport is thus pivotal to the future of tourism. However, transport is pivotal not only to tourism. It is pivotal also to the economy and indeed to society. As a result it has always attracted the interest of politicians and rulers. The earliest road systems of the Roman Empire – and indeed of most, if not all, later empires – were built for strategic reasons, without thought for tourism. The Duke of Wellington opposed the construction of railways on the grounds that it would result in the working class becoming ungovernable. Construction of a Channel Tunnel was obstructed for a century on the grounds that it would facilitate any invasion of Britain. The roads of Scotland were built by the English army to uphold Union. The first canal network of Europe was built to allow rapid Spanish troop movement throughout the mutinous Netherlands. The first aeroplanes were conceived a hundred years ago as weapons of war and it was not until the middle of the 20th century that governments finally recognised that they should be mainly considered as instruments of peace. More recently, the 747 jumbo jet only came about in the 1970s because the US government had already funded its massive engines to power a giant military freighter.

It is precisely because transport developments invariably come about for reasons that have nothing to do with tourism that it is notoriously difficult to predict far ahead how the transport tail is going to wag the tourism dog. This is abundantly evident in the inaccuracy of any transport-related predictions. As a result, serious transport forecasters seldom look more than ten years ahead. And the most far-sighted serious prediction of which I am aware is that for airport capacity in the south east of England – 30 years ahead, with any data beyond 20 years being viewed with extreme caution.

In the past the political interference with the transport market has been mainly directed at promoting or protecting particular aspects of the transport system which are considered to be either in the public interest or in vote-catching interest. Two very recent examples can be offered from the UK. To encourage private funding of the bridge connecting the island of Skye to the Scottish mainland, the government obliged the state-owned ferry operator to withdraw its Skye service, despite the fact that the profits from this service supported the loss-making services on the rest of its network. A condition attached to the latest extension of Eurotunnel's concession was that no other tunnel operator would be permitted by the governments of the UK and France for a period of 50 years. However, transport predictors are now faced with a new generation of 'Iron Dukes' who would like to suppress transport in some way or other. Despite the awful experience of Montreal's Mirabelle, more governments are insisting on developing airports which are too remote to be of interest to air travellers or to airport workers; Oslo is one recent example Addis Ababa is probably another. Milan might well prove yet another. A recent example from Britain was the last Conservative government's capitulation, apparently on vote-catching grounds, to the environmental lobby and scrapping its long-overdue road improvement programme.

This chronic, built-in habit by governments of interfering in transport matters, and thus distorting the working of the market, is the basic reason why predictions on future developments have to be taken with great suspicion. But even if this habit were to be curbed, prediction would still be dubious, except in the short-term, because of the peculiarly complex nature of both demand and supply which together form the transport market.

**Demand**

It is often wrongly supposed that transport demand is all about people being moved from one place to another, from A to B, and then, in the case of tourism, back from B to A. This error is often evident in academic discussions on air transport where airlines are viewed as offering a single homogeneous product and are then accused of superficially 'differentiating' their products in order to establish a distinct identity in the marketplace. In real life the demand for any transport service is extremely complex. To start off, it is essentially a derived demand in the sense that it is only demanded as a response to demand for something else. In the case of tourism this is the demand to do something in a place other than the normal place of work or residence. This immediately introduces an unpredictable variable for the transport forecaster: how will people split their time in the future between in-home or in-office activities and out-home or out-office activities? The poor forecaster can only be sure of one thing: that the split will change one way or another. But which way it will change, when and how much; these defy prediction simply because there are too many unknowns. So the forecaster assumes that the split will remain as it is even though it does not, thus creating another reason why so many forecasts are wrong. This tells us that we should all be placing much higher priority on distinguishing between demand for tourism products and demand for alternative non-tourism products. A start has been taken by the World Tourism Organisation (WTO), whose preliminary view is that increasing pressure on people's personal time is going to tilt the balance in favour of non-tourism products. For what it is worth, my view is that this particular prediction is wrong.

### Supply

To some extent this fundamental split between tourism demand and non-tourism demand will be determined by the view taken in the marketplace on the other features of transport service which together will not only determine whether we travel but also which travel mode we choose, should we decide to travel, and indeed which particular service and carrier we choose. Principal among these features, other than physical transplant, are the following: speed, frequency, comfort, safety, availability, information, access and – last but not least – price. Before briefly examining each of these in turn it is worth nothing that on balance – with the possible exception of price – the overall quality of transport is likely to continue to improve significantly. This suggests that the tourism versus non-tourism demand spit is more likely to be determined by the relative prices of tourism and non-tourism products rather than by the pressure felt by people on their time.

### Speed

In assessing the value placed on speed it is important to take account not only of time saved but also of reduced journey time. For most people the ideal is instantaneous travel, not only because it would release more time for doing other things – including doing nothing – but also because it would remove the many unpleasant aspects of travel that have to be endured in order to be transplanted. This means that we all display a stronger preference for speed, and for paying a premium price for speed, than can be explained by the value placed on time saved. My favourite example of this is Sydney harbour, where it is evident that many people choose to pay extra for a faster ferry, only to spend the time saved enjoying doing little or nothing. Most of the unpleasant features, like the expense of travel as compared with non-travel, are self-evident. However, one feature deserves to be better understood: it is the dislike of not being in control. Transport planners everywhere fail to give enough weight to this factor. It is the main reason why the motor car has become the dominant mode of transport for tourism. And it explains why forecasts for rail travel are persistently over-optimistic. Again, my prediction is that this preference for personal control – as opposed to being under the control of others – is certain to become an increasingly important factor in transport and this is bound to favour the car over the train or the aeroplane.

**Frequency**

Frequency is another feature of transport that is often misunderstood by planners. Frequency seen as being low is not only seen as being inconvenient, it is also a potential waste of time and therefore equivalent to slow service. Most public service vehicles, notably trains, are so large in relation to expected traffic that economic operation can usually be achieved – except on a few high-volume routes – only by reducing frequencies to levels that are often unacceptable in the marketplace. This is going to become a major problem for airlines at the ever rising number of points where inadequate airport capacity obliges the use of aircraft so large that frequency suffers.

**Comfort and Safety**

In an effort to compensate for the innate unpleasantness of travel, vehicle manufacturers and operators over the past decade have gone to great lengths to improve travel comfort and safety. In terms of comfort, the results have been spectacularly successful, particularly in the case of the motor car where the occupant today is often more comfortable than he or she would have been at home! Perhaps the main failure in terms of comfort has been failure by public service operators to match seat-pitch to customer expectations. Whereas the typical car seat has become an armchair, the seat in a modern aeroplane or coach is increasingly akin to a barstool. For those unwilling to pay the normally excessive price of business class travel, this factor is already driving traffic away from air travel to surface travel. As far as safety is concerned, the actual improvements which are going on in surface travel, and which are likely to continue in the future, are not being matched on the aviation front where safety rates appear at best to have stabilised. Airline leaders are now becoming alarmed by the threatened public perception that air travel is unacceptably dangerous. As railway operators have recently discovered in Britain, public perceptions of safety have more to do with media coverage than with actual safety levels.

**Availability**

The actual presence of a convenient seat to the desired destination – a situation covered by the jargon term 'availability' – is obviously a basic element in any transport service. Here the future prospect is dominated by funding, in particular of infrastructure. Until now governments in one way or another have funded virtually all transport infrastructure. This investment has seldom yielded an economic return to the governments concerned, and in many cases it has even been proved intrinsically uneconomic. The TanZam railway is perhaps the most spectacular recent example of such a white elephant. But any transport economist is ready to provide any number of disturbing examples. However, there is no doubt that governments almost everywhere are increasingly reluctant to pour money into transport infrastructure. A topical example is the great difficulty being experienced by its sponsors in raising funds for the ultra high-speed magnetic railway between Berlin and Hamburg. Despite the great attraction of this project, if only as a working model for later applications, the current prospect facing the sponsors is not optimistic. On a smaller scale, there are now similar doubts about the viability of earlier plans to modernise the trunk railway linking London and Glasgow *via* Britain's west coast. This reluctance to invest in transport infrastructure reflects several converging forces: pressure on governments to achieve balanced budgets and low levels of indebtedness; growing realisation that the private sector – and this means, ultimately the travelling public – can and should bear the costs of infrastructure; and finally, that a growing body of voters are ready to vote against any transport project which they consider to be against the public interest, regardless of whether or not it is actually against the public interest! The net effect is that in the coming decades it is certain that transport infrastructure will either be lacking or will result in transport services becoming more expensive. This effect will not be evenly felt. My guess is that this problem of infrastructural constraint is going to be most severely felt in the most developed so-called Western world; this could lead within 20 years to major change in the global distribution of tourism.

The same forces, which are encouraging governments to behave less generously over provision of transport infrastructure, are persuading governments to be less generous in their subsidy of uneconomic state-run or state-backed transport services. Western governments have now, with few exceptions, withdrawn from the subsidy of operations by their national airlines. It is most unlikely that Western governments will continue pouring subsidy into rail operations other than for metropolitan commuters (where the sheer number of affected voters would result in a politically unacceptable outcry). An early casualty of this could well be Amtrak. Heavily subsidised rail operations of most European states – notably. France, Germany, Spain and Italy – are surely bound to be curtailed. It is no coincidence that it is these same countries which are busy persuading the European Commission to shoulder the burden of rail funding. It needs a bold forecaster to predict the future tourism implications of this particular situation.

## Marketing

In contrast to the political uncertainties over infrastructure, there is little doubt that the prospects in regard to two other essential elements of transport service – provision of advance information to potential customers and facilitation of purchase (known as access in the jargon) – are both certain and positive. Thanks to electronic technology we are standing at the dawn of a new and improved era, a true paradigm. More than any other aspect of transport operation, these two elements – which can perhaps be better described jointly as marketing – are already resulting in a transformation of the quality of the entire transport product. A good example can be seen in Berlin, where it will soon be possible for intending passengers to discover immediately by mobile phone in how many minutes the next bus of their choice will reach the nearest stopping point. Because tourism more than any other economic activity involves communication over relatively long distance, it is a reasonable guess that tourism in general – and transport in particular – will become a primary beneficiary of the electronic revolution. The impact of this is already being felt but it is as yet too diffused to show up in statistics. It is not too fanciful to hazard a guess that this factor alone could account in the long-term – i.e. more than ten years ahead – for an extra one per cent growth per annum. If other factors were broadly balanced this would mean a jump upward in the long-term annual growth of world tourism from say four to five per cent.

## Price

The final essential element in transport to consider is price. Here the critical factor would appear to be the cost of fuel. Despite two major so-called fuel crises, first in the early 1970s and again in the early 1980s, we went through the 1990s living through a period of relatively cheap fuel prices. Paradoxically, this was the result of the two 'crises' which brought about a desperate but astonishingly successful search for new fuel reserves. This in turn created a relatively short-term excess of supply over demand from which the world economy is now starting to retreat. As the most price-sensitive user of fuel, airlines are again proving to be the first to suffer. In the case of surface transport, the effects are masked by discriminatory taxation which so distorts the market that accurate forecasting requires advance knowledge of how politicians are going to tax (as well as subsidise) the various competing forms of transport. However, it is reasonable to guess that conventional fuels are slowly going to become less readily availabie and will tend to become more expensive. This means that transport products will generally become more expensive, and therefore less economically attractive, than non-transport products, until alternative fuels become available in abundance, as is certain to happen within our 30-year time frame. Unfortunately for the forecaster, nobody yet knows exactly when this will happen!

**Vehicles**

Last to consider among the mysterious variables that confront the forecaster are the changing characteristics of vehicles and indeed the emergence of new forms of vehicle. It is interesting to reflect that few of the significant vehicular changes that have actually taken place were accurately predicted in advance. When these fundamental changes take place, it is invariably the result of an invention aimed at solving a non-transport problem. The application of coal and later of oil and most recently of gas to generate power; the invention and development of electricity; the development of the train and the aeroplane: none of these started life as projects to promote passenger travel. One of the very few exceptions is the reciprocating engine, which immediately spawned the motor car, and which is still today in its many derivative forms the foundation stone of the transport industry. In contrast there is no shortage of forecasts for exciting new devices that have in fact failed to work as passenger vehicles. Vertical take-off, Hovercraft, Rockets. My guess is that in the coming 10 – 20-year time frame, beyond which it is imprudent to look, there will be no revolutionary changes on the vehicle front. I am quite sure that space travel, even in the limited form of recreational space stations, will not become of any significant commercial importance. What in fact will happen is a slow, gradual, steady adaptation of existing technology to take advantage of new materials and processes – which will usually have evolved in areas other than transport – and to respond to the changes which I have attempted to describe. The many different forms of vehicle which will surely emerge in the next 10 or 20 years are indeed the subject for another occasion. For this chapter, the main message is that the realistic future will be determined not by the vehicle but by the political and economic environment it which it is allowed to operate.

As indicated in my introductory remarks, my assessment of the overall situation is that we now stand at a turning point. Throughout the past century we enjoyed dramatic improvements both in vehicles and in the way they can be used by tourists. In contrast, looking a quarter of a century ahead, we see few dramatic improvements in vehicles and many possible limitations on the use of vehicles. We may well therefore find ourselves in a new situation where improvements in our vehicles are outweighed by restrictions inflicted by governments on the use of our vehicles. This possibility – of transport becoming a hindrance rather than a help – will ultimately turn on our success at persuading the makers of laws, regulations and infrastructure that tourism is so politically important that it must not be restrained by inadequate transport. From now on the dog must take control of its tail.

# 18

# THE FUTURE OF TIMESHARING

## Introduction

Over the 1990s alone, timeshare has come a long way. New markets and consumers are coming on stream, sales are buoyant, legislation is in place in most markets, satisfaction levels amongst purchasers are high, and the public image of the product has improved considerably. Moreover, timeshare has now reached the point where it is becoming ever more an integrated part of the 'mainstream' holiday market. Integration is a theme that runs through this chapter; for whilst timeshare is a distinct product with unique properties, requiring specialist skills and knowledge to bring to the market, its long-term future is inextricably linked to that of the broader hospitality and travel sectors wherein vertical and horizontal integration are reshaping supply and distribution channels. Implicit in the above is the spectre of consolidation, branding, segmentation and other drivers of change.

## A Global Industry

Timeshare is a global industry, with more than 5000 resorts and 4 million owners spanning all continents. Although timeshare emerged first in Europe during the 1960s, it was in the United States where it burgeoned, especially after the introduction of the exchange function in the mid-1970s. The United States currently accounts for 35% of all timeshare resorts and 48% of all timeshare owners, though its percentage share of the world totals will inevitably decline as the industry continues its geographical expansion. Indeed, growth in the European market has ben particularly strong throughout the late 1980s and 1990s, making it the second largest market with 31.5% and 26% of timeshare resorts and owners respectively (RCI Consulting, 1999). These two key regions are annexed by a number of smaller established markets and, moreover, the emergence of new markets: India and Asia, Central and Eastern Europe, and the Middle East, for example.

At a global level, growth throughout the 1980s and 1990s was considerable, albeit from a low base in the early stages. In the late 1990s, growth in resorts and owners has levelled off to more sustainable figures of around 7–8%. Although not strictly comparable, as a point of reference it represents twice the growth rate of supply in the hotel sector in 1998. In terms of sales, the worldwide industry totalled over US$ 6 billion in 1998, double the volume processed in 1990 at the start of the decade.

Whilst the aggregate figures give a broad overview of the industry as a whole, it is important to recognise that they mask differences between markets. It is difficult to categorise Europe, for example, as one market, when in reality growth rates vary between constituent countries, reflecting their different and particular characteristics and nuances. In some cases the performance of the timeshare industry in a given country is linked to general macro economic conditions and Russia is perhaps an obvious, albeit extreme example. More often than not, however, there is no direct correlation between economic growth and that of sales in an industry that is overwhelmingly supply-driven.

### A Changing Industry Structure

The composition of the industry is changing, and the pace of change looks set to increase in the coming years. Key drivers of change include the entry of branded hospitality corporations and vertically integrated travel companies linked to a general trend towards consolidation.

***Consolidation, Hospitality Groups and Clubs***

The recent takeover of US timeshare group Vistana by Starwood Hotels & Resorts is symptomatic of timeshare's transition from an industry comprising large numbers of localised independent companies to one comprising a smaller number of branded global players. To date, this has been a gradual and largely US-centred process: timeshare has been home to a number of large branded companies, including the oft-quoted hospitality groups such as Hilton, Hyatt, Disney and Marriott, for some time. Over the next five years or so, however, the pace of change is likely to increase and, moreover, embrace more fully regions outside of North America. It is no coincidence that virtually all of the leading hospitality companies have looked at, or are looking at, formally entering the timeshare industry. The obvious question to ask is: 'What is motivating these companies to enter the timeshare business?' And the answer is simple: new revenue streams and new profits. Of course, the viability of each project has to be viewed on its merits, and the operational nuances of a mixed-use or separately run site are manifold. Yet, on a general level the hotel and timeshare products are a good fit, and the natural overlap between many operational and promotional functions means that the two businesses complement rather than compete with each other. (For a detailed review of the issues pertaining to hotels and timeshare see, for example. Dean, 1993; Sweeney, 1993; RCI Consulting, 1999). This trend is set to intensify in the foreseeable future, proving mutually beneficial to hospitality and timeshare industries alike. For the timeshare industry, the association of well-known brands not only brings credibility, it also provides a sustainable platform for future growth.

But the consolidation process currently under way in the timeshare industry is not exclusively hospitality-driven. Growth *via* acquisition and merger is a strategy being pursued by a number of specialist timeshare developing companies, the most obvious example being the Sunterra Corporation. Sunterra is a relatively new company, which has grown ten-fold between 1995 and 1998, largely through acquisition. Last year it sold US$ 352 million worth of inventory, making it second only to Marriott in terms of global timeshare sales (Vacation Ownership World, 1997, 1999). These are US-based companies with global reach and inventory – so they operate in Europe and other regions as well as North America. Further, they are also companies that operate club products utilising 'points'.

### *The Move Towards Holiday Clubs and Points*

Of course, points-based products and holiday clubs are nothing new. Hapimag, a pioneer of European timeshare, has operated a points-based product since the mid-1960s and points have dominated the South African market for several years, for example. But the move towards this form of product has gathered momentum in recent years, especially in the major markets. There are currently many successful clubs operating in Europe in addition to the aforementioned US-based concerns. Generally, the clubs grow not in an organic fashion, but by acquisition and merger – that is to say, they acquire specific inventory or whole resorts, which then become part of a club's network of inventory, which, in turn, is made available to its members. The larger the number of resorts and resort destinations the club has, the greater the choice offered to the member and potential member. Coupled with the flexibility of points, which enables members to vary their vacation patterns according to needs and lifestyle, the club concept has much appeal.

Whilst this shift presents potential difficulties for small developers – in terms of maintaining an independently successful operation – it does not mean that large and small operators cannot co-exist. But co-existence for independent operators will probably entail a re-focusing of business strategy and a review of options such as segmentation and niche marketing, perhaps.

One thing is clear, however: holiday clubs and the points-based timeshare product is here to stay. And these are not hollow words; for we at RCI Europe have already shown our commitment to the points club product through the acquisition of Club Resorts International (CRI) earlier this year. CRI is now up and running, and forms the European arm of RCI's Global Points Network (GPN) which is to be rolled out in full in the near future. GPN will not only ensure that RCI continues to operate at the heart of the industry, but it also provides an opportunity for smaller developers to embrace the club concept and continue to compete in an increasingly competitive marketplace.

***Travel Trade Distribution***

Timeshare is also attracting interest from major vertically integrated travel groups, which are set to initiate a new wave of change in product delivery. Groups such as Thomas Cook and Airtours bring to the product additional brand visibility and increased public awareness and acceptance. To date, the exposure to timeshare of tour operators and the high street travel agents has been limited, but what activity there has been has proved successful. Indeed, RCI Europe recently established a programme to promote timeshare-based holidays with Seligo, the UK's leading worldwide accommodation reservation specialist. The promotion is then distributed through independent travel agents. The initial stages of the project suggest that it will be a promising venture.

And this is the central message with regard to travel trade groups – that the potential here is vast, and could transform the way in which timeshare is sold. The retail branch networks of the major travel chains are a powerful distribution channel that could bring the timeshare product to a much larger and more diverse consumer base. This, in turn, integrates timeshare still further into the mainstream holiday market and increases the potential for cross-marketing activity for all concerned. Most important of all, however, the consumer is afforded easy access to the timeshare product *via* familiar and trusted mechanism – the agent in the High Street.

***Moving more Towards a Customer-driven Market?***

Over time, the increased sophistication and diversity of distribution channels will bring the timeshare product more in line with traditional holiday products by eroding the dominance of supply over demand. At present, applying the traditional concept of a market to timeshare is problematic because the notion of 'natural' demand does not apply. That is to say that the product is 'sold' rather than 'sought', meaning that the size of given countries' customer bases are largely a function of sales and marketing activity by developers and marketing companies as opposed to indicators of consumer demand. And, price competition is something that the industry has hitherto lacked courtesy of limited supply outlets and a lack of pricing transparency. Of course, this system has worked spectacularly well for many companies, in many regions, and for many years – and, generally, the very high quality of the product has ultimately converted prospects into sales. But as the industry matures, so it embraces the trappings that accrue to mature markets everywhere, including greater competition, price transparency and concomitant developments such as a vibrant resale market. The latter is already growing, proliferation being speeded *via* the Internet, technology that will, in turn, increase the ability of consumers to 'comparison-shop' with regards to new as well as second-hand goods.

**Product Trends**

It is not just the way the product is sold and distributed that is changing, the timeshare product itself is becoming more diverse and segmented. The traditional beach, mountain or country club product will always be mainstays of timeshare, just as they are mainstays of holiday products in general, but timeshare is evolving ever more into a lifestyle product, catering to activity-based and niche markets. Indeed, the products now embraced by timeshare include cruise ships, golf, skiing, narrow boats, hotels, villas and even caravans courtesy of Resort Parks International (RPI), a subsidiary of RCI Europe.

Another avenue proving increasingly attractive to developers is the urban market. High profile examples here include the Manhattan Club in New York and the Edinburgh residence in Scotland, allied to a number of properties in London, Paris, and other cities across the globe. The urban sector thus far has grown quite modestly, perhaps because the increased profile and attractiveness of timeshare has coincided with a property boom in the major cities, and the return on investment has to be measured against that generated from other options such as serviced apartments (Anthony, 1998). Clearly, both of these factors act as broad constraints on the cumulative expansion of the urban market, but they need to be set alongside the potential benefits such as all year round seasons and the possibility of attracting corporate customers. One thing is clear – the city locations currently operating timeshare are both popular and successful, and I believe that the urban market is set to be a major growth sector over the next five years, fuelled in part by the involvement of the hospitality companies noted earlier.

Then there are the points-based products mentioned earlier. Points are essentially currency: owners can choose the number of points they want to purchase and, because they know in advance the number of points needed to secure their desired holiday experience, they can use them in a flexible way. Whereas traditional timeshare has operated around predominantly fixed weekly intervals, points open up new permutations, enabling owners to choose the number of trips – and combinations (e.g. short breaks mixed with longer holidays) – taken per year, which can be varied to the full value of points held. Ultimately, points are a vehicle for the delivery of a true integrated lifestyle product, where timeshare becomes one piece of a larger jigsaw embracing hotels, cruises, car rentals, package deals and a whole raft of other products and services that can be accessed by a universal points currency. Some leading hospitality companies have operated points systems for some time. The associated loyalty schemes, and those of airlines, operate around transferable currency. In the future, it is likely that timeshare will become an integrated part of an expanded currency-based system, offering consumers ever more choice and control over their holiday experiences.

And then there is the service that is most associated with my own company, RCI – exchange. This will continue to be the oil that lubricates the industry, operating at the very heart of the timeshare business as it has since the early days back in the mid-1970s. The ability to exchange was the catalyst for the growth of timeshare in the late 1970s and 1980s. This continued through the 1990s, and the exchange function will continue to add value to the timeshare product in the future. Of course, no business can afford to stand still, and that is why RCI has embraced the points business. This will complement our core exchange business and provide a solid platform for future growth. Both of the two major exchange companies have vast timeshare experience and knowledge, growing resort networks and member bases, and exchange will continue to be a major factor in the success of the industry as it heads towards maturity.

**Public Image, Satisfaction and the Consumer**

It is no secret that, throughout its short life, timeshare has attracted negative coverage from the media, resulting in public wariness concerning the product. This has largely been due to a focus on isolated sales abuses by a minority of companies in the early years, obscuring the positives such as product quality and high satisfaction amongst owners. However, the image is improving. In the United States, the combination of effective consumer legislation, the entrance of well-known brands, the efforts of a well-funded and organised trade body – American Resort Development Agency (ARDA) – and a high quality product backed by efficient exchange networks, has effectively refreshed the image of timeshare. The most recent survey by RCI Consulting (1998a) into the public image of timeshare in the

United States, found that 31.6% of consumers were interested in purchasing a timeshare interval, up from 27% in 1992. Although direct survey data for other regions are limited, this gradual improvement in public perception is also evident.

In Europe, we have worked closely with the new trade body – Organisation for Timeshare in Europe (OTE) – in promoting the industry and educating the consumer about the product. Virtually all of the EU countries have now passed the Timeshare Directive, affording consumer protection to potential purchasers, and the press coverage of timeshare is much more balanced and positive than was once the case. A good example of this is Germany, a market in which the image problem had been particularly pronounced. In 1996, over 80% of press coverage of timeshare in Germany was negative; by 1998 it was just under 60%; we project that the positive will outweigh the negative over the next few years (figures based on circulation: according to unpublished internal RCI research). Of course, the German market still represents an ongoing challenge, as do many other markets, but the point to emphasise is that the image of timeshare is moving in the right direction. As to the future, strong and well-funded trade bodies are essential to ensuring that this continues – and I believe that, over time, OTE will do for the industry in Europe what ARDA has done for it on North America.

### *Consumer Profiles, Product Penetration and Satisfaction*

Typically, timeshare consumers have tended to be well-educated married couples between the ages of 40 to 60 with above-average incomes. The key purchase motivations are the opportunity to exchange, quality of accommodation, value for money (e.g. RCI Consulting, 1998b). Penetration levels tend to be higher in the upper income brackets. In the United States, for instance, penetration rates vary from 1.8% amongst purchasers with incomes of US$ 35 – 50000 up to almost 6% amongst buyers with incomes of over US$ 100,000 (RCI Consulting, 1998c). In general, this reflects the fact that it is not until later in life that most people have the disposable income to purchase the product. But the demographics of new buyers may change over time, with a larger percentage of younger buyers possibly coming on stream as (a) the availability of consumer finance increases, rendering the product more affordable, and (b) more diverse 'lifestyle' products attract hitherto untargeted sections of the population (e.g. singles, sports/activity-oriented buyers, double-income families with no children, etc.). In addition, the consumer is becoming better educated and more sophisticated. In part, this is linked to the educational and awareness programmes of the trade bodies and exchange companies allied to an improving press mentioned earlier. More than this, however, the customer of the future will benefit from, amongst other things, the Internet and other technology that will facilitate easier comparison shopping and aid informed choice.

One thing above all is clear, and that is the vast size of the potential market for the product in all corners of the globe. Even in countries with the highest penetration levels, such as the United States and the UK, less than 5% of all households with a minimum income of £22,000 currently own timeshare (RCI Consulting, 1998c; UK figures based on unpublished RCI research). And this is potential growth in a product that achieves very high satisfaction rates amongst owners. Numerous studies over the past five years have pointed to satisfaction rates of between 80 and 90% ('satisfaction' here referring to the combination of 'very' and 'somewhat' satisfied results from questionnaire – based surveys) across all regions (e.g. Ragatz Associates, 1995; RCI Consulting, 1997, 1998b).

## Conclusion

Summing up, it is clear that timeshare is an industry witnessing considerable change. It is becoming more global, attracting larger, sophisticated and well-capitalised players. In conjunction with technological advances that enable consumers to compare prices, this will lead to a more competitive business climate, forcing smaller players to review strategies or succumb to consolidation. This process is inextricably linked to the growth of points and holiday clubs, and the ability of companies to capture niche and sheltered markets. Moreover, the future is a regulated place – if Europe and the other regions that have enacted consumer legislation mimic the experience of the United States then regulation may have a short-term impact on sales, but will serve as a solid platform for long-term growth.

Last, but by no means least, penetration rates are still relatively low even in the major markets, and new markets are coming on stream across the globe each year. This is good news for an industry that is becoming more integrated into the mainstream travel and tourism market, leading to improvements in product delivery. This, in tandem with the already high quality of the timeshare product, bodes well for the industry. Ultimately, I believe that the changes currently under way will benefit the customer – and providing the industry does not lose sight of that, it faces a bright and profitable future.

# 19

# NEW CHALLENGES IN TOURISM TODAY

## The Travel Market: Main Features

### *A Growth Market With Intensive Competition*

Leisure travel today has become a basic need and turned into a commodity. The desire and urge to travel and 'go some place' is nowadays viewed as a matter of course. By and large, it can be said, no matter what the circumstances, people will make time and means available to travel. They may undertake a short trip, an extended vacation some other time, vary the standards and so on, but travel they will.

The growing demand has led to a rapid expansion of the travel industry. Today we are facing substantial excess capacities. Air and other transportation capacities are available in abundance. Tour operators produce travel packages in ever larger quantities and at the destinations guests, decision-makers and product managers are lured not only with attractive rates, but with promotional support and a range of incentives as stimulants to fill the wide offers of accommodations. Holiday prices show a clear downward trend; it is noteworthy in this context to recall the availability of travel and its cost some 30 years ago compared to today's virtually limitless possibilities and low costs.

In line with the development of increasing volumes of vacationers and tourism in general, the industry has undergone and still is undergoing a process of change and concentration. Different skills and competences are required to succeed in the highly competitive volume market in the lower and mid range than in the segment of niche markets for the more discerning traveller.

While operators of niche products continue successfully to occupy their positions and hold their own markets, a process of concentration in the volume market has been initiated among a handful of large internationally operating travel groups. Given the fierce price war taking place in the high volume market and the big investments and competences required in IT for processing and distribution, significant volumes and turnovers are needed for a profitable operation. These are not feasible without concentration and though this process has been going on for some time, it will continue even further.

### *IT – Motor in Competition*

The dramatic development in the IT field has also had its impact on the travel industry and is a major motor to stimulate competition. In the volume business it is today without a doubt the single biggest factor that contributes to an operator's competitiveness, in fact a high degree of IT know-how can assure the competitive edge over the competition.

IT is not only the key to lower operational costs and higher productivity, it opens new avenues in marketing and sales, be it direct sales, interactive TV travel shops or transactions and ultimately one-to-one marketing *via* the Internet. To implement these new technologies, which are here to stay, and make them work by giving the consumer extra value and convenience, requires substantial know-how and competence in IT technology and the skill to combine these new technologies with the requirements and mechanics of the travel business as well as with the changing consumer behaviour.

### *Pressure to Change by Changing Consumer Behaviour*

Consumers for any type of product or service are today vastly different from what they were not long ago. The relentless flow of information to which we are all exposed on a daily basis, the readily available information, facts and details, literally available at our fingertips, on almost any topic, provides today's consumers with a competence not existing in earlier times and confidence in defining their requirements and making their choices and decisions. And they make use of this increased self-reliance by letting the markets know. They buy what they want, or do not buy if it is not there, rather than simply buying what the market suggests one should buy.

This combined with the strong trend to individualism, or individual lifestyles, by the modern consumer, has not left the travel industry without impact. The increasing amount of spare time and growing importance of leisure activities, the desire for more frequent but shorter trips and holidays, have caused the travel industry to adapt. New travel products are on the market; flexible individual travel programmes have out-ranked the regimented group travel packages, which at one time formed the bulk of leisure travel. In addition the increased transparency of market and product information has enhanced price awareness among consumers and as a result further raised price competition in the industry.

**Tourism Market Workflow**

Through changing consumer behaviour and the entry of new technologies, the traditional workflow link in the travel market is also undergoing decisive changes and the once clearly separated roles and functions of its principal participants are being redefined. The borderlines of their respective activities and market audiences are getting more and more blurred with increasing overlapping.

Electronic platforms, like global distribution systems (GDS) and other booking systems, are not only the line of contact to tour operators and travel agents; new technologies offer new opportunities for new channels of information, marketing and sales straight to the end consumers. This will shift the established balances of the workflow in the industry. On the downside, by pursuing this option, suppliers will have to add significantly to their marketing and advertising budgets as well as work on their IT competence and exposure. Widening the marketplace, dealing through more channels and selling to a larger number of buyers in different segments will increase the importance of yield management for best use of capacities and maximising revenues.

What goes for one participant in the change process of the workflow will of course apply to others, too: tour operators will equally take full advantage of the newly available technologies in their efforts for most effective distribution, including direct marketing to end consumers. With growing complexity of the markets and the consumers being overwhelmed by a multitude of information sources and a continuous barrage of direct marketing *via* conventional and electronic channels, consumers will have fewer ties and emotions toward a specific product, service or brand. Apart from the many ways and means to foster customer relationships, a precisely defined and strictly followed brand policy will become a key criterion. A strong brand underlies perceptions and signals reliability and stability – elements by which the vast majority of consumers are, to a greater or lesser extent, mostly unwittingly, influenced, and will be more so in the future. Strong brands will also in our business increasingly make the difference between making or losing a sale.

Despite commission capping and the threat of direct sales by tour operators and suppliers, the retail industry will not be forced out. In fact, through the new technologies new opportunities arise beyond merely reducing operational costs. The range and depth of available information on products and services in combination with the retailer's skill to draw on this immense pool of data and render it quickly at the customer's disposal highlights the strength and added value of the retailer's advisory competence and care. The new media are perfectly suited to provide individual, custom-made and yet efficient advice and recommendations to the retail clientele, and complete transactions on their behalf, any place, any time and over distance. The speed of communication can be accelerated to the customer's own pace. The challenge for the retail industry is to profile itself as a 'counsellor' and service provider, away from the image of a mere outlet.

**Tomorrow's Consumer**

Tomorrow's consumer will not only add further to his or her personal know-how and competence, but become also more and more demanding and expectant. Market transparencies will increase and knowing that information is available, consumers will expect to be given the relevant details and information without having to gather it on their own. The times when selections and decisions are made on price alone are – apart from specific bargain offers – largely gone.

'Best value for time and money' is not just a buzzword, though it can have different meanings for different people. With the increasing individual lifestyle mentioned earlier, the trend for individualism in travel is also growing. As travellers gain more routine, they become receptive to and eager for new innovative products and look more often now for new experiences and adventures rather than just 'another vacation'.

In general, public trends, moods and value thinking will have to be taken more and more into account. On the issues of ecology, for example, there is a slowly awakening trend detectable, putting eventually if not a halt, a brake on certain developments in world-wide tourism. Apart from a minority, people are hardly yet at the point where they would refrain from buying a specific travel programme for ecological considerations unless it would severely affect their own personal comfort and experience during their travel. But what is likely to happen when an operator's reputation suffers on environmental grounds is that consumers might stay away from an entire brand. Such developments are impossible to predict, but nowadays they must not be ignored.

**Challenges of the New Tourism Marketplace**

Let me summarize the key issues ahead of us. The direct access to everyone, the wealth of information and density of communication made possible by new technologies and the changing consumer behaviour will place the customer at the centre of the new marketplace. All active participants in the market, suppliers, tour operators, retailers and new industry entrants, will be increasingly vying directly for consumers' attention. For consumers this development is two-sided, yet the additional benefits of more choices and options and of low prices outweigh the extra task of sifting through the information, separating the unwanted from the useful and desirable and making appropriate comparisons. The decision-making process may not always become simpler.

The highly competitive business environment with its low elasticity of prices in the market together with the new consumer expectations, force tour operators to generate high volumes and come up with products at attractive prices. These products have to be flexible so that they can be tailored individually to a complete holiday programme according to the clients' liking.

The complexity of the handling of such products requires sophisticated IT systems. Quick and easy access to a tour operator's products and uncomplicated, 'user-friendly' booking and order-processing through innovative IT systems are becoming as decisive for success as a good travel product at a fair price. IT issues become of utmost strategic importance.

In the growing myriad of propositions and choices in the market, consumers will look for orientation and guidance, a spot with which they can identify and find some common values. A strong brand will stand out as a marker and have a drawing effect. Weak brands will go by largely unnoticed and its products and services will consequently be in low demand.

Finally, there is an increasing awareness of health and security. While it seems accepted that certain risks and hazards in travel like anywhere else, be it through 'force majeure' or otherwise, can never be ruled out entirely, the tolerance and willingness to accept mishaps and incidents and bear the brunt of the consequences are diminishing. Risks to the travellers' well-being and safety may arise anywhere through political developments, dangers to public health or natural forces. Consumers want to know in unambiguous terms that someone is responsible for their respective activities and that they are accountable. Obligations and responsibilities of suppliers, providers and intermediaries will increase, as well as expectations by the public that all realistically feasible considerations and precautions are taken and appropriate information is provided. It is evident and must be understood that product liability on the part of all of us in the travel industry and its inherent risks and implications will continue to rise.

# 20

# CONCLUSIONS

The previous chapters in this book have addressed many aspects of tourism and hospitality in the 21st century. This concluding chapter begins with a discussion of what we regard as over-riding problems of tourism and hospitality in the new century, followed by a review of major challenges which the industry will face. We conclude the chapter with some thoughts on the likely nature of tourism and hospitality in the future.

## Problems

While the world faces many problems, most of which affect tourism and hospitality to a greater or lesser degree, there are four significant general problems that emerge from the chapters to be of particular relevance to tourism and hospitality.

### *The Problem of Definitions*

Despite the fact that the terms 'tourism' and 'hospitality' are widely used there continues to be a lack of agreement as to exactly what each of these encompasses and as to the relationship between them. In this discussion, we take tourism to be an all-encompassing term covering every aspect of people staying away from home, and hospitality to be a specific aspect of this, dealing with accommodation and feeding tourists. One difficulty, of course, is that the hospitality industry also feeds and accommodates many people who are not tourists.

In reality 'tourism' is often interpreted quite narrowly, i.e. as the flow of visitors from one country to another. This is because, like many of the authors of chapters in this book, academics and researchers generally rely heavily on the World Tourism Organisation (WTO) as their principal source of data. Yet in many parts of the world, particularly the United States and China, there are very high levels of domestic tourism. Even today only about 10% of the US population has a passport.

This problem of differentiating between international and domestic tourism is likely to become even more severe. If the European Union should become the United States of Europe, intra-regional travel within the Union will cease to be international tourism regardless of its purpose. (Travel between Hong Kong and PRC has already ceased to be international tourist travel, although the volume of traffic has increased and the purpose changed little.)

It is clear there is also a great deal of inconsistency between data, which is largely due to the problems of definition. Purpose of visit is one such definitional problem. When tourism is not defined it generally means pleasure tourism, people on holidays, but formal definitions (like that of the WTO) tend to include anyone travelling. Witt and Song state that 70% of worldwide trips were holidays, 15% were business and 10% were related to visiting friends and relatives (VFR). Yet the most recent Horwath International global hotel study (1999) identifies only 50% of occupancy deriving from the leisure traveller and 46% from business guests. From the hospitality and airline industries' point of view the business traveller is extremely important and often the major focus of attention and effort.

The apparent inconsistency in figures is partly because so many pleasure tourists stay in less conventional accommodation. In Scotland, for example, Scottish Tourist Board figures published in 1999 show that hotel accommodation makes up only about 40% of total tourist accommodation excluding VFR beds. Rather too many surveys concentrate solely on hotel guests, thus much less is known about other staying visitors. Domestic tourists are more likely than international tourists to use accommodation other than hotels as they are better placed to know about alternatives. Until the problems relating to the definitions of tourism and hospitality are resolved and the definitions become all-encompassing, applying with equal validity to all regions, there are likely to be continued difficulties and inconsistencies in understanding tourism and travel data and statistics.

### *The Problem of Forecasting and Predicting Growth and Change*

A feature of this text has been the forecasts about tourism's future. Witt and Song are clear about which methods work, and Frechtling makes some telling points about which factors will influence tourism in the next decade. But most econometric and statistical trend projections are based on the principle of *ceteris paribus* – all things remaining equal. What if they do not? A feature of the 20th century, especially the second half of the century, was relative stability in many aspects of tourism, but this may not be true for the 21st century.

Global tourism is forecast to grow, but overall growth forecasts hide tremendous differences between regions and countries. According to Teye Africa receives only 4% of all international tourists and only 2% of total international tourism receipts. He shows that many African countries are economically worse off now than they were 40 years ago, still over-reliant on agricultural and/or mineral production, with tourism presenting both cultural and environmental challenges. He concludes that there have been and still are a myriad of obstacles to tourism development, such as political instability, economic restructuring, human resource constraints, lack of regional co-operation and a lack of basic infrastructure.

An optimistic view of Europe and North America is that at best their tourism industries are stable. Cook states that short-term growth in US arrivals will be slow, whilst Cleverdon suggests tourism in Europe is growing at a rate of

3% compared with a global rate of 4%, and its market share is forecast to decline from 59% (1995) to 47% by 2020. On the other hand South America looks set for a period of sustained tourism growth. Arrivals have been growing at an annual rate of 9% and receipts at 12%. It has some tremendous advantages, including its relative proximity to lucrative North American markets, historic and language links with Europe, and excellent natural resources (rainforest/Andes/beaches).

Asia Pacific also seems to be on an upturn. Chamberlain quotes the WTO as forecasting that this region will 'grow faster than any other' and will pass the Americas to become second to Europe in the number of visitor arrivals. This means five times as many visitors in 2020 as in 1998 – admittedly a low year – although there may be some difficulty in accommodating that number of visitors and it might pose strains on the infrastructure in the region. Asia Pacific illustrates perfectly how vulnerable these industries are to unexpected events. The recent financial crisis in this region led to dramatic falls in arrivals, hotel rates and hotel occupancies, not only in the Pacific region but globally. This kind of event makes forecasting tourism performance in some regions almost impossible. No one can predict what might happen in the Middle East, the Indian sub-continent and the Russian Federation. Political instability, economic turbulence and religious differences could all have negative effects on potential tourism development and growth.

Overall there is evidence of extremely rapid growth in some regions, that this growth will continue, and that other regions will begin to attain a greater share of tourism in the years ahead. But there is really no such thing as a 'fair share' despite what ministers and NTOs say. Not everywhere needs or can expect to attract large numbers of tourists. Those places that have not grown significantly or do not have major tourism industries generally are in that position for good reasons. Cetron identified some of these reasons – a lack of perceived attractions compared to other areas, relative or absolute inaccessibility, unsuitable climate, political regimes which discourage tourism, problems of security, health and safety, relatively high cost and often a combination of several of these.

What is needed is an examination of which, if any, of these elements are likely to change significantly in the short- to medium-term future, to understand if those regions are likely to see major increases in tourism. Even then, should such a change in situation come about, we need to see whether and region is appropriately equipped to handle such an increase effectively. Rapid percentage growth is rather easy from a low base, but long-term sustained growth is what is important, if indeed it is growth that is desired. If the world is serious about sustainable development and living within the limits of the resources available, then growth, especially rapid growth, may not be the pattern desired or acceptable in all regions. This aspect is rarely tackled in forecasts, where the focus is normally on growth.

***The Problem of Industry Characteristics***

It seems clear there is going to be continued growth of global brands such as McDonalds and Burger King, Hilton and Holiday Inn, British Airways, One World Alliance, Thomas Cook and American Express, Avis and Hertz. Despite the fact that the Internet makes some people suggest the brand is dead, big firms will continue. There are still economies of scale to be achieved by being big, even in a world of e-commerce, as the AOL–Time Warner merger demonstrates. But the industries will continue to have many small operators managing unique operations on a local basis. One of the comments frequently made about tourism is its fragmentation and the difficulty this poses for instituting controls, particularly self-regulation by the industry. It often results in multiple, sometimes opposing, objectives among different players, which require different solutions in different locations. This is one of the reasons for the frequent lack of application and success of national master plans. Despite the globalisation trends to which Chamberlain and others refer in this volume, there is likely to remain a large element of the tourism industry made up of very small players. The web should encourage and assist the maintenance of some of this diversity.

The tourism workforce is typically described as having low ability and few skills. Large numbers of young people are employed in these industries, expected to work long, unsociable hours, paid below average wages resulting in extremely high levels of staff turnover. This pattern may not be able to continue, if only because in many countries in the developed world there will be fewer young people to be employed under these or any conditions because of changing demographics. Changes in the composition of populations, nationally and globally, are likely to have major, if still uncertain effects on all aspects of tourism and hospitality in the coming century.

***The Problem of Climate Change***

A key problem that tourism and hospitality has to face is climate change. This issue could have greater effects on tomorrow's world and tourism and hospitality in particular than anything else discussed so far. Two islands have disappeared already because of rising sea levels, and the effects of El Nino and weather instability throughout the world have been terrible in recent years. The most worrying aspect is that very little is known about the full nature or level of these effects. To all intents and purposes the tourism and hospitality industries appear to have buried their heads in the sand and seem intent on ignoring what could be *the* major problem of the century.

Some of the likely effects as well as rising sea levels, include negative effects on ski areas with fewer days of snow-cover, increased could and rainfall in some areas, and increased temperatures and greater sun exposure in other parts of the world, with general increased turbulence and unpredictability of weather. Lohmann showed that many of these are serious enough to at least threaten, if not change, the patterns of tourism and to have significant impacts on hospitality operations.

If sea levels do rise significantly as forecast, many world cities including London, Tokyo, Los Angeles, Washington, Sydney and Singapore would be under water, as well as Bangladesh, the Maldives, the Seychelles, the Netherlands and Florida among others. There would be economic, political and social turmoil. Tourism depends on global economic well-being and this would not exist if this scenario became reality.

At this time, however, it seems that only the insurance and banking industries have begun to take real notice of what is likely to be a significant problem, not just for our industries but the world as a whole. Even if serious steps are taken to reduce the problem, it will be decades before the process is reversed, if indeed, it can be reversed.

It is worrying that in general the problem is being ignored by forecasters and by planners. It seems rather naive, for example, to produce a tourism master plan for a place that might be under water by the time the plan is ready to be implemented.

## Challenges

The tourism and hospitality industries face a large number of challenges caused by the general nature of global dynamics, as well as the specific problems noted above.

### *The Challenge of Demographics*

There is considerable evidence that tourism is linked to population size and GDP, so in some respects the future of tourism would seem assured. Demographics is a key element of most forecasting models of tourism. Throughout the 20th century trends were clear and predictable. It was a period during which the average life expectancy of people living in the developed world increased from 47 years to 75. This was due to improved economic conditions, to advances in medicine, especially antibiotics and vaccines, health care and better diet generally and, in the past 50 years, a decline in mass conflicts and wars.

Some believe that our exponential growth in knowledge will accelerate this trend. Mapping the human genome could lead to advances in gene therapies, such as cell replacement and gene scrubbing, so that human life might be extended almost indefinitely. The development of human stem cell technology may enable individuals to grow in a laboratory their own spare parts – already blood vessels are produced in this way. Some experts are predicting that human life span could certainly be extended to 150 years of age, or even indefinitely.

On the other hand, while science has solved many problems, a great many still remain and others are being created. Only one virus – smallpox – has been eradicated to date, although polio may become the second very shortly. Antibiotics, while allowing a reduction in disease, are becoming less and less effective. Antibiotic-resistant TB is now commonplace. In the UK and the United States patients who fail to follow the strict, complex and long-term regime required to cure this disease are forcibly hospitalised to ensure they do so. There are already restrictions on food exports and we may well see restrictions on people who have certain symptoms or illnesses from travelling.

In addition, new infections and diseases, such as Ebola, Lassa, AIDS and CJD, have developed to which there are no known cures. Forty million people worldwide have HIV. In 20 years, AIDS has moved from being undocumented to being one of the largest causes of death in the world. The origin of these diseases is often unknown, although it is increasingly recognised that viruses can cross the species barrier. The world has yet to see another pandemic like the flu outbreak in 1918/19, which killed at least 18 million people, but such a pandemic is almost certain according to academics. The 1918 flu pandemic spread globally through the movement of large numbers of troops following the end of the First World War. Today the travel industry, alongwith a global food distribution system, could have the same effect.

### *The Challenge of the Internet*

The Internet is changing the way many businesses are conducted. The appearance of e-commerce would be as significant an event in this century as the agrarian revolution of the 17th century, the industrial revolution of the 18th century, and the information revolution of the late 20th century. Shares in e-businesses are the fastest growing stocks on the stock market, even though many have yet to make a profit. Currently only 2% of the world's population has Internet access, but this is changing rapidly.

One scenario is that demand for goods and services will increase as distribution costs come down, entrepreneurship will thrive as individuals are given access to global markets, and overall economic growth will raise living standards and wealth everywhere. But there is a downside to the Internet. It is not only a tool for empowering entrepreneurship and businesses, but also a tool for empowering and informing the dispossessed, the outsiders, the have-nots and the extremists. Bombs exploded by Basques in Spain, Tamils in Sri Lanka and Hesbollah in the Middle East can all be made by following instructions available on the worldwide web. Instructions for making weapons of mass destruction – chemical, biological, atomic – will soon be available to any such individual or group. If used, such weapons would create a world that would be in economic chaos as industrial output was disrupted by events affecting energy supplies, production, labour and likely political stability. In such a world tourism and hospitality would suffer more than most industries.

New technology could make moving around the world much safer. Microchips on credit cards can store millions of bits of information about their owner and their owner's preferences. Currently these are used mainly to facilitate transactions, but they can just as easily facilitate personal interactions. These microchips, and even cellular phone technology, will become implantable beneath the skin, which could greatly facilitate security scanning and passport control at airports. It also enables people to use voice commands to interact with their surroundings, controlling items of electrical equipment such as doors, curtains, lights and thermostats by voice alone. Of some interest is the extent to which resort accommodation should become a haven of respite from this 'wired world' or be as technically sophisticated as other living environments. They will probably have to be wired, leaving the choice with the guest as to what use is made of the technology.

### *The Challenges of Travel and Leisure*

Even if e-commerce thrives, the Internet may have an adverse effect on business travel. In the so-called 'wired-world', business travel may actually decline. A global infrastructure of low orbit satellites, asymmetric digital subscriber lines (ASDL) and other new technologies will enable business people to interact, rather than just communicate, in real time, thereby negating the need physically to travel. In many large cities the speed of ground travel has remained almost unchanged in the past 100 years as the advantage of the internal combustion engine over the horse has been confounded by the problem of congestion. Whilst technology will allow business travellers to 'work' on trains and aeroplanes, it is possible to foresee the day that using a mobile phone in public will become as distasteful, both socially and medically, as smoking is now, thus removing this 'benefit' of travel.

Indeed, firms may wish staff to avoid travelling on grounds of efficiency and security and may come to see travel as undesirable for other reasons. First, travel to other countries may be a health risk. Travel to some countries has always required vaccination or protection against established diseases such as hepatitis, typhoid and malaria, but new diseases for which there is no protection and no cure have raised the stakes. Second, business travellers who represent wealthy global firms may be the target of criminals or extremists. Bodyguards already accompany business people travelling in certain countries due to the risk of kidnapping or worse.

The Internet could, therefore, be bad for business travel, but what about leisure travel? These customers differ from business travellers in two main ways. First, they are spending their own disposable income which makes them particularly value conscious, so the Internet driving down prices is something that will stimulate such demand. Second, they have an ever-wider choice as to where they can go and what they can do when they get there. The Internet provides much more information about destinations, facilities, infrastructure and transport options, although already there appear to be signs of information overload for some consumers.

It can be argued that the technologies that make it unnecessary for the business person to travel, will also enable the leisure traveller to stay at home. Virtual reality offers a high degree of stimulation and simulated danger without any of the actual physical risk. Egyptian and other tourism industries have been devastated by the impact of terrorism. Such fears and concerns are likely to heighten demand for holidays in apparently secure environments such as cruise ships and closed integrated resorts combining timeshare, hotels, self-catering, restaurants and leisure facilities such as South Seas Plantation, Club Méditerranée and Center Parcs.

### *The Challenges of Perception and Awareness*

Despite the real risks noted above, human behaviour is based less on actual risk and more on the perception of risk, a feature we are very bad at calculating. The effects of a disaster seem to take about 18 – 36 months to be forgotten at a national level. Acts of terrorism or health scales tend to be viewed as one-off events and providing they do not appear with great regularity in the same place, seem to be accepted by tourists as being unpredictable and unlikely to happen at the destination to which they are going at the time they are going. This philosophy views Egypt is one of the safest places immediately after the last terrorist attack. A single occurrence, however bad, seems to slip memories fairly quickly, a feature the tourism and hospitality industries assist if they can.

Reality is that such events as terrorist acts are of high magnitude but low frequency. For any individual, while results could be fatal, the odds are rather small if one is sensible and does not go to obvious problem spots. On the other hand, potential disasters like climate change are of low personal magnitude but of high or constant frequency, that is, the specific effects are not life-threatening, but the overall likelihood of being affected by the phenomenon is very high or constant. If tourists worry, they seem to worry more about the disasters least likely to affect them in probability terms. The industry does not seem to worry, or does not want to be seen to worry. Air safety is a good example – a lap belt will not significantly increase one's chance of surviving an air crash compared to where one sits in an aircraft but it is given great attention, while the most valuable and highest paying passengers are normally placed in the most dangerous part of the plane!

As well as perception of risk, there is the question of perception and awareness of opportunity for leisure, tourism and travel. The influence of the Internet and new forms of communication in this area have already been noted. Changes in cost and availability of services will also have significant effects on what is perceived of as opportunity and potential destinations for many tourists and travellers.

### *The Challenge of the 'Dark Side' of Travel*

The tourism and hospitality industries are generally poor at catering for disabled populations. Figures in the United States suggest that the disabled or challenged sector is a very large one and despite difficulties, is travelling more and likely to place specific demands on all elements of the tourism and hospitality sectors. There is a great deal of money to be made by meeting the demands of specific groups, and these sectors are no exceptions. Security and user-friendly infrastructure is not cheap, but is not only necessary and fair, but also good business sense. The disabled rarely feature in any forecasts or predictions as a specific group, but it is a large group and one which is likely to get larger and more vocal in expressing its needs and commenting on the industry's shortcomings as members of this group travel or try to travel more in the future.

Tourism also has other dark sides. Tourists can be attracted by the macabre to locations associated with tragedy and death, such as sites of massacres, death camps and war in general. The weird, the extreme, the bizarre also attract visitors in considerable numbers. There are contemporary destinations that have a reputation for sex tourism of all kinds, some extremely undesirable and illegal. Sex tourism is just one aspect that tends to be ignored by most respectable, middle-class academics and industry professionals. It is also one example of the economic activity derived from tourism that is not captured by the statistics. It is unlikely that anyone has any idea of what the true economic value of tourism and hospitality would be if all the undeclared, untaxed activity was included.

### *The Challenge for Research*

Finally, there is the state of tourism and hospitality research, a subject that should be of concern to all involved in these industries. Both Weiler and Olsen were critical in the state of the art. Weiler claimed that tourism researchers had removed themselves psychologically and physically from research consumers, i.e., industry. She argued that much research is not meeting industry needs, there is too much low quality research published, much of the output is written in a way that makes it difficult for industry to access and/or understand, and there are huge gaps in the body of knowledge. Olsen identified hospitality research as being eclectic, the body of knowledge poorly defined, journals having a very mixed review process and conferences being even worse. He claimed there is too much replicative work and too much theory-building, with very few people, especially doctoral candidates, answering the 'so what' questions. These charges are serious and if correct, have major implications for the future of the industries since inadequate research is likely to lead to inappropriate or incorrect decisions about investment, development and operations. The tourism and hospitality industries have poor reputations with respect to investing in research, compounding the problem.

## Conclusions

A level of agreement emerges from the chapters with respect to some likely characteristics of the tourism and hospitality industries in the coming century. It seems clear that there is going to be greater polarisation in the industries in all kinds of ways:

- the 'haves' *vs.* the 'have nots' in terms of consumers as well as destination areas;
- large, global firms *vs.* small, niche players;
- increased mass tourism *vs.* increased elite tourism;
- domestic *vs.* international tourism;
- business *vs.* pleasure tourism, often with extremely different requirements;
- full service *vs.* no frills commodity service/products.

There may be less seasonality for many reasons:

- congestion and supply saturation in peak periods will reduce attractiveness;
- growth in self-employment will drive low-cost and thus off-peak demand;
- increased numbers of retirees free of work-related time constraints;
- changes in patterns of leisure time – short breaks;
- climate change, altering climatic seasonality in some locations.

The notion of 'blur' will apply not only to e-commerce but also to the world generally:

- between business and leisure (travel, activity, time);
- between provider and consumer;
- between operational types.

There is likely to be increased homogeneity in many areas of travel:

- no frontiers and hence no need for passports;
- countries will become less distinguishable from each other;
- urban architecture and imagery will be increasingly uniform (golden arches syndrome);

- many more tourism products – airline seats, bookings, rooms – will become sold as perishable commodities.

These predictions have to be placed in the context of a lack of knowledge about a number of things. We really do not know about:

- key tourism sectors – religious, business, sex, medical, shopping;
- the true economic value of tourism;
- tourist motivations – whether they are tribal, or spiritual;
- the real reasons for travel and destination choice, rather than simple market research categories;
- environmental forces – how green will society have to be, or choose to be?
- e-commerce and the 'wired world', in particular its penetration and level of acceptance;
- climate change, its magnitude, its effects and its time scale, as well as possible solutions.

Industry has to take a number of steps in response to these factors. First, to satisfy the business traveller tourism providers – airlines, car hire, hotels, restaurants – must become completely 'wired'. They must make it possible for their customers to interface with every type of global communication system at the fastest speed possible with utter reliability and meeting all of their needs.

Second, suppliers must provide a totally secure environment, free from both health and security risks, in light of the culture of fear Todd speaks about. This may involve the necessity to develop a totally integrated service that protects the customer from their point of arrival at a destination to their point of departure, even if this means even more tourist ghettos for those who place a high importance on peace of mind.

Third, industry is going to have a become more flexible. Short breaks will be even more popular and may be more common than long holidays. Most of the growth in intra-regional travel arrivals in Europe will be due to this. This will place an enormous strain on the travel industry, even though it may be good for hospitality and may become heavily dependent on the web to facilitate this.

Fourth, brands and branding will need to be rethought. We need to determine if and for what elements brands are still important, whether brand loyalty is still important, and how to constantly renew the attraction of a brand.

Fifth, there will be some real issues with regard to labour supply and quality, not the least being where the cleaners, waiters and chefs will come from in the future. More importantly perhaps, whether they will be able to deliver the ever-more consistent and high standards that customers will expect.

Sixth, the industries are very bad at understanding risk and managing crises, and if tomorrow's world is more unstable, with increased storms, catastrophic flooding and increased terrorism, insurance companies and legal necessity will require tourism and hospitality providers to become sophisticated crisis managers.

Finally, there is clearly a need for academics to do relevant work and share the findings with industry colleagues in a way they can be understood. However, both Weiler's and Olsen's comments also apply equally to research done in the private sector and the government sector. Academics are often justifiably critical of research in tourism and hospitality undertaken by non-academics. However much we might try to educate and train our students in appropriate research methodologies and techniques, once they leave university they are often unable to use the knowledge they have gained. Many of the Terms of Reference for projects mean consultants and others have to conduct research under unrealistic time scales and with unachievable objectives, which they feel unable to criticise if they want to stay in business or keep their jobs. The results often include unusable National Tourism Plans as several contributors have noted, and inaccurate predictions. The need for quick and simple answers to complex problems for government political decisions or short-term industry planning makes this sort of situation for too common to be acceptable.

Olsen said that because research in our field is so diverse and applied 'it demands visionaries from across the spectrum of industry and academic stakeholders who are capable of taking it to the next level'. That is a mighty challenge, but it might be possible. All it takes is getting all the best minds in the field to recognise the need for improvement and create the will for it to happen. This text, and the conference on which it was based, has tried to do just that.

# BIBLIOGRAPHY


Adelson, C. (1976) Tanzania: Western tourism and African socialism. *Africa Report*. September–October.

Ankomah, P.K. and Crompton, J.L. (1990) Unrealised tourism potential: the case of sub-Saharan Africa. *Tourism Management,* 11 (1): 11 – 28.

Anthony, D.S. (1998) Urban timeshare . . . a new wave in the industry?, *Hospitality and Leisure Executive Report,* 5 (3).

Ascanio, A. (1997) El programma de posadas y campanmentos turisticos venezolanos. *Estudios y Perspectivas en Turismo,* 6: 157 – 16.

Ascanio, M. (1999) Una aproximaction al ecoturismo en Venezuela. El Parque Nacional Henri Pittier, *Estudieos y Perspectivas en Turismo,* 8: 274 – 90.

Ayi, N. (1974) Are we Ghanaians or semi-Europeans?, *Daily Graphic,* 3 January, p. 5.

Barnes, J. (1988) African makes a hard choice. *US News and World Report* June 27, 28 – 32.

Bell, D. (1999) *The Coming of Post-Industrial Society.* New York: Basic Books.

Bell, R. (1987) Conservation with a human face: conflict and reconclliation in African land use planning. In *Conservation in Africa: People, Policies and Practice.* Cambridge: Cambridge University Press.

BFK (Bundesamt für Konjunkturfragen) (1991) *Schweiz morgen: vier Szenarien zur scheweizerischen Zukunft: Bericht der Eidgenössischen Expertenkommision an den Bundesra:* Berne: Bundesamt für Konjunkturfragen: Vertrieb: Edig. Drucksachen- und Materialzentrale.

Brotherton, B. (ed.) (1999) *The Handbook of Contemporary Hospitality Research.* Chichester: John Wiley and Sons.

Britton, S. (1982) The political economy of tourism in the third world. *Annals of Tourism Research,* 9 (3): 331 – 58.

Brewn, D.O. (1998) In search of an appropriate form of tourism for Africa: lessons from the past and suggestions for the future. *Tourism Management,* 19(3): 237 – 45.

Bruner, E.D. (1996) Tourism in Ghana – the representation of slavery and the return of the black diaspore, *American Anthropologist*, 98 (2): 290 – 304.

Busnell, R., Faulkner, B. and Jafari, J. (eds) (1997) ARC *Report Tourism Research in Australia: A Strategy to Mobilise National Research Capabilities.* Occasional Paper, Bureau of Tourism Research, Canberra.

Butcher, J. (1997) Sustainable development or development?, In M.J. Stabler (ed.), *Tourism and Sustainability: Principles to Practice.* New York: CAB International, pp. 27 – 38.

Carter, S. (1998) Tourists' and travellers' social construction of Africa and Asia as risky locations. *Tourism Management*, 19 (4): 349 – 58.

Chun, M. (1995) The future model rainforest lodge. IICT training academic native craft center. In D.E. Hawkins, M. Epler Wood and M. Bittman (eds), *The Ecolodge Source Book for Planners and Developers.* North Bennington: TES, pp. 107 – 9.

Coriolano, L. (1996) Turismo e degradacaö ambiental no litoral do Ceará. In A. Lemos (ed.), *Turismo: Impactos Socioambientais.* Sao Paulo: Editora Hucitec, pp. 93 – 103.

Crouch, Geoffrey I. (1994a) A study of international tourism demand: a survey of practice, *Journal of Travel Research*, XXXII (4): 41 – 55.

Crouch, Geoffrey I. (1994b) A study of international tourism demand: a review of findings, *Journal of Travel Research*, XXXIII (1): 12 – 23.

Davidson, J., Hendry, D.F., Saba, F. and Yeo, S. (1978) Econometric modelling of the aggregate time series relationships between consumers' expenditure and income in the United Kingdom. *Economic Journal*, 88: 661 – 92.

Davis, S. and Meyer, C. (1998) *Blur, the Speed of Change in the Connected Economy.* Reading, MA: Addison Wesley Longman.

de Kadt, E (1979) *Tourism: Passport to Development?* New York: Oxford University Press.

Delupes, I.D. (1969) *The East African Economic Community and Common Market.* London: Longman.

Dean, P. (1993) Timesharing opportunities for the hotel sector. *Travel & Tourism Analyst.* 4.

Dieke, P.U.C. (1993) Cross-national comparisons of tourism development: lessons from Kenya and the Gambia. *Journal of Tourism Studies*, 4(1): 2 – 18.

Dieke, P.U.C. (1995) Tourism and structural adjustment programmes in the African economy. *Tourism Economics* 1(1): 71 – 93.

Dieke, P.U.C. (1998) Regional tourism in Africa – scope and critical issues. In Laws *et al.* (eds), *Embracing and Managing Change in tourism-International Case Studies.* New York: Routledge, pp. 29 – 48.

ECA (1986) *Development of Tourism in Africa: the intra-African Tourism Promotion of Tourist Product.* Addis Ababa, Ethiopia: UN Economic Commission for Africa.

ECA (1992) *Directory of Vocational Training Facilities in tourism in Africa.* Addis Ababa, Ethiopia: UN Economic Commission for Africa.

ECA/WTO (1984) Intra-Africa tourism cooperation, joint presentation to the regional conference on intra-African tourism cooperation by the ECA and WTO, Naimey, Niger, October 2 – 5.

Economist Intelligence Unit (1995) *International Tourism Forecasts to 2005.* London: EIU.

Erbes, R. (1973) *International Tourism and the Economy of Developing Countries.* Paris: Organisation for Economic Cooperation and Development.

Esh, T. and Rosenblum, I. (1975) *Tourism in Developing Countries – Trick or Treat?: A Report from the Gambia.* Uppsala, Sweden: The Scandinavian Institute of African Studies, Research Report 31.

European Travel Commission (1999) Megatrends of Tourism in Europe (to the year 2005 and beyond). Unpublished draft. ETC.

European Travel and Tourism Action Group (1998) *Marketing Intelliegence for Planning the Further Europe in the Global Context:* ETAG/ETC/BTA.

Frechtling, Douglas C. (1996) *Practical Tourism Forecasting.* Oxford: Butterworth-Heinemann.

Friedman, T.L. (1999) *The Lexus and the Olive Tree.* New York: Farmer, Straus and Giroux.

Go, F.M. and Jenkins, L.K. (eds) (1997) *Tourism and Economic Development in Asia and Australasia.* London: Cassell.

Goeldner, C.R. (1999) Directions and trends in tourism research: past, present and future, in V.C.S. Heung, J. App and K.F. Wong (eds), *Proceedings of Asia Pacific Tourism Association Fifth Annual Conference,* Hong Kong, pp. 33 – 43.

González, P. and Moral, P. (1995) An analysis of the international tourism demand in Spain. *International Journal of Forecasting,* 11: 233 – 51.

González, P. and Moral, P. (1996) Analysis of tourism trends in Spain. *Annals of Tourism Research,* 23: 739 – 54.

Graburn, N.H.H. and Jafari, J. (1991) Introduction: tourism social science, *Annals of Tourism Research,* 18 (1): 1 – 11.

Haworth, J. (1997) *Work Leisure and Well-being.* London: Routledge.

Hay, B./Scottish Tourist Board (2000) Conference Interventions. Tourism and Hospitality in the 21st century. University of Surrey.

Hendry, D.F. and von Ungern-Sternberg, t. (1981) Liquidity and inflation effects on consumers' expenditure, in A.S. Deaton (ed.), *Essays in the Theory and Measurement of Consumer Behaviour.* Cambridge: Cambridge University Press, pp. 237 – 60.

Horx, Matthias (1995) *Megatrends für die späten neanziger Jahre.* Düsseldorf: ECON-Verlag.

Jafari, J. (1990) Research and scholarship: the basis of tourism education. *Journa of Tourism Studies*, 1 (1): 33 – 41.

Jones, P. (ed.) (1998) Special Issue: Hospitality Research: The State of the Art. *International Journal of Hospitality Management*, 17(2).

Khan, M., Olsen, M.D. and Var, T. (1993) *VNRs Encyclopedia of Hospitality and Tourism*. New York: Van Nostrand Reinhold.

Kim, S. and Song, H. (1998) An empirical analysis of demand for Korean tourism: a cointegration and error correction approach. *Tourism Analysis*, 3: 25 – 41.

Kulendran, N. and King, M.L. (1997) Forecasting international quarterly tourist flows using error correction and time series models *International Journal of Forecasting*, 13: 319 – 27.

Kulendran, N. and Witt, S.F. (2001) Cointegration versus least squares regression. *Annals of Tourism Research*, 28 (forthcoming).

Law, R. and Au, N. (1999) A neural network model to forecast Japanese demand for travel to Hong Kong. *Tourism Management*, 20: 89 – 97.

Lea, J. (1988) *Tourism and Development in the Third World*. London: Routledge.

Lee, G. (1987) Future of national and regional tourism in developing countries. *Tourism Management*, 8: 2.

Linden, E. (1998) *The Future in Plain Sight*. New York: Simon and Schuster.

Lynch, R. and Brown, P. (1999) Utility of large-scale leisure research agendas. *Managing Leisure*, 4: 63 – 77.

Machado, E.V. (1996) Festas de outubro em Santa Catarina. Notas para compreensäo de suas influencias na (re) organizacäo do espaco. In A. Lemos (ed.), *Turismo: Impactos Socioambientais*. Sao Paulo: Editora Hucitec, pp. 241 – 60.

Martin, W. and Mason, S. (1998) *Transforming the Future: Rethinking Free Time and Work*. Sudbury: Leisure Consultants.

Martin, C.A. and Witt, S.F. (1987) tourism demand forecasting models: choice of appropriate variable to represent tourists' cost of living. *Tourism Management*, 8: 233 – 46.

Martin, C.A. and Witt, S.F. (1989) Forecasting tourism demand: a comparison of the accuracy of several quantitative methods. *International Journal of Forecasting*, 5: 1 – 13.

Masri de Achar, S. and Robles-Ponce, L. (1997) *La industria turistica hacia la sustentabilidad*. Mexico: Editorial Diana.

Middleton, V.T.C. (1990) *New Visions for Independent Museums in the UK*. Chichester: Association of Independent Museums.

Middleton, V.T.C. (1998) *New Visions for Museums in the 21st Century*. London: Association of Independent Museums.

Middleton, V.T.C. (1999) The new resorts for the 21st century? In *Insights*. London: English Tourist Board.

Mizon, G.E. and Richard, J.F. (1986) The encompassing principle and its application to testing non-nested hypotheses. *Econometrica*, 54: 657 – 78.

Morales-Arnao, C. (1994) El turismo de aventura en el Perú. *Estudios y Perspectivas en Turismo*, 3: 162 – 71.

Museums & Galleries Commission (1998) *The Domus Database*.

Naisbitt, J. (1994) *Global Paradox: the Bigger the World Economy, the More Powerful its Smallest Players*. London: NIcholas Brealey Publishing.

Novicki, M. (1983) Zimbabwe: tourism with a socialist slant. *Africa Report*, January – February, 49 – 53.

Nyerere, J. (1969) Essay, *The House Magazine*, Dar-es-Salaam, Tanzania: National Development Corporation.

Olsen, M.D. and Connolly, D.J. (1999) Antecedents of technological change in the hospitality industry. *Tourism Analysis*, 4(1): 19 – 28.

Olsen, M.D., West, J. and Tse, E. (1999) *Strategic Management in the Hospitality Industry*. New York: John Wiley and Sons.

Opaschowski, Horst W. (1995) *Tourismus mit Zukunft*. Urlaub 94/95, Hrsg.: BAT-Freizeit-Forschungsinstitut, Hamburg.

Opaschowski, Horst W. (1999) *Tourismus and Freizeit 2000 – Wohin die Reise geht*. Address given at the 'Tourism and Leisure' economic event organised by the Industrie and Handelskammer Schwarzwald on 24 April 1999 in Bad Dürrheim.

Organisation for Economic Co-operation and Development (1999) *National Accounts, Main Aggregates 1960 – 1997*, Volume 1, Washington, DC: OECD.

Organisation of African Unity (OAU) (1981) *Lagos Plan of Action for the Economic Development of Africa: 1980 – 2000*. Geneva, Switzerland: International Institute of Labour Studies.

Patterson, J. (1998) *The Oxford History of the Twentieth Century*. Oxford: Oxford University Press.

Pattie, D.C. and Snyder, J. (1996) Using a neural network to forecast visitor behaviour. *Annals of Tourism Research*, 23: 151 – 64.

Pina Mendonca, E. (1995) Bahia – leading tourism development in Brazil: investment opportunities. In Ministry of tourism of Israel (ed.), *Investments and Financing in the Tourism Industry*. Madrid: WTO, pp. 174 – 8.

Pine, B.J. II and Gilmore, J.H. (1998) Welcome to the experience economy. *Harvard Business Review*, 76(4): 97 – 105.

Pires, C.C. (1999) Management in ecotourism agencies and their insertion in the context of sustainability. *Turismo: Visão E Acáo*, 1(2): 45 – 6.

Ragatz Associates (1995) *The World Wide Resort Timeshare Industry*. American Resort Development Agency.

RCI Consulting (1997) *Timeshare Purchasers in France, Germany, Italy and Spain: Who They Are, Why They Buy*. Eugene, Kettering: RCI Consulting Inc. Europe.

RCI Consulting (1998a) *The Public Image of Resort Timesharing*. Eugene, Oregon: RCI Consulting Inc.
RCI Consulting. (1998b) *The Benefits of Owning Resort Timesharing: A National Survey of Resort Timeshare Owners*, 1998 edition. Eugene, Oregon: RCI consulting Inc.
RCI Consulting (1998c) *Timeshare Purchasers: Who They Are, Why They Buy*, 1998 edition Eugene, Oregon: RCI Consulting Inc.
RCI Consulting (1999) *Timeshare Industry Overview '99*. Eugene, Oregon: RCI Consulting Inc.
Rifkin, J. (1995) *The End of Work*. London: Tarder Putnam.
Rivera, J. (1993) Project for regulating and developing ecotourism in Amazonia. Proceedings of the World Congress on Adventure Travel and Ecotourism, Manaus.
Roberts, K. (1999) *Leisure in Contemporary Society*. Wallingford, Oxfordshire: CABI Publishing.
Romero-Mayo, R. (1997) Dilemas del turismo ecológico en el Caribe Mexicano, *Revista Mexicana del Caribe*, 2(4): 80 – 129.
Ruschmann, D. (1997) O ecoturismo no Brasil. Proceedings of the World Ecotour '96, Rio de Janeiro.
Sako, F. (1990) Tourism in Africa: an expanding industry. *The Courier*, 122: 62 – 72.
Sargan, J.D. (1964) Wages and prices in the United Kingdom, in P.E. Hart, G. Mills and J.K. Whittaker (eds), *Econometric Analysis of National Economic Planning*. London: Butterworths, pp. 25 – 64.
Schlüter, R. (1998) Tourism development: a Latin American perspective. In W. Theobald (ed.), *Global Tourism*. Oxford: Butterworth-Heinemann, pp. 216 – 30.
Schlüter, R. (1999) Sustainable tourism development in South America. The case of Patagonia. Argentina. In D. Pearce and R. Butler (eds), *Contemporary Issues in Tourism Development*. London: Routledge, pp. 176 – 91.
Schor, J. (1991) *The Overworked American. The Unexpected Decline of Leisure*. New York: Basic Books.
Schor, J. (1998) *The Overspent American*. New York: Basic Books.
Schor, J. (1999) *A Sustainable Economy for the 21st Century* New York: Seven Stories Press.
Sheldon, P. (1993) Forecasting tourism: expenditures versus arrivals *Journal of Travel Research*, XXXII (1): 13 – 20.
Sims, C. (1980) Macroeconomics and reality. *Econometrics*, 48, 1 – 48.
Smeral, Egon (1998) Tourism demand, economic theory and econometrics: an integrated approach, *Journal of Travel Research*, XXVI(4): 38 – 43.
Song, H. and Witt, S.F. (2000) *Tourism Demand Modelling and Forecasting Modern Econometric Approaches*. Oxford: Flsevier.

Song, H., Romilly, P. and Liu, X. (2000) An empirical study of UK outbound tourism demand. *Applied Economics,* 32 (5): 611 – 24.

Song, H., Witt, S.F. and Jensen, T. (1999) Forecasting performance of tourism demand models: the case of Denmark. Paper presented at the Nineteenth International Symposium on Forecasting, Washington, DC.

South East England Tourist Board (1998) *Bluewater: Retail Tourism in the South East.* Tunbridge Wells: SEETB.

SUDAM/OEA (1994a) *Oferta touristica da regiäo Amazonia brasileira.* Belem: Para.

SUDAM/OEA (1994b) *Diagnóstico do desenvolvimento de ecoturismo no Pantanal brasilerio.* Belem: Pará.

SUDAM/OEA (1997) *Recursos Naturais na Amazonia.* Belem: Pará.

Summary, R. (1987) Tourism's contribution to the economy of Kenya. *Annals of Tourism Research,* 14: 531 – 40.

Sweeney, J.F. (1993) Hotel and timesharing mixed use. *Developments,* November (American Resort Development Agency).

Szmulewicz, P. (1995) Agroturismo en el sur de Chile. *Estudios y Perspectivas en Turismo,* 4: 201 – 15.

Tapecott, D. (1995) *The Digital Economy.* New York: McGraw–Hill, pp. 58 – 59.

Teye, V.B. (1986) Liberation wars and tourism development in Africa – the case of Zambia. *Annals of Tourism Research,* 13 (4): 589 – 608.

Teye, V.B. (1987) Developing Africa's tourism potential: prospects and issues. *Tourism Recreation Research,* 12 (1): 9 – 14.

Teye, V.B. (1988) Coups d'etat and African tourism: a study of Ghana. *Annals of Tourism Research,* 15 (3): 329 – 56.

Teye, V.B. (1991) Prospects for regional tourism cooperation in Africa. In S. Medlik (ed.), *Managing Tourism.* Oxford: Butterworth – Heinemann, pp. 286 – 96.

Thiem, Marion (1994) Tourismus and kulturelle Identität, *berner Studien zu Freizeit and Tourismus.* No. 30.

Thomas, R.L. (1997) *Modern Econometrics: An Introduction.* Harlow: Addison – Wesley.

Todd, G. (2000) World Travel and Tourism Today. Conference Paper. Tourism and Hospitality in the 21st Century, University of Surrey.

Tourism Trendspotter (1999) Eight trends for Europe. *Tourism Trendspotter* (Crusader Publications), 1(4): 2 – 4.

Travel Industry Association of America (1999) Travel Industry Association of Amercia's Market Share IndicatorSM. Washington, DC: Travel Industry Association of America.

UN/WTO (United Nations and World Tourism Organisation) (1994) *Recommendations on Tourism Statistics.* New York: United Nations.

United Nations (UN) (1986) *Africa's submission to the special session of the UN General Assembly on Africa's economic and social crisis.* New York: UN General Assembly.

Uweche, R. (ed.) (1975) Tourism, peace and sunshine. *Africa,* February, 73–74.

*Vacation Ownership World,* January 1997.

*Vacation Ownership World,* January 1999.

Vera-Mendia, J. (1999) Turismo en Bolivia. Propuesta para categorizar la profesión del guia de turismo: *Estudios y Perspectivas en Turismo,* 8: 351 – 65.

Wahal, S. and Pigram, J. eds (1997) *Tourism Development and Growth.* London: Routledge.

Williams, D. (ed.) (1974) Matchet diary . . . . from Ada. *West Africa,* 19 August, pp. 10–11.

Willmott, M. (2000) The World of Today and Tommorrow. Conference paper. Tourism and Hospitality in the 21st Century, University of Surrey.

Witt, C.A. Witt, S.F. and Wilson, N. (1994) Forecasting international tourist flows. *Annals of Tourism Research,* 21: 612 – 28.

Witt, S.F. (1980) An abstract mode – abstract (destination) node model of foreign holiday demand: *Applied Economics,* 12: 163 – 80.

Witt, S.F. and Martin, C.A. (1987) Measuring the impacts of mega-events on tourism flows, in ALEST (ed.), *The Role and Impact of Mega-Events and Attractions on Regional and National Tourism Development.* St Gallen: AIEST, pp. 213 – 21.

Witt, C.A. and Witt, S.F. (1989) Measures of forecasting accuracy: turning point error v. size of error. *Tourism Management,* 10: 255 – 60.

Witt, S.F. and Witt, C.A. (1991) Tourism forecasting: error magnitude, direction of change error and trend change error. *Journal of Travel Research,* XXX(2): 26 – 33.

Witt, S.F. and Witt, C.A. (1992) *Modelling and Forecasting Demand in Tourism.* London: Academic Press.

Witt, S.F. and Witt, C.A. (1995) forecasting tourism demand: a review of empirical research. *International Journal of Forecasting.* 11: 447 – 75.

World Bank (1996) *Annual Report 1996.* Washington, DC: The World Bank. http://www.worldbank.org/html/extpb/annrep96/.

World Tourism Organisation (WTO) (1991) *Impact of the Gulf Crisis on International Tourism.* Madrid: WTO Special Report.

World Tourism Organisation (WTO) (1994) *Global Tourism Forecasts to the year 2000 and Beyond: Africa Volume* 2. Madrid. WTO.

World Tourism Organisation (1997a) *Compendium of Tourism Statistics, 1991 – 1995,* 17the edn. Madrid: WTO.

World Tourism Organisation (1997b) *Tourism Economic Report.* Madrid: WTO.

World Tourism Organisation (1998) *Turismo: Panorama 2020. Nuevas Tendencias.* Madrid: WTO.

World Tourism Organisation (1999) *Changes in Leisure Time: The Impact on Tourism.* madrid: WTO.

World Tourism Organisation (1999) *Compendium of Tourism Statistics, 1993 – 1997*, 19th edn. Madrid: WTO.

World Tourism Organisation (1999) *Tendencias del mercado turistico: Las Américas:* Madrid: WTO.

World Tourism Organisation (WTO) (1999) *Tourism Market Trends, Africa 1989 – 1998.* Madrid: WTO Commission for Africa.

World Tourism Organisation (WTO) (2000) *Compendium of Tourism Statistics 1994 – 1998.* Madrid: WTO.

WTO Leadership Forum of Advisers of the WTO Business Council (1998). *Conclusions: Strategic Issues for Europe.* Madrid: World Tourism Organisation.

WTO (1998) *Tourism Market Trends 1998.* Madrid: World Tourism Organisation.

WTO (2000) *Tourism 2020 Vision: Intraregional and Long Haul Flows*, Volume 4, *Europe.* Madrid: World Tourism Organisation.